Praise for *Levittown*

"[An] absorbing study of racial politics in America's model postwar suburb . . . Written as a sort of novelistic narrative history, *Levittown* traces the stories of two sets of disparate protagonists . . . Kushner relates [the drama] with judicious economy and an eye for the effective image."

—*Bookforum*

"In 1957, the event immediately recognized as a watershed moment in civil rights was the attempted integration of Central High School in Little Rock . . . But, in 1957, there was also Levittown. The equally harrowing story of how one black family tried to break the color line in that suburb outside of Philadelphia . . . [has] largely been forgotten by history. In *Levittown*, David Kushner rectifies that with a spare, brisk but always indignant account of another watershed moment that, while overshadowed by Little Rock and other events, was in many ways more consequential."

—*Los Angeles Times*

"A gripping, beautifully written history of a hot summer in one town where so many threads of postwar American history came together—suburbanization, segregation, the civil rights movement, McCarthyism. A real page-turner."

—Stephanie Coontz, author of
The Way We Never Were* and *Marriage, a History

"This is a multilayered tale of public policy, personal desire for a better life, McCarthyism, and Communist Party support for civil rights . . . Kushner expertly recounts the events and places them in a broader historical context. The book is a valuable contribution to the literature on suburbia. It is a story of racial backlash but also of the Myer courage and the enormous outburst of support of neighbors a across the country who recognized the injustice they challenged

—*Jewish Boo*

"[Kushner's] storytelling techniques capture a drama that is ofte in academic studies . . . A compelling read."

—*Chicago*

"A mesmerizing account of the efforts to integrate America's most famous suburb."   —*AARP The Magazine*

"Kushner has gathered a mass of material and organized it effectively to tell a gripping story. After reading it, Americans will understand how suburbs became so white in the first place and what two families—one black, one white—did to remedy the situation."

—**James W. Loewen, author of**
Lies My Teacher Told Me* and *Sundown Towns

"Kushner skillfully pieces together a shameful chronicle of racial discrimination during the American postwar economic boom . . . The Levittown fracas, he demonstrates, was a crucial moment in the overall struggle [for civil rights]. A remarkable story fashioned into a dramatic narrative."   —*Kirkus Reviews*

"Riveting . . . Kushner's fast-paced account deftly re-creates the drama, which, though largely forgotten today, received nationwide coverage as it unfolded."   —***Barnes and Noble Review***

"A dramatic social history of the Pennsylvania suburb."   —*USA Today*

"In his stirring new book . . . Kushner employs a low-key, journalistic style and never becomes polemical or judgmental . . . This is a story well worth telling and one well told in an affecting account of humanity at its worst and ultimately triumphant best."   —**Bookreporter.com**

"Kushner frames the Myers's story within the rise of self-assured entrepreneur developer Bill Levitt, who built wildly successful postwar suburbs and was an unrepentant defender of racially exclusive policies . . . The tension of that summer is still palpable in this gripping account."
—*Library Journal*

LEVITTOWN

Two Families, One Tycoon, and the Fight for Civil Rights in America's Legendary Suburb

DAVID KUSHNER

Walker & Company
New York

Published by Walker Publishing Company, Inc., New York

All papers used by Walker & Company are natural,
recyclable products made from wood grown in well-managed forests.
The manufacturing processes conform to the environmental
regulations of the country of origin.

LIBRARY OF CONGRESS CATALOGING-IN-PUBLICATION DATA

Kushner, David, 1968–
Levittown : two families, one tycoon, and the fight for civil rights
in America's legendary suburb / David Kushner.—1st U.S. ed.
        p. cm.
Includes bibliographical references.
ISBN-13: 978-0-8027-1619-4 (hardcover)
ISBN-10: 0-8027-1619-9 (hardcover)
1. Levittown (Pa.)—History—20th century.   2. African Americans—Civil rights—
Pennsylvania—Levittown—History—20th century.   3. Segregation—
Pennsylvania—Levittown—History—20th century.
4. Levittown (Pa.)—Race relations.   5. Levitt, William, 1907–1994.   I. Title.

F159.L6K87 2009
305.896'073074821—dc22
2008026319

Visit Walker & Company's Web site at www.walkerbooks.com

First published by Walker & Company in 2009
This paperback edition published in 2010

Paperback ISBN: 978-0-8027-1795-5

1 3 5 7 9 10 8 6 4 2

Typeset by Westchester Book Group
Printed in the United States of America by Worldcolor Fairfield

For Sue, Sami, and Mia

Contents

AUTHOR'S NOTE

YOU NEVER KNOW what stories your neighbor might have to tell. My mother-in-law, Harriett, urged me to sit down and talk with her neighbors, Bea and Lew Wechsler, about their experience in Levittown, Pennsylvania. Finally one day I listened. Bea came out of her house carrying a small dusty cardboard box for me. When I opened it that night, I found yellowed newspaper articles, fading black-and-white photographs, handwritten letters from around the world, and a copy of her husband Lew's riveting self-published memoir, *The First Stone*.

There was more. The Wechsler's former Levittown neighbor Daisy Myers had also written a powerful memoir, but it had languished in her attic for nearly fifty years without publication. It turned out Daisy was alive and well in York, Pennsylvania. After I drove to meet with her, she had something else to share with me in addition to her manuscript (later published as *Sticks 'n Stones* by the York County Heritage Trust): another dusty old box. Inside there was a thick tattered transcript of the trial that had become so central to their lives nearly a half century before.

I began to investigate the lives of the Levitts, the creators of the town, their ambitions, their plans, their conflicts. The more I explored, the more a larger story began to take shape—from the creation of Levittown through the battle of 1957 and its aftermath. And it was one, to my surprise, that had never completely been told. Though I'm not a historian, there was something I could do: tell it. I spoke with Bea, Lew, and Daisy about my interest, and they agreed to relive their part of the story with me over many long afternoons. For the rest, I spent four years reporting, interviewing, and researching, talking with surviving members of the Levitt family and others, and taking many trips to Levittown, Pennsylvania, where the Myers' house still stands at 43 Deepgreen Lane. This book is the result. The scenes, events, and dialogue are culled directly from my research. Everything is real. I did my best to tell it as it happened, and get out of the way.

PROLOGUE

THERE ARE STORIES that are true, and stories we want to believe. One day not long ago, a group of people discovered that one of their favorite stories might not be so true after all. It happened one bright morning in Stony Brook, New York, a rolling, wooded town on the North Shore of Long Island. The sky was swimming-pool blue, the lawns, AstroTurf green. Inside an old red carriage house on a hilltop, a few dozen locals chose to spend this gorgeous day indoors for a conference entitled "Suburbia at Sixty."

On a small stage, a young professor pointed his remote-control clicker at a projector screen behind him and said they were going to play a game. He would show them four slides and they would tell him which one didn't belong with the rest. The attendees adjusted their glasses and inched forward in their seats.

Click. The first slide showed a black-and-white aerial view of a cookie-cutter suburb with winding streets of identical houses in perfect lines. *Click.* The second, also black-and-white, captured a happy nuclear family from the 1950s standing in front of a boxy house. *Click.* The third slide triggered chuckles of recognition from the crowd; it was a promotional photo of the Cleaver family from the popular 1950s sitcom *Leave It to Beaver*. The final *click* brought up the last shot: a color picture of a McMansion, one of those sprawling new suburban castles taking over the land.

"It's that one!" an older woman shouted from her seat.

"The McMansion," concurred another.

The professor brandished his clicker. "Actually, I was thinking of this one," he said, in a tone that suggested he was sorry to disappoint them. Then he booted up the picture of the Cleavers again. "This one sticks out because it's an image of *make-believe*."

But given the topic of the day's conference, the audience couldn't help but blur the line. The conference title "Suburbia at Sixty" was both a misnomer and bit of good old American mythmaking. In fact, the suburbs are way older than sixty years and began far from these shores. Historian Kenneth Jackson traced the dream back to the days of Babylon B.C. Clay tablets found in Iraq show a letter to the king of Persia from 539 B.C. in which the writer effuses about his new home outside town. "Our property seems to me the most beautiful in the world," he wrote. "It is so close to Babylon that we enjoy all the advantages of the city, and yet when we come home we are away from all the noise and dust."

But for most Americans, including those gathered here, the fairy tale begins thirty miles down the road. It's the story of the model town that sprouted up from the potato fields when the nation's greatest heroes, the veterans returning from World War II, desperately needed homes. It's the legend of Levittown, the community often called the "original suburb," and that's what the neighbors had come to celebrate this day.

Across the road at the small, one-story Long Island Museum, the story unfolded in three rooms of newsreels, artifacts, and black-and-white photos. And as the visitors noted, it had much to say about their modern world. It started with a people in crisis. Despite the booming postwar economy, there weren't enough affordable homes to go around. Young veterans and their families were forced to sleep in trolley cars in Chicago and surplus bins in North Dakota. In Omaha, someone took out an ad: "Big Ice Box, 7×17 feet, could be fixed to live in." An editorial cartoon on one wall of the museum showed a family looking up longingly at a home on a puffy cloud. "How can we expect to sell democracy in Europe," read a quote by Harry Truman, "until we prove that . . . we can provide decent homes for our people?"

But thanks to one entrepreneurial family, the American Dream of a good home in a good town would soon come true. Down the hall at the museum hung a life-size photo of these men, the Levitts: two dapper young brothers, William and Alfred, and their diminutive father, Abe. In contemporary terms, they had the kinetic chemistry and renegade brash of a Silicon Valley start-up. Abe, a self-made immigrant and passionate horticulturalist, provided the springboard and the grass seed. Alfred, a self-taught architect (and sci-fi geek), designed the homes. And Bill, a Barnumesque promoter and marketing whiz, built the business and sold the dream.

Though there had been suburbs before theirs, the Levitts delivered something new: an inexpensive home with state-of-the-art gadgets in a seemingly perfect storybook town. With the federal government's subsidies for vets, the Levitts applied the innovations of mass production to building their houses. They didn't invent their product, but they mastered something dazzling: how to swiftly make and sell it. As the veterans watched in wonder, the Levitts churned out inexpensive Cape Cod houses by the dozens with assembly-line precision. Levittowns in Pennsylvania and New Jersey later followed.

And the builders were heroes. Bill Levitt, the front man, was a national icon and titan on the scale of Henry Ford and Walt Disney. *Time* magazine put him on the cover and ordained Levittown "as much an achievement of its cultural moment as Venice or Jerusalem." The opening of Levittown triggered the greatest migration in modern American history. During the 1950s, twenty million Americans would move to suburbs, the largest movement since the westward expansion of the 1880s. As the rest of the exhibit showed—from the *I Love Lucy* film clips on the vintage TV to the faded Levittown Boosters Little League uniform tacked on the wall—Levittown would become synonymous not just with the prosperity and hope of the 1950s, but the enduring vision of the suburbs that would draw families for decades.

At the beginning of the twenty-first century, when the Long Island conference took place, suburbia remained a national obsession. Two thirds of Americans lived in the suburbs. Over thirteen million new homes, including many in cookie-cutter suburban and McMansion developments, had been built in the last decade alone. Over seven million were tucked away behind walls and pristine lawns of gated communities.

Suburbia shaped our culture, landscape, and industry, from the fast food we ate on the way to and from work, to the shows we watched when we got home.

Why the fascination? From war to global warming, Americans felt increasingly under siege. As threats rose, a house in the suburbs represented the ultimate in security and community, a picture-perfect plan in a world that seems increasingly without one. Just as in the 1940s, parents still wanted good schools for the kids, friendly neighbors, immaculate lawns. And they were working harder, commuting longer, and striving higher to have it all.

But, as the "Suburbia at Sixty" conference got under way, the attendees learned that their dream could be over. With oil prices and global warming on the rise, speaker Ted Steinberg, a Pulitzer-nominated historian, said the story of suburbs may be ending. "Is the idea of suburbia an ecologically sustainable one over the long term?" he asked the crowd. "Will there be a symposium like this two generations from now? Or, as some people argue, have we reached as the end of suburbia? Is it possible this high-energy lifestyle—the automobile lifestyle—will disappear in some ways, and we'll have maybe a string of ghost towns? I think that's the central issue of our time."

As the end of this story loomed, it called the beginning into question. The answer could be found by digging—with new light—into the past. Because while the dream of Levittown had embedded itself into the popular culture and imagination, a darker, but no less American, story lurked inside. And it was nowhere to be found on the walls of the museum this day.

America's model town was built not just on hope, but on fear. In part, it was meant to ward off the widespread terror of a foreign threat: Communism. "No man who owns his own home and lot can be a Communist," Bill Levitt once said, "he has too much to do." And "the most perfectly planned community in America," as Levitt described it, was also built to keep out African-Americans. Levitt excluded African-Americans for decades after the Supreme Court ruled it unconstitutional to do so. It wasn't the first suburb to do this and it wouldn't be the last. But it epitomizes how systematically people can be shut out of a dream—and yet how heroically they can take it back.

This is the story that unfolded one unseasonably hot summer in 1957 on Deepgreen Lane, a quiet street in Levittown, Pennsylvania. There, a white, Jewish, Communist family named the Wechslers secretly arranged for an African-American family, the Myerses, to buy the little pink house next door. What followed was an explosive summer of violence that would transform their lives, and the nation. It would lead to the downfall of a titan and the integration of the most famous suburb in the world. It's a story of hope and fear, invention and rebellion, and the power that comes when ordinary people take an extraordinary stand. And, unlike the legend, this was real.

This is the story of Levittown.

One

THE CAPTAIN AND THE KIDS

ONCE UPON A time on a cold, dark night, a terrible sea lashed the boat of the notorious Captain Kidd. Lightning sliced darkness. Thunder clapped. Water crashed. Brash and bold, Kidd acted as though he had invented piracy and the search for treasure. But now, all around him, a mutinous lot of rebels set out to break him. Sickness had overtaken his men, a plague of cholera ravishing their bodies. And they wanted Kidd dead. They were closing in on him with their cleavers and pistols. Captain Kidd needed help quickly. "Abraham!" he howled into the wind.

From out below the deck shot his trusty sidekick: a slight man with a large nose and a hump on his back. Abraham fought the dastardly crew one by one, picking them off with deftness and ease. When the waves stilled, and the clouds parted, he stood by his captain's side, eyeing a lush island on the horizon. It was a new frontier. And not a pirate in the world could stand in their way.

As Abraham Levitt finished telling this tale, he looked down warmly upon his two young boys—William and Alfred—listening raptly at his feet. They sat in the well-furnished living room of a brownstone in Brooklyn, New York. Musty hardcover books from history to horticulture lined the shelves. The sweet smell of stuffed cabbage rose from the kitchen, as their bosomy mother, Pauline, labored at the stove. A smile spread across Abe's face.

"And of course you remember my pursuit of Wild Ike Mike in the jungles of Africa!" Abe continued. "And how I rescued Buffalo Bill from the clutches of that villain! How I cut open the body of that monstrous whale and found Jimmy, our cabin boy—swallowed by that creature—sitting on a crate of oranges playing 'Happy Days Are Here Again!' All of which is as true as the Gospel."

How was it possible that this diminutive man in his thirties had sailed the high seas with Captain Kidd two hundreds years before? Abe was slender with a wide, balding head, narrow eyes, large, pointy ears, and a slight hunch on his back. Little, nearsighted Alfred in his thick glasses thought of his comic books, and science fiction novels. Had his father invented some new technology to control the space/time continuum? His brother, Bill, four years older, couldn't care less about such things. Bill's mind filled with dreams of swashbuckling instead. They had heard enough of Abe's stories before to get the moral: Anything is possible. This world can be mean and awful. It can suck the marrow from your bones and replace it with fear. But it is up to you to live your dreams and share your bounty with the world. As their father liked to say, "The way to be happy is to make others happy. All else is trivial."

Though he may never have battled alongside Captain Kidd, Abraham Levitt, like most immigrants, had fought hard to get here. His father, a rabbi named Lewis, had fled anti-Semitism in Russia for America in the 1860s. But Lewis's life in the new land with his Austrian wife, Nellie Groden, was tough. The family was desperately poor, and Abe, the youngest of five, was born in the kitchen of his family's home in Williamsburg, Brooklyn, on August 2, 1880.

Despite his unceremonious beginnings, Abe sought the best for himself at an early age. While the other kids played stickball in the street, he dropped out of school at age ten to earn money washing dishes at restaurants and selling newspapers at the foot of the World Building on Park Row. But he was also a dreamer. In his spare moments, he'd take to the city's parks and gardens, where he'd spend hours losing himself in the natural beauty. His love of nature rivaled only his passion for reading. He started with magazines and newspapers, but soon moved on to books with wide-ranging subjects—history, economics, science, and, of course, the stories of Captain Kidd.

By his teens, Abe had joined literary and scientific societies and would venture over the river to Manhattan to attend classes at Cooper Union in the East Village. The more he learned, the more he began to reject the orthodox religious views of his father, whom he saw as domineering. Among the writings he enjoyed was the work of Ernst Haeckel, a German zoologist and comparative anatomist. In addition to naming thousands of species, Haeckel was a philosopher who posited a controversial and racist theory called recapitulation. In his view, an individual's biological development mirrored the evolution of its species. "In order to be convinced of this important result, it is above all things necessary to study and compare the mental life of wild savages and of children," he wrote. "At the lowest stage of human mental development are the Australians, some tribes of the Polynesians, and the Bushmen, Hottentots, and some of the Negro tribes."

In lieu of a high school degree, Abe took the state regents exam and passed. At the turn of the century, he was twenty and ready to put his self-taught brains to professional use. He entered law school at New York University, where he stood out for his drive and gumption. As a sophomore, he wrote a book on real estate called *Levitt's Notes on Law* and used the proceeds to pay off his tuition. Abe completed his degree in just two years and conquered the bar exam the next year, in 1903. Abe specialized in real estate law and earned enough to buy a four-story brownstone on leafy Macon Street in Brooklyn.

Though a quiet and contemplative young man, he chose a large and outgoing woman for his wife—Pauline A. Biederman. As his family would later joke, Abe started his marriage at six foot three, but ended up ground down to five four by the time Pauline was done with him. Though not wealthy, the Levitts had enough money to have domestic help and the leisure to stroll through the nearby parks. The once poor immigrant had finally come into his own small piece of the American Dream. It was time to have children. When their first son was born on February 11, 1907, they named him William Jaird.

Brothers fight. And, after Abe and Pauline had their second child, Alfred Stuart, on March 12, 1911, there was plenty of fighting—good-natured and otherwise—in the Levitt home. Abe set the tone. As in building a start-up business, he wanted a snappy, do-it-yourself, bootstrapping crew on his ship. Arguing—both to defend a point and to build one's character—was encouraged. "It is generally a good thing to have a lawyer father who will kick you into college and present you with some social arguments once in a while," Alfred later said. "Self-confidence waxed mightily," Bill recalled. Bill, bold and outgoing, gravitated to the lectures on baseball, particularly on the family's favorite team, the Dodgers. Alfred, introspective and reserved, took to the discussions of art.

From an early age, the boys possessed competitive, though complementary, differences. One day, the brothers snuck up to the attic and found some antique swords. They dueled with each other until Bill inadvertently took a slice out of Alfred's thumb. The thumb was sewn back up, but the split between the brothers would always remain.

Bill had his mother's tough streak. He never hesitated to speak his mind. Upon overhearing his father's business escapades, he would pipe in to say, "You'll never get rich that way." Abe marveled that his eleven-year-old son thought he needed his advice. At PS 44 and Boys High School in Bedford-Stuyvesant, Bill competed in lacrosse and swimming. In his teens, Bill gravitated to the high life, with a taste for money, attractive women, and sports cars. He wore the latest fashions, like tailored plus-four pants, cut four inches below the knees. In one photo, he posed in his plus fours, cockily, leaning against a Model T. One morning, he arrived at breakfast dressed to the nines. "Where you going all dressed up like that?" his parents asked. "I'm off to Manhattan," he replied. "I'm going to buy the Chrysler Building!"

While his older brother chased his dreams of power and fortune, Alfred preferred more intellectual pursuits such as chess, and reading. Fascinated by technology, he'd spend hours reading science-fiction and fantasy stories, particularly those in the pioneering sci-fi magazine *Amazing Stories*. Before long, the family would find him alone in his room, sketching futuristic buildings on an artist's pad. "Alfred is a genius," his father would say, "and I use that term advisedly." But, at times, it seemed as though their mother, Pauline, played favorites. On occasion, she would call for Alfred from across the brownstone. It's me she wants, he would think. She would pull Alfred close and bring his little ear to her lips. "Where's your brother, Bill?" she would whisper.

But Bill was off. At sixteen, he entered his father's alma mater, New York University, where he made a go at studying English and math. The distractions proved too strong. Bill began dating a pretty girl, Rhoda Kirshner, from the Bronx. He grew restless and dropped out of NYU in his third year at age nineteen in 1927. When later asked why, he replied, "I got itchy, I wanted to make a lot of money. I wanted a big car and a lot of clothes."

His father obliged, taking his eldest son under his wing at his law firm. Around that time, Abe acquired land in Rockville Centre, Long Island, an up-and-coming commuter area on the South Shore, from a client who had defaulted on his payments. The housing market of the 1920s had reached a high point of $4.5 billion in 1925 and had been falling since— as far down as $2.45 billion by 1929. With many losing money, it was a time, as one writer put it, "when anyone who even mentioned building a home for sale was ripe for the booby hatch."

But the Levitts had the guts to roll the dice. In a project that branched out beyond the law firm's ordinary activities, the Levitts completed and sold forty homes on the Rockville property. The experience invigorated young Bill, who had, as he said, been itching to get into industry. It also intrigued his brother, Alfred. After studying art for a year at NYU, he had marched into his dean's office and announced that he was dropping out because the school had nothing to teach him. Designing and selling homes, on the other hand, could let both him and Bill both explore their interests, hands-on. All they had to do was make it official. So they created a company with their father devoted to building: Levitt & Sons.

At just twenty-two, Bill became president and designated front man— tasked with advertising, sales, and financing. He had matured into a tall, handsome young man, with bushy eyebrows, tight, curly black hair, and sad, droopy eyes. Alfred, eager to flex his nascent interest in architecture and art, became the eighteen-year-old vice president of design. He had the look of an artist, with fashionable glasses and a wry smile. Though their differences were still profound, their father saw in them, as a team, something dynamic. "Bill wouldn't be a success without Alfred, and

Alfred wouldn't be a success without Bill," Abe would say. "Together they are terrific."

Alfred, with no architectural training, took to the task like a nerd to a chemistry set. He sketched a six-room, two-bath, Tudor-style, half-timbered home, then watched with delight as the house went up over the summer of 1929. Bill brought it to market for a high price of $14,500. On August 2, Abe's forty-ninth birthday, his sons gave him the ultimate present: the company's first sale. Levitt & Sons was in business. And they saw their new frontier: suburbia.

Suburbia was an invention, like any other, but it was hardly new. Through and long past the Middle Ages, the dream of a country home near the city was the domain of the elite. English manor homes in the 1600s gave way to sprawling estates for dukes and duchesses in the 1800s. The dream spread to North America. Thomas Jefferson said, "I view large cities as pestilential to the morals, the health, and the liberties of man."

Starting in 1815, innovations in transportation—steamboats, railroads, and horse-drawn carts—gave city dwellers new ways to escape the urban noise and dust. And they did, heading off in droves for what would become the first wave of planned suburbs. Cambridge and Somerville bloomed outside Boston. Brooklyn Heights absorbed movers and shakers from across the river in New York City. Llewellyn Park, New Jersey, would soon define some of the essential features for suburban communities— from the curvilinear roads to the green parks in the center of the developments.

And there were more and more reasons to leave the city. Outbreaks of diseases such as cholera and smallpox ravaged the crowded cities, adding to the appeal of living in a spacious, natural environment nearby. As the nineteenth century progressed, life in suburbia took on more allure. Brooklyn bard Walt Whitman wrote, "A man is not a whole and complete man unless he owns a house and the ground it stands on." Frederick Law Olmsted, the designer of Central Park in New York, said, "No great town can long exist without great suburbs."

Books on landscaping and lawn care—aimed at the suburban homeowner—hit the shelves. One scribe, Frank J. Scott, author of *The*

Art of Beautifying Suburban Home Grounds, wrote, "A smooth, closely-shaven surface of grass is by far the most essential element of beauty on the grounds of a suburban house." Again, new technologies met the demands, as lawn-mowing machines hit the market in the mid-1800s. And so that homeowners didn't have to busy themselves watering their grass, a patent was issued in 1871 for the first lawn sprinkler.

Suburbia was a desirable destination for those who could afford it. Railroads enabled a new commuting culture, but only the wealthy could have a horse and driver greet them at the station and take them home. With the invention of electricity, their suburban homes were soon filled with gadgets from radios to washing machines. When Henry Ford invented the Model T, they had cars to get them there. "The city is doomed," Ford warned, "we shall solve the city problem by leaving the city."

People heeded such calls, triggering a suburban boom in the 1920s. At the beginning of the decade, less than half of families in the country owned homes. But between 1920 and 1927, an average of 883,000 new homes went up each year—more than double the rate of any other seven-year period in history. Suburbia began to spread rapidly outside the major cities throughout the decade—hitting over 700 percent growth in communities outside Detroit and Chicago alone. One of the greatest booms ran throughout Long Island; Nassau County's population nearly tripled. As the end of the decade neared, one out of six Americans lived in the suburbs.

Speculators, eager to cash in, began to buy up land with hopes of riding the wave. But, despite the boom, the housing market had reached its peak in 1925 and slowly swan-dived from there. New housing plummeted to 509,000 units by 1929. Prognosticators saw the beginning of the end, and they were right. On October 29, 1929, three months after the Levitts went into business, the stock market crashed. The Great Depression had begun.

It was hard times in America in 1933, and twenty-six-year-old Bill Levitt needed a shave. As he sat lathered up in a barbershop in Rockville Centre, Long Island, the man with the blade asked him how business was going. "Damn tough," Bill replied, "we can't get a dime of mortgage money."

At first, it hadn't been so bad. As the head of Levitt & Sons, Bill had built and sold eighteen homes for $18,000 apiece in their first year of business and went on to sell forty more in their second year. But with banks in trouble, the times were growing tough, as Bill lamented. He had more than real estate on his mind. He was a father now. The previous year, he had had his first son, William Levitt Jr., with the girlfriend he had married in November 1929, the raven-haired beauty Rhoda. He had a family to support. He needed mortgage money, and fast, he told his barber.

But then, from the stool next to him, came a voice. "Better come in and see me," said the man wrapped in a face towel, "I might be able to help." The man was a local banker, and, as it turned out, a family friend. The next day Bill walked into the bank and left with the loans he needed. While the Depression loomed, he would go on to build six hundred houses in Rockville Centre. By 1934, Levitt & Sons had sold over 250 homes for a total of $2,750,000. Bill was back on track and knew exactly what to do next. He would bring the centuries-old dream of the suburban country estate to the upper-middle-class people of New York.

Bill secured land from a millionaire judge in Manhasset, on Long Island's so-called Gold Coast, a ritzy suburb on the North Shore, just twenty miles east of Manhattan. Levitt & Sons called their first full-blown community Strathmore-at-Manhasset, a name that conjured up visions of English manors and rolling countryside. They weren't just selling homes, they knew, they were selling the *idea* of a fantasy home—and drawing on each of their skills, they went about bringing that dream to life.

Alfred was just twenty-three when the Levitts began work in Manhasset, but the self-taught whiz-kid architect was at no loss for ideas—despite his father's good-natured teasing. "Alfred loves to draw," Abe joked, "but he doesn't know what a two-by-four is." In fact, the boy wonder had a keen sense for innovation and the promise of the future. He was the first on the block to buy an electric razor and to drive a Studebaker. The idea for Manhasset was to deliver luxury at a reasonable price or, as the Levitts liked to put it, "swank at low cost." No home would go for more than $20,000, and the average price would be $11,000.

On the surface, the plan seemed easy enough. Alfred began with tried-and-true English and colonial designs. The homes were built on curvilinear roads, with no two looking alike, and staggered setbacks. But he didn't stop there. No idea was too outlandish for the young designer. After flying to the Bahamas to look at home designs, Alfred came back with a host of new ideas. The first home he built in Manhasset looked like something out of his father's fictitious seafaring adventures. It included a child's room designed to look like a cabin on a steamship—complete with knotty-pine walls, a compass on the floor, and lanterns.

The homes weren't just quirky, they were showcases for the future. "General Motors doesn't build the simplest and cheapest vehicle that will provide transportation," Alfred said. "It packs a lot of chrome right up front where everyone can see it, and chromes sells cars." Alfred worked with his flashy big brother, Bill, to make sure the houses were, as he said, "all gooed up" with the latest gadgets inside. Bill cut deals with manufacturers such as General Electric to include all the sexy gizmos inside the home.

Alfred designed a whitewashed brick Georgian home with seven rooms, and three baths to show off their stuff. They called it the Metropolitan Home. Visitors filed through the model home as if they were witnessing a future-world exhibit at some theme park. The kitchen, to their delight, was fully electric. Instead of wooden cabinets, they saw recessed steel. The General Electric sinks sported garbage disposals and, as promised in Levitt's ads, a "dishwashing and drying apparatus." The Levitts even trumpeted the color of their plumbing—not the usual yellow brass pipes but only the finest "Anaconda red-brass." They converted a former Vanderbilt mansion and its grounds into a clubhouse for the residents—complete with a swimming pool, billiards room, cocktail lounge, and gym. They weren't just building homes, as Bill stressed, they were creating a community.

With Alfred tending to the designs, Abraham, now semiretired, obsessed over the landscaping. Abe brought in trees, evergreens, flowering shrubs, annuals, and perennials from around the country. But it wasn't just to beautify the homes, it was to preserve their value and offset the faux English and Norman-French architecture, as Alfred was quick to note: "Father had the foresight to realize that by intelligent landscaping the normal depreciation of our houses could be offset. The magnificence of Father's planting is not to be put in words . . . every social idea this company has is the result of Father's pressing and persuading. Now he has two adherents—my brother and me. We finally began to appreciate."

Abe even micromanaged the outdoor lighting. "Almost everything we have learned about improving the appearance of our communities we have learned from Father," Alfred told a reporter one day. "He was the one, for example, who always insisted that no telephone poles be allowed on our streets. If you allow poles on the street, the town will hang those terrible streetlights on them that don't light the street but light the second stories of houses."

The meticulousness spilled over into the rules the Levitts set for their residents. Every Strathmore homeowner would have to agree to strict regimen of lawn maintenance. Flowers could only be planted in the backyard. Grass had to be cut once a week, and if a resident failed to perform the duty, the Levitts would dispatch someone to do the job—and send a bill. Laundry was not allowed to be hung outside on Sundays or holidays. Even doghouses had to conform with the accompanying designs of the homes.

As the plan grew, Bill demonstrated his prowess for marketing and sales. "He can't draw a line on a plane nor does he know how to build anything," Alfred joked, ". . . but [has] extraordinary talent. This talent displays itself in all those phases that architects are not trained in and weren't given an inheritance in—such as money." Bill controlled every possible bit of the construction—from the design and landscaping to selling furnishings to the buyers. Though they didn't invent the technique, the Levitts brought the assembly line to the site—with specialized workers building up to twenty homes at once.

But Bill, a lifelong playboy with a keen sense of panache and story, knew he wasn't just selling brick and mortar—he was selling a dream. As the Levitts' chief advertising and marketing man, he got busy penning the script. The story played out not on the silver screen, but in his flamboyant newspaper ads. Every Sunday after breakfast, he would retire to his study, take pen in hand, and write out an ad for the next weekend's *New York Times*. The prose read more like a fairy tale than a real estate pitch.

"Once upon a time—October 29th, 1929, to be exact," he scribbled one morning, "there was a stock market crash. A great many people who like to speculate, and a great many more who thought they were investing, were wiped out. Business began to get worse and worse, until finally there just wasn't any business at all—or practically none, anyway. But this company decided to pay no attention to the prevailing pessimism. We reasoned that as long as man existed he needed a roof over his head. And we reasoned further: If that roof, and the plaster, and the floors, and the walls could be made into a more attractive home than ever before, it would be bought." And, of course, as Bill noted in the ad, the Levitts were correct.

The media, hungry for good news, eagerly picked up the inspiring tale of the boot-strapped boys from Brooklyn who made good when all the country seemed to be going bad. The *Saturday Evening Post* called the Levitts "outstanding among the unnumbered thousands of housebuilders in America" and marveled at their prodigal success. "They were extraordinarily young when they started, and made an almost fabulous success at a time when practically all over the country the housebulding industry was in the doldrums." The *New York Times* trumpeted in a headline for a story in 1934 about the Levitts: DEVELOPERS DEFY DEPRESSION YEARS.

Abe Levitt and his kids—not even thirty years old—had become heroes and soon joined the ranks of the biggest builders in America. Word spread, and, as one reporter put it, Bill Levitt became "the young man to see for high-end housing along Long Island's North Shore." Assorted lawyers, bankers, engineers, and tobacco magnates of New York snatched up the Levitts' two hundred Manhasset homes. Bill even boasted as much in his ads, citing "a good cross section" who had found happiness in his communities. But, under the radar, the cross section had its limits.

As was commonly practiced in ritzy enclaves, Bill barred Jews from buying in Strathmore. He was a builder, and so what if they were the descendants of a rabbi; this is what builders did, they resolved. One Sunday after breakfast, Bill retired to his study, took pen in hand, and began to write his weekly copy. "No one realizes better than Levitt that an undesirable class can quickly ruin a community," he wrote.

Bill often told the legend of his own migration to suburbia in the 1930s. He would speak of Haeckel, his father's favorite philosopher, and his thoughts on the essential way in which the world worked, the absence of free will, the cause and effect. "Okay," Bill once explained to a reporter in the back of a limousine, "in the seventeenth century, in 1624 exactly, a man by the name of Captain John Hawkins, an Englishman, brought the first boatload of slaves to Virginia. Up until then there were no black people on this continent. By now the black people were here, they multiplied geometrically until finally a couple of centuries later, as they moved into the North, they moved onto the same street we lived on in Brooklyn. Next to us a black assistant DA moved in. Fearing a diminution of values if too many came in, we picked up and moved out. We then got into the suburbs, into building . . ."

"Which started everything," the reporter asked, "the whole—"

"Exactly," Bill replied.

Two

THE OTHER HARLEM

EIGHT-YEAR-OLD DAISY DAILEY skipped out her front door one morning in 1933, schoolbooks in hand, took one look around, and thought, There's no better community to live in the world than this one: Jackson Ward. Every block in this neighborhood where she lived near downtown Richmond, Virginia, promised a different architectural wonder. Redbrick homes and colorful awnings. Cast-iron porches as in New Orleans. A building shaped like a castle. And, most fantastic of all, the Richmond Dairy—a towering brick building on West Marshal with three gleaming white sixteen-foot-high milk bottles on three of the corners.

Around the way on Second Street was the Hippodrome Theater, the bustling venue that would draw the biggest names in African-American entertainment: Duke Ellington, Ethel Waters, and Ella Fitzgerald. The tap-dancing pioneer Bill "Bojangles" Robinson, another Hippodrome regular, was a local who'd grown up just around the corner from Daisy on Third Street. The Hippodrome scene was such a sensation that people began calling Jackson Ward "the Harlem of the South."

Jackson Ward didn't happen by accident. While whites fled the cities for manufactured suburbs, freed slaves left their masters far behind to create a rich and robust community in the early 1800s built on innovation and pride. Former slave Giles Jackson became the first black lawyer to address the Supreme Court of Virginia. Abner Clay, a green-thumbed civic leader, tended to the area's parks.

One of the America's first black newspapers, the *Richmond Planet*, launched in 1894. The Southern Aid Society of Virginia, the first black-owned insurance company in the country, came soon after. The Ward's most famous entrepreneur was Maggie L. Walker, the first African-American woman to become the president of a bank in U.S. history. Just as Jackson Ward thrived as an artistic center, its role as a center of commerce earned it the moniker "the Wall Street of Black America." By the 1920s, 94 percent of Richmond's black population lived here.

For Daisy, who was born here on February 10, 1925, the spirit of community and enterprise was infectious. The only child of William Lester and Alma Hockett, a teenage domestic worker who was unable to care for her, Daisy was raised by a couple who lived across the street from her mother named the Daileys. Despite being the outsider, Daisy thrived in the two-story, three-bedroom house with her ten new brothers and sisters.

The Dailey house bustled with activity. The man Daisy called her father, Myers Dailey, worked as a cooper on the Richmond, Fredericksburg & Potomac Railroad. On weekends, Daisy's father would use his free train passes to take the kids on trips to Washington, D.C., or other sites. His wife, Lottie, tended to the house and took great pride in her garden. She also made sure her kids stayed in line. All she had to do was cast "the look," as Daisy called it, and everyone behaved. One time Daisy made the mistake of asking her mother why she was looking at her in such a stern way—and, after a swift punishment, never made that error again.

Meals were boisterous and good-naturedly argumentative. On Sundays, the family would attend the Moore Street Baptist Church, where Myers Dailey worked as a deacon. On Sunday nights, they'd cozy up around the radio to hear the latest horror broadcast on the popular radio show *Inner Sanctum Mysteries*. On Christmas Daisy got exactly what she wanted: a red-and-white-striped bike with fat tires.

Daisy, a bright, attentive, and sometimes precocious student, found just as strong a community at school. Because she was nearsighted, she sat close to the front of the class and grew to admire her teachers—whom she hoped one day to emulate. The kids playfully called her the "teacher's pet." Daisy delighted in her teachers' sometimes eccentric personalities and quirks: the teacher who could never find his glasses because they were always on top of his head, the football coach who told her she looked better without red nail polish or lipstick, the cute but dim instructor whom all the boys pranked.

Daisy played basketball, studied piano, and went to Girl Scout meetings every other week. The kids voted her the most popular in class. With her body changing, she began to worry more about how she looked, whether her clothes matched or fit the latest style, whether her hair was in place. Boys began paying more attention to her, and the attraction was mutual. Soon, she was old enough to be trusted by her parents to go visit their relative's farm in Amelia, Virginia, by herself. There, she learned all the ways of the farm—churning butter from milk, feeding cows, riding horses. On sunny days, she'd run to the henhouse to gather eggs, then sell them to the local grocer for twelve cents a dozen, taking five cents to spring on a soda or candy bar.

But despite her love of her home and neighborhood, Daisy knew a larger and more mysterious world was outside. She would catch glimpses of it flashing by on Fifth Street. Occasionally, a foreign vessel would appear and vanish—a trolley full of white people passing quickly through the neighborhood. Though she viewed her life in Jackson Ward as a kind of childhood paradise, the blur of white faces on the trolley suggested another reality.

One day when her mother woke her to go get a new outfit for Easter, Daisy caught her first glimpse. From the moment she boarded the trolley, everything changed. The world inverted like the negative of a photo. Stoic white faces stared up at her and her mother from the seats, while the conductor waited indifferently. Daisy saw open seats in the front, but her mother took her firmly by the arm and walked her, instead, to the back. Why couldn't they just take the seats up front? Daisy wondered innocently.

As they pulled out of Jackson Ward, the African-American faces in the street were soon replaced by white. Daisy looked out the window and saw signs over water fountain labeled Colored. She saw whites sitting at lunch counters, while blacks ate their food outside. As they got off the trolley, they too went to lunch and had to join the other African-Americans away from the counters.

By the time Daisy and her mother got to the clothing shop, Daisy became excited again to get her new threads. The shop was filled with all the fashions of the day, and she could picture herself walking into church and the boys taking notice. When a hat caught her attention on a rack, she reached for it eagerly. But the white clerk swiped it away and said, "She can't try that on." Though just a child, Daisy didn't feel afraid, she felt bewildered. Why couldn't she try on the hat? My head is round like anyone else's, she thought. But the rules outside Jackson Ward were different, and arbitrary. Daisy's mother looked the clerk in the eye and said, "If she can't try it on, then we're not buying it." And they left.

Though Daisy never dreamed of leaving her city behind, if she had, she couldn't go far. Unlike the legions of wealthy whites who fled to the romantic suburbs during and after the housing boom of the 1920s, black Americans were routinely excluded from participating in the suburban dream. It started at the level of "gentlemen's agreements" to restrict blacks from buying in white neighborhoods and soon became established in federally mandated guidelines.

While the U.S. Supreme Court had ruled against municipal and residential segregation laws in 1917, an ugly but well-oiled machine churned behind the white-picket-fenced towns. The National Association of Real Estate Boards provided the power in 1914 when it implemented an ethics code that forbid members from "introducing into a neighborhood . . . members of any race or nationality . . . whose presence will clearly be detrimental to property values." Facing heavy fines for violations, those in the realty industry dutifully played along. Banks refused to provide mortgages to blacks, and community members signed contracts agreeing not to rent or sell their homes to "any person other than one of the Caucasian race."

Fines weren't the only method of enforcement. Other practices also thrived in the burgeoning suburbs up North. One of the most egregious locations was just outside New York City on Long Island. There, Robert Moses, who had become president of the Long Island State Park Commission, kept African-Americans out of the beaches and public parks by requiring special permits. Believing that blacks were dirty and afraid of cold water, he had the pool at Jones Beach kept extracold to keep them out.

The burgeoning Ku Klux Klan drove the sentiment home. In the early 1920s, one of eight white residents in Nassau and Suffolk counties in Long Island were members of the KKK—including the ministers and chief of police in Freeport. One Long Island march of the KKK drew more than thirty thousand people; it was held on July 4, Independence Day, 1924.

As the Depression swept across America in the early 1930s, the exclusion of blacks from suburbia became more institutionalized. It started on June 13, 1933, when Franklin Delano Roosevelt signed the Home Owners Loan Corporation into law to protect homeowners from foreclosure. The HOLC pumped billions of dollars into the market, refinancing tens of thousands of mortgages, long term and low interest. But it left a devastating legacy.

As part of its due diligence, the HOLC implemented an elaborate means of appraising the communities in which the mortgages were financed. The plan assigned a letter grade corresponding to the determined value of a particular area. High marks were given to neighborhoods that were homogeneous, which was defined as containing "American business and professional men." The lowest grade—assigned the letter *D* or the color red—went to neighborhoods that had declined with "an undesirable element."

Predominantly African-American inner-city communities such as Jackson Ward were redlined. A mixed-race section of Pasadena, California, for example, earned the lowest grade, despite the appraiser's assessment of its having "all conveniences" and being "favorably located," because of the presence of ten black homeowners. "Although the Negroes are said to be of the better class their presence has caused a wave of selling in the area and it seems inevitable that ownership and property values will drift to lower levels," the report noted. A community in St. Louis without a "single foreigner or Negro" got the highest marks. Scholars and real-estate-textbook authors codified this notion that an influx of African-Americans would devalue a community. "Inharmonious groups of people," as one popular textbook put it, was considered a "blighting influence" for a neighborhood on par with being built next to a factory.

While the HOLC nevertheless provided financing for these low-grade communities, the damage was done—and racist beliefs, already deeply ingrained throughout the country, leached with even greater credence into business practices. Bankers and Realtors who completed the HOLC questionnaires evaluating their communities absorbed the equation that redlined areas were bad investments and denied mortgages accordingly.

With the Federal Housing Administration's creation in 1934, it adopted the HOLC plan, becoming, as one historian put it, "the most important single cause of residential segregation." The FHA was established to protect and expand the housing industry. It did this by rescuing lenders and builders, issuing low-interest, long-term mortgages—as long as the recipients adhered to their HOLC-inspired standards.

In its *Underwriting Manual* from 1936, the FHA mandated, "If a neighborhood is to retain stability, it is necessary that its properties shall continue to be occupied by the same social and racial classes. A change in social or racial occupancy generally leads to instability and a reduction in values." The FHA had specific suggestions about how to enforce this. One way was with physical barriers. "Natural or artificially established barriers will prove effective in protecting a neighborhood and the locations within it from adverse influences. Usually the protection against adverse influences afforded by these means include prevention of the infiltration of business and industrial uses, lower-class occupancy, and inharmonious racial groups."

The FHA also recommended restrictive covenants. In 1938, there were eight suggested provisions. The seventh prohibited stables and pigpens. The next provision prohibited "the occupancy of properties except by the race for which they are intended." While the HOLC insured mixed-race neighborhoods despite its findings, the FHA wore its prejudices on its sleeves—in the simplest terms, those who didn't play by the rules would not have their loans guaranteed.

It was a sad turning point in American history, as Kenneth Jackson would note: "For perhaps the first time, the federal government embraced the discriminatory attitudes of the marketplace. Previously, prejudices were personalized and individualized; FHA exhorted segregation and enshrined it as public policy." And the legacy would remain. "The national government . . . put its seal of approval on ethnic and racial discrimination and developed policies which had the result of the practical

abandonment of large sections of older, industrial cities . . . The financial community saw blighted neighborhoods as physical evidence of the
melting-pot mistake."

Daisy's school had no cafeteria. No library. No gym. When the kids
wanted to exercise, the teachers pushed aside the desks and let them
jump around the classroom. As much as Daisy loved Jackson Ward, the
older she grew—the more trips to the white part of town she took, the
more she studied African-American history in school, the more train
rides she rode through the suburbs of Virginia—the more she realized
how differently people lived.

While Daisy was familiar with the Jim Crow laws that called for "separate but equal" lives for black Americans, she struggled with that idea. She
would hear people say that "the Virginia Negro seemed happiest," but
that rang untrue. She knew plenty of people who were bitter and resent-
ful, but without, as she put it, "an escape hatch." She would often think
How we could sit anywhere in the North, but not here? What's the difference? When she'd talk about it with her parents, they'd say, "There will be
a time when this will all break down. One day, segregation will be over."

And they were going to take part in the fight. When her father was
denied a promotion because he was African-American, Daisy's parents
became more active in the community—signing up as early supporters
of the National Association for the Advancement of Colored People, and
urging others to pay the poll tax so that they could vote. Leading up to
Elections Days, her parents would work the rows of her father's church:
"Are you making sure to vote?" Her parents would ask people, "Do you
need transportation?" On Election Day, her parents would pile people
into their car and take them to the voting sites. Her parents instilled their
values in the girl. When Daisy complained that all her friends were going to a free dentist, her mother stood firm. "When I can't afford something," she said, "we do without."

At the same time, Daisy was growing into a strong young woman with
a bright smile and easy laugh. She played basketball and piano, had
plenty of friends, participated actively in the church. She struggled not

to pine for the things she didn't have. "People who long to be like some-one else aren't satisfied with who they are," she'd say, "and I'm quite sat-isfied with who I am." While the white people had a world at their disposal, Jackson Ward had its own black-run taxis and stores. "Every-thing they have," she said, "we have too."

But it was hard to maintain her resolve for long. In 1945, after gradu-ating from Virginia Union College, where she studied education and so-ciology and became the first in her family to get a college degree, she got a taste of life outside Jackson Ward. Just twenty, Daisy went to teach sixth grade in Amelia, where her mother had grown up. Kids played craps in the back of her classroom. Most students couldn't afford books. The parents struggled to feed their families, working on farms long and hard to pay the bills.

Surrounded by these conditions, Daisy's childhood dream of being a teacher took on new meaning. One day, a student confessed that instead of drinking from the water fountain labeled Colored, he drank from the one marked White. He wanted to see if the water tasted different. Daisy taught the students black history, about the NAACP and the poll tax. She delighted in seeing a larger world open up in the children's minds, and it soon became time for her to expand her world too.

In the fall of 1947, Daisy received a scholarship to pursue a master's degree in social work at New York University in New York City and made plans to go with two of her girlfriends. Her parents had heard hor-ror stories about the big city and lectured her about "bad influences" to avoid. "Don't get caught up in that Venus flytrap," they warned.

But Daisy couldn't get there fast enough—and read all about the city in anticipation. From the moment she stepped out of her friend's car on the morning she arrived, New York exceeded all of her expectations. It was fast and big and loud, tall buildings, honking horns, and activity. On her first day of classes at NYU, she eagerly took her seat near the front—and was surprised when a white student took the chair to her left, and another to her right.

After a lifetime of segregation, it was a shock to her system, and a new world unfolded with every step. By day, she wandered Greenwich Vil-lage between classes, past the artists and musicians, of many colors and ethnicities. When she boarded a bus, she would sit anywhere she wanted, no questions asked. Most exciting of all was just seeing all these different people together—talking with each other, cooperating, laughing, having a good time regardless of their skin color. She took a job at a publishing company, where blacks worked equally with whites. To her amazement, one of the African-American foremen had more white people working under him than blacks.

At night, Daisy would ride the subway up to the YWCA on 135th Street. While she grew up in Jackson Ward when it was known as the Southern Harlem, this other Harlem was a totally different scene. Her roommate, an effervescent young African-American woman named Nan, was a musician with a white boyfriend named Claude. At first, Daisy was taken aback by the interracial relationship, but her trepidation soon melted away.

While her mind broadened, she was able to resolve something in her personal life too: her relationship with her biological mother. The two had lost touch years before, but now her mother was living in an apartment with her eleven children and new family in Brooklyn. The reunion was emotional, and her mother made up for lost time—filling her in on all her years, and reconnecting with her daughter. She explained how terrible she had felt about having to give Daisy away, but because she was so young and working so hard, she thought it was the best option. However, she reminded Daisy, she was adamant about never putting her daughter up for adoption, and she remained Daisy's legal mother to that day.

By the end of her first semester, Daisy was a changed person. She said it felt as if she had been living her whole life in a coal mine, but had finally come up for air. She began to reexamine her childhood and community, trying to understand how segregation had, as she put it, "handicapped" her. After her semester at NYU, she boarded a bus for her home and had one thought: "If integration works here, why not everywhere?"

When Daisy came back to Virginia in 1948, it was with a new energy, and soon enough, she met a young man who shared her dreams: William Edward Myers Jr. Daisy met him at the Hampton Institute, where she had enrolled to take classes. Six foot tall, 192 pounds, athletically built with a warm smile and pencil-thin mustache, Bill was walking down the hall with a belt full of tools when she first laid eyes on him. At twenty-five, he was a Hampton Institute graduate and, now, chief engineer—teaching classes in industrial arts and overseeing maintenance. Bill was a dedicated repairman who could bring a wrench to an air conditioner or a transmission with equal gusto. As Daisy discovered after a few dates, Bill was even more passionate about the promise of racial equality in the North—and the troubles facing blacks in the South. And he had his own fix-it for the problem: leave.

As he enthusiastically told her during long, slow strolls across campus, the place he dreamed of going back to was his childhood hometown up North: York, Pennsylvania. Bill regaled Daisy with starry-eyed descriptions of his life in this model town. Born on November 16, 1923, Bill had grown up among whites. His father, William, worked for years as a bellman at the Yorktown hotel and became close with the white family who owned it. He was said to be the first black man in York to own his own car.

The Myerses were the only African-American family living in a white neighborhood near the hotel, but Bill told Daisy he had never felt out of place. In fact, he became known for his willingness to cross racial lines. A gifted clarinetist, Bill's favorite musician was Benny Goodman, the white player, and Bill became the first black person to join his all-white high school band. The other kids nicknamed him Benny. Bill was also a star basketball player and earned a sports scholarship to attend Hampton Institute.

After such a happy childhood in York, he despised the restrictive life in Virginia. When he went to buy a car, the salesman ignored him despite the money he had to spend. When he inquired about joining an engineering union, he was told he couldn't because he was black. Even after two and one-half years away serving in the Army Quartermaster Corps in World War II, it felt bittersweet to come back.

The worst experience happened when his mother, Minerva, came for a visit—her first to the South. Unfamiliar with the local ways, Minerva boarded a bus and sat in a seat in the front, only to have the white man next to her push her off the seat. No one rose to help. Bill was outraged when he heard the story, and his mother vowed never to return. He couldn't blame her and promised to head back to York at his first opportunity.

Daisy listened to Bill's stories with mixed emotions. They had so much in common—their love of music and sports. They'd shoot baskets together. Daisy would play the piano, and Bill would accompany her on the clarinet. She saw how sweetly he treated his mother, a good sign. "A man who is good to his mother is usually good to his lady friend," she'd say. Even better, she thought, he never says no to me. Daisy was falling in love, but this man wanted nothing to do with the community she held so close to her heart. At the same time, she had experienced life up North, and Bill's passion inspired her.

One day, they were parked together at their favorite spot—a bluff overlooking the copper blue waters of Chesapeake Bay. Bill looked at Daisy and said, "I'm going to marry you." Daisy agreed. They would leave the past behind and find their new home, a freer life, they resolved, up North.

Three

DODGERS FANS

IT WAS APRIL 15, 1947, and the radio was on. Inside a modest apartment in the Bronx, the announcer said that Jackie Robinson, the first African-American baseball player in the major leagues, had stepped out onto Ebbets Field in Brooklyn. He had just broken the color barrier in America's favorite game by joining the Brooklyn Dodgers. Despite being lifelong Yankees fans, Lew Wechsler, a stocky twenty-eight-year-old with close-cropped hair and deep-set eyes, and his spry curly-haired, twenty-seven-year-old wife, Bea, eight months pregnant, let out a cheer. "Why did you do that, Daddy?" asked Katy, their three-year-old daughter. "Because, honey," replied Lew in his thick New York accent, "we don't like the Yankees anymore. We like the Dodgers. They're our team."

For Bea and Lew, switching allegiances was a no-brainer—even though Lew had grown up just outside Yankee Stadium. As die-hard activists, they had risked everything—their jobs, their security, even their lives—for the sake of social causes. Their vision of the American Dream was built on the conviction that they could change the world, and they were young enough to believe it. The Levitts built and sold the fantasy of a perfect home for the wealthy. Daisy and Bill Myers struggled to find happiness despite exclusion. And the Wechslers—for generations—had been fighting to tear the divide down, just as Robinson had done this day in Brooklyn.

For Bea, the revolutionary spirit was in her DNA. Both her parents were radicals. As a boy in Latvia, her father, Moses Chasanov, faced mandatory military service for a cause in which he didn't believe. The army representatives came to his family's house to get him. Chasanov's trunk waited for them at the door. When they stooped to pick it up, the heavy trunk couldn't be moved. They opened it to find it filled with rocks. Eighteen-year-old Chasanov watched the comical display from a nearby tree. Let them struggle! he chuckled to himself. Then he scurried down and ran off for a boat headed to America—never to return.

In Ukraine, Bea's mother, Eva Schwartz, had even more trouble with the authorities. By sixteen, she was imprisoned as an anarchist in the revolutionary movement. Just as she was to be sent to Siberia, she got smuggled out of prison by the underground. But her mother warned her to stay away—the czarists, she said, had captured and killed her younger brother. Her mother eventually met her, and they went to New York City, seeking freedom too.

Bea was born on September 5, 1919, and raised in the East Bronx. But her own fighting spirit was not just a matter of genetics. Her father left the family when she was five to live in Florida, and Bea, the youngest of three kids, relied on her fiery streak and Bronx-fed street smarts to get by. At Hunter College High School, she stood out as both a skilled modern dancer and a budding radical just like her mom. The lunchroom sold potatoes for five cents apiece, a fortune for poor families such as Bea's. But she found a way to fight back—by leading a protest as part of a controversial new organization, the National Student League.

Formed in 1931, the National Student League was a Communist-led, student-run organization that had risen from the ashes of the Depression. It grew out of the Student League for Industrial Democracy, a socialist group founded by Upton Sinclair, Jack London, and others. The stock market crash had shattered student support of Republicans after the boom years of the previous decade. As employment and loans vanished, the National Student League provided a more active means of protesting the problems—from student and worker rights to racial equality. But because it was linked with socialists and Communists, being a member of this group was to make oneself an easy target. One letter writer to the *New*

York Times compared the activist students and their "Communist propaganda" to mosquitoes that needed to be exterminated.

On April 12, 1935, fifteen-year-old Bea got her first taste of the limelight. The occasion was a student strike for peace, a national day of protest that had brought the National Student League and its members to the forefront. Thousands of students from around the country rallied against war and fascism. Despite their links with Communism, they had supporters, including Albert Einstein, who heralded the students fight for world peace. "The creation of the deeply felt good-will is the first important step to attain that goal," Einstein said.

Not everyone agreed. As the students crowded into the streets with their ABOLISH the ROTC protest signs, they were met with flying eggs. Most of the protesters were in college; few high school students had the nerve to join the ranks. But Bea was among them. Outside Hunter College, the streets teemed with young people—hoisting signs, singing protest songs, and chanting antiwar slogans. College students took turns on a soapbox, and Bea felt that unique electricity of being a young person, surrounded by other young people, rallying together for a cause.

What she didn't expect was to be the center of attention. "We have a student from the high school who'd like to speak," announced one of the college kids on the soapbox to Bea's surprise. He was volunteering Bea, who reluctantly took the stage. "Greetings from high school!" Bea said, as the crowd cheered. Her speech against the war was brief, but successful, and she was met with a wave of accolades. Then she was taken straight to the principal's office.

"You betrayed me," said the principal.

"I just wanted to talk to the other students," Bea replied.

But the principal wasn't having any of it and told Bea she was swimming into dangerous waters filled with criminals and murderers. When Bea's mother heard that the school was threatening disciplinary action, she stormed past the principal's secretary into the office. "Don't you ever call my daughter a murderer again!" her mother snapped. If Bea was going to continue her activities with the National Student League, she realized she would need help taking on this administration. One day she looked up and saw just the guy: a stocky West Bronx boy from City

College of New York with a fistful of yellow leaflets and a warm, wide smile, Lew.

Like Bea, Lew Wechsler was raised with the conviction that he could make the world a better place. His mother, Ray, a teacher and social worker, and his father, Maurice, a fur tradesman, were socially active. When poor tenants were evicted from their apartments in the Bronx, Maurice was the first one helping them move their furniture back into their homes from the street. Born on November 25, 1918, young Lew quickly became aware of the discrepancies in people's living conditions. The African-American kids in his school told stories of their families paying as much for a run-down one-bedroom apartment as his family was paying for a three-bedroom.

Lew became just as strong-willed as his father. At DeWitt Clinton High School in the Bronx in the 1930s, an English-literature teacher began making pro-Nazi statements in class. Jews were a minority in the school of Italians and African-Americans. But Lew and his buddies weren't having any of it, and they defiantly spoke against the rising tides of fascism whenever the teacher aired her views. But there would be a price. The teacher was also Lew's faculty adviser, and she wrote a scathing assessment of the boy, describing him as "an agitator of an extremely obnoxious type."

But after graduation, Lew found like-minded activists in the 1930s as a nonmatriculated student at the City College of New York in the Bronx. Lew became a leader in the National Student League and would venture far into Manhattan just to make inexpensive yellow leaflets to pass out to his peers—including Bea, whom he had briefly met. In December 1935, however, they would again meet, at a national convention in Columbus, Ohio, to announce the merging of two left-wing student groups— the National Student League and the Student League for Industrial Democracy—into the American Student Union.

The ASU drew up rallying points: forming an alliance between the union and labor, fighting fascism, and defending civil rights. "It condemns the 'southern system' of keeping the Negro in servitude by denying him an education," wrote the *New York Times*. Lew organized the buses of those attending from New York, and when Bea came on board, the two rekindled their friendship and became inseparable. They married in 1940 in a Bronx courthouse.

Before long, they were meeting as a team with radicals from around the region. On one trip, they went up to a secret meeting place in Canada and were ushered into a back room of a building with blackened windows. They collected money to send activists to fight in the war in Spain. Many of their friends died in battle. They would go to rallies and be physically attacked. Lew got a job as a waiter in the Catskills and fought to organize a union. The hot-button issue: housing. Waiters were being shacked up in run-down cottages nicknamed the doghouses, with twelve people jammed in three tiny rooms. Lew's efforts led to better living and working conditions, but not without repercussions.

One day, when Bea was home alone pregnant, there was a loud pounding at the door. She opened it to find two thuggish representatives from the right-wing International Waiters Union who didn't like her husband's ways. "We gotta convert your husband into a good person," one of the big tough guys told her in a thick New York accent. Bea was characteristically firm. "Why don't you leave my husband alone?" she said, and slammed the door.

In 1944, Lew would get called away for another reason: to serve as a rifleman in World War II. Though the Wechslers were not pacifists—they believed in the war against the fascists and the need to fight—it was difficult to have Lew go. Bea, who had the year before given birth to Katy, remained in New York with her sister, Florence, and the two raised their children together while their husbands fought overseas. After her brother-in-law was killed, Bea could only dream of the day when Lew would come home to build their new life together.

The Wechslers weren't the only ones hanging on to this hope. As the war dragged brutally on, the fantasy of a dream house in the suburbs took on an even greater role in the popular imagination. It wasn't just a matter of escape from reality; home ownership was an explicit way, American leaders suggested, to keep the nation strong. There was just one problem.

People like the Wechslers wouldn't share in this future if the dream makers could help it.

"Ownership of homes is the best guarantee against communism and socialism and the various bad 'isms' of life," wrote one social scientist in 1938. "I do not say that it is an infallible guarantee, but I do say that owners of homes usually are more interested in the safeguarding of our national history than are renters and tenants." President Franklin Roosevelt echoed the sentiment four years later when addressing the United States Savings and Loan League: "A nation of homeowners, of people who own a real share in their land, is unconquerable."

Popular culture began reflecting a utopian vision of life in the suburbs. At the New York World's Fair in 1939, army wives and their children strolled through twenty-one homes in an artificial suburb called the Town of Tomorrow. Pop songs such as "My Blue Heaven" and "We'll Build a Bungalow Big Enough for Two" hit the radio. The book *Mr. Blandings Builds His Dream House*, the story of new suburbanites, was a bestseller and a film starring Cary Grant. Magazines such as *Ladies' Home Journal* began churning out glossy spreads on "dream homes" designed by top architects.

Accompanying ads happily sold the idea of a home. "All the fighting power of their nation is directed toward securing, for [soldiers] and their children, the one thing in life they value most: a happy and livable home . . . ," read an ad in *Better Homes and Gardens*. "The home is the sound and constructive force, the builder of national characters . . . and what, for them makes up such a home? Love, freedom and human kindness of course. But also a host of little things—a new better room for Junior, a den for dad. New furniture for the living room. A glassed in porch . . . A housewife's faith that gay flowers can continue to bloom, year after year, in a little garden forever safe from the violation of a conqueror's boots."

The government created the Servicemen's Readjustment Act, including the GI Bill of Rights, in 1944 as a way of making those flowers bloom. The GI Bill offered veterans a real dream: a low-interest no-money-down mortgage. Affording a home was one thing; finding one to buy, however, was another. By the time the war ended in 1945, veterans found that coming back alive was one matter—coming back to a home, something else entirely. The country was in a housing crisis. It came after the perfect storm of the highest birth rate in twenty years along with a plunge in new home construction. Nineteen forty-five would be the sixteenth year in a row that new construction fell short of housing demand.

As a result, vets and their clans had to shack up wherever, and however, they could. Six million moved in with family and friends. And they were the lucky ones. "Most veterans said they were doubling up with in-laws and . . . said they would take anything with four walls," reported the *New York Times*. Literally. Trailers and trolley cars, iceboxes and grain bins, became makeshift homes. A half million families lived in Quonset huts. One senator, an amateur country singer, took the cause to the steps of the U.S. Capitol when, with his wife and kids, he sang, "Oh, give me a home near the Capitol dome, with a yard where the little children can play. Just one room or two, any old thing will do, oh, we cain't find a pla-ace to stay."

While the picture of veterans living in chicken coops had become a national tragedy, a battle was waging over public versus private housing solutions—and the fear of Communism took center stage. In 1945, supporters of multifamily housing introduced the Taft-Ellender-Wagner housing bill as a means of jump-starting public housing projects. But their so-called "un-American" plot garnered high-profile opponents. One day in 1947, a gaggle of reporters trailed after a brisk junior senator through the Rego Park Veterans Housing Project in Queens, New York. It was "a deliberately created slum area, at federal expense," said the thirty-eight-year-old junior senator from Wisconsin, "a breeding ground for Communists." His name was Joseph McCarthy.

Years before he was known on a national stage, McCarthy had glommed on to the issue of public housing as a way of kick-starting his political career. His platform: running hearings for the U.S. Senate Joint Committee Study and Investigation of Housing. Over five months from 1947 to 1948, 1,286 witnesses testified in thirty-three cities as a means, ostensibly, to figure out the roots of the housing problems. McCarthy made no bones about where he put his hopes: builders. "There are those who maintain that because private enterprise has not solved the entire problem, we should scrap private enterprise and socialize housing," he said. "But it seems logical that instead of attempting to scrap private enterprise we should furnish the necessary aids to make it work."

That he hired a publicity firm that also backed the National Association of Home Builders, the National Association of Real Estate Boards, and the U.S. Savings and Loan League was not lost on his opponents. Planes dropped flyers over Lubbock, Texas, with the words "Do You Believe in Socialism? No! Is Public Housing Socialism? Yes!" Magazines and newsreels took up the cause and a target: unions. Painters and bricklayers were criticized for not working fast enough, and thwarting the path of progress. The hotbed of unions and activists was New York City. When Lew came back to city in 1945 after eighteen months on the front lines in Europe, he and Bea were ready to fight.

Bea was sitting in the offices of the Bronx Tenants Council when a young African-American woman, Sophie Decatur, came through the door. Bea had joined the council as a way of dealing with landlord disputes, but Decatur's story was hardly the usual. The young mother of two explained that she and her husband, a railroad porter, lived in Parkchester, a housing development in the Bronx owned by the Metropolitan Life Insurance Company. Met Life was among those embroiled in the housing crisis and had been a McCarthyesque example of how private industry could step up to the plate. But Met Life's plan was not all that it seemed.

Decatur told Bea that her family was being evicted simply because they were black. Met Life had a policy of not selling or renting to African-Americans in New York. But because the Decaturs had been subletting their apartment from a white family, they had gone unnoticed—until now. And because of the color of their skin, this young mother and her children were being thrown out onto the street. Decatur wanted to know if Bea and the Bronx Tenants Council could do anything to help.

Decatur had come to the right woman. After a lifetime of activism, Bea and Lew had stepped up in their causes since his return from the war. They were not teenagers fighting against higher lunchroom prices anymore, they were adults, and true believers in their fights. No cause was too big or too small. And despite now having two children, they were more committed than ever to changing the world, even if their safety in the rising tide of red-baiting was at stake.

Before one rally, Lew put on his best suit, and Bea and the kids also dressed to the nines. They were going to be photographed and attacked, they knew, and they had to look good. Katy and Nick, their second child, who arrived in 1947, heard the crowd rallying for peace. They and the other kids started chanting for ice cream. Then the eggs started flying from the crowd, pelting their finest threads. Such events became a regular occurrence. While other kids were sitting on Santa's lap, Katy and Nick were at a rally on the knee of activist Paul Robeson. In summers, Katy and Nick attended camps with other "red diaper babies." At the end of the Korean War, the camp released symbolic pigeons in the mess hall.

Peace was the topic at the kids' schools too. One day, the children were told that they had to wear dog tags so that, if the school was bombed by the Russians, they could be identified. This terrified Katy so much that she refused to put them on. "Sorry," she informed a school administrator, "I'm not wearing this dog tag because it means they're going to bomb me."

The administrator looked condescendingly upon this plucky, curly-haired girl. "Take it home and show you mother," he replied curtly.

Katy arched a brow and said, "You don't know my mother." Sure enough, Bea marched into school, and after that, Katy never had to wear the dog tags again.

The Wechslers' associations and activities, however, came at a price. From as long as the kids could remember, strange men in dark suits would show up at their front door: the FBI. After enough visits, little Katy opened the door to a man in a suit and said matter-of-factly, "Oh, you want to see my daddy." When Bea heard the commotion, she slammed the door in the guy's face and told Katy she was never to speak with such men. Lew soon began losing jobs because of his political activities. When Lew came home with his toolbox, the family knew he'd been fired that day.

During the trial of suspected Communists Julius and Ethel Rosenberg, the Wechsler family took to the streets in their support. "These were good people who believed in peace and justice and were arrested for their beliefs," Bea and Lew told their kids. But it was to no avail. On June 19, 1953, the family sat in their apartment listening to the radio as news came of the Rosenbergs' execution. Katy looked out the window and saw a bloodred sun setting in the distance. A chill shot through her body. It could have been Mom and Dad, she thought.

But nothing could keep the Wechslers from their fights. And the fight for the Decaturs was on. On the day of the family's scheduled eviction, Bea showed up at their home with other representatives from the Tenants Council. The eviction team came in as Sophie Decatur was cooking dinner for her two kids. But that didn't stop them. When Bea and her team refused to move, the tough guys closed in—grabbing them and throwing them down a flight of steps.

Bea was bruised and, worse, defeated. All these protests, all these fights, and for what? But she picked herself right up and hatched a plan. She knew of a perfect place where the Decaturs could move: the Wechslers' house. The time had come, Bea and Lew decided, to move from the Bronx. Lew had recently completed a master's degree in social work at Columbia and wanted to join the workers in a steel mill outside the city. Bea's sister, Florence, and her family had already left for similar pursuits, and Bea agreed to move. With the Wechslers out, the Decaturs could take over their lease and get back to their lives once and for all.

There was just one problem: Nick and Katy didn't want to leave. They were happy with their friends and school. But Bea and Lew cut them a deal. If the kids would move, they would get two things they always wanted: a dog, and a trip to see the family hero Jackie Robinson play ball. Nick and Katy considered the offer and accepted. The Wechslers would go to the suburbs. And they knew just the place.

Four

THE PERFECT PLAN

BILL LEVITT KNEW just where to find his little brother, Alfred: deep down inside "the Hole." The Hole was Alfred's family's nickname for the home office bunker he had designed for himself. To get there, Bill had to squeeze through what used to be Alfred's wife Sylvia's walk-in closet, through a hole in the wall that Alfred had punched for a door, and down a narrow stairwell into the darkness. There, Alfred sat in his bathrobe in his cozy little room, coffee in hand, science fiction magazines on the floor, dreaming up the homes of tomorrow. As one journalist put it, for Alfred inspiration was never lacking. Alfred would "wake up at 3 a.m. with an idea for a movable storage wall."

The Hole was located partially underground in the new home thirty-year-old Alfred had designed for his family in Cedarhurst, Long Island. It sat on 3.5 acres with a tennis court and a swimming pool. Like the rest of America, the Levitts were consumed with the fantasy of their dream home—the difference: while most lost their shirts in the Depression, the Levitts earned enough money to realize their goals. By 1940, Levitt & Sons was already a great success—but not without its problems. A palpable tension existed between the ambitious young brothers. Bill craved the spotlight, and Alfred felt his innovations were either overshadowed or claimed by his big brother. But, as in many great partnerships, the conflict fueled advancement.

The Levitts had completed more than two thousand homes in the upper-crust neighborhoods of Long Island's Gold Coast. Life was good.

Abe was known to walk down the street and toss coins to children. Bill, thirty-four, had fulfilled his lifelong dream of having "a big car and a lot of clothes." Alfred disappeared into his lair to sketch, read pulp magazines, and play chess. To celebrate their success, Alfred and Bill built homes of their own down the block from each other on an aptly named regal spot, King's Point Road.

But the good times would come to an end on December 7, 1941, when the bombs fell on Pearl Harbor. With World War II on, the government put an end to almost all building except for war-related projects. The Levitts weighed the choices: lose their business or make a pact with Uncle Sam. Seeing an opportunity, they struck a deal to build 750 rental homes for naval officers in Norfolk, Virginia. There was just one problem: it had to be done in a year, nearly a quarter of the time they figured it would take them to complete. The best discoveries come under pressure. And for the young, self-taught builders the solution was simple; as Bill put it, "We have to dream up new methods."

They found inspiration in mass production. Ford had brought the assembly line to the automotive industry with great success. As Alfred well knew, they weren't the only home builders paying attention. In 1936, he had spent months watching and learning from famed architect Frank Lloyd Wright, who was building a home in Great Neck. "He told me about certain houses that he had in mind for mass production in this country," Alfred recalled, ". . . built of brick and steel rod. The roof was to be flat. And when I did slip in 'How would that be finished?' he said, 'A half dozen or two dozen shovels of topsoil, but then there's the problem of weeds' . . . The noncompromising attitude of topsoil on the roof or high skill in detail that 99 per cent of American architects draw and insist upon is so unrealistic that if this is the form in which they believe that their sense of art appreciation can be passed on to the American people, they are up in the clouds in their dreams."

The Levitts determined to bring mass production more down to earth. They framed an entire wall on the ground, then raised it up in place. They churned out their own precast concrete septic tanks, allowing them to make twenty in a day instead of the usual one. They poured long strips of concrete floor slabs and hoisted a plumbing tree and prebuilt chimney from the muck. With Bill selling the plan and Alfred engineering the production, Abe, the horticulturalist, focused on bringing the homes to life. He made sure that each home came with a variety of trees—apple, crab apple, chestnut—and shrubs. "It is part of my special department, landscaping," Abe said, ". . . and it's one special thing which we intend to do always hereafter." Some in the company jokingly called him Levitt & Sons' "vice president in charge of grass seed."

Not only did they complete the Norfolk job, they shaved two months off the deadline—and were rewarded with more homes to build. By the end of the war, they would build 2,350 homes for the federal government in record time. It convinced them of something that would shape their futures: inexpensive homes could be mass-produced. When Bill shipped off to serve during the war, he only grew in confidence. In 1944, Bill went to Oahu to join the Seabees, the navy's construction division, as a lieutenant. As he later bragged, the military had more to learn from him than the other way around: "That little branch of the Navy that had the pleasure of my company learned much more about building from me than I did from them."

Bill's ego swelled in the company of the 260 servicemen he managed. As the press later recounted, in the navy he learned how to "disobey orders and ignore red tape." Levitt made sure his men had the best accommodations—and would hustle to get them, striking deals for vodka, the finest chocolate, or Johnnie Walker Red. They would stay up all hours singing Hawaiian songs as he played the piano and sipped a dry martini.

Back at home, his brother, Alfred, tended to the business because he was flat-footed and unable to serve. As the war raged on, he saw the need for housing reach crisis proportions. "How can we expect to sell democracy in Europe until we prove that within the democratic system we can provide decent homes for our people?" President Truman would later say. Alfred read ads in the pages of architecture magazines urging builders to get ready for the postwar efforts. "Are you doodling or planning for that building boom?" one advertisement read, over a sketch of a spherical science fiction home on a farm. For Alfred, there would be no dreaming of fantastical utopias anymore. As the homes in Norfolk popped up around him, he realized the fantasy houses could become a reality.

Bill agreed. All the elements were in place: the demand, sixteen million veterans were coming back to America in need of homes; the government subsidies provided by the GI Bill; the innovations in mass production; and banks "busting with money," as Bill put it. The time was ripe for the Levitts to cash in. While sitting with companions at Pearl Harbor, Bill said, "Do you fellows realize that for five years, the year before the war and four more for us, there's been literally no housing built for people. Some defense housing, but that's all. And when we get home, there's going to be a mad rush." So he made the troops a promise. When I get back, he told them, I'm going to build you your homes.

Then he telegrammed his father, Abe, and his brother, Alfred: "Buy all the land you possibly can . . . Beg, borrow or steal the money and then build and build."

Like some great science fiction movie, it started with an invasion and ended with heroes. The invasion came in the form of a tiny parasite called the golden nematode, which was ravaging the potato crops over thousands of acres in Island Trees, a farming community in Long Island. In 1946 the Levitts came to the farmers with cash and the offer of a lifetime: Sell us your land. Before long, they had amassed over thirty-five hundred acres of potato fields. And the Levitts hatched their ambitious plan: to mass-produce the American dream for the common people, the veterans coming home from the war. They would build a town.

With pencil in hand, Alfred descended into his Hole and got to work. They weren't just constructing homes, he resolved, they were building a community. As Alfred put it, "Intelligent planning of communities is not a Utopian dream. It is just plain common sense." He drafted up the vision—"a suburban community of several thousand homes, with its own shopping centers, churches, swimming pools, parks, and recreational facilities." There would be winding, curvilinear streets for a rural feel, and culs-de-sac where the kids could play and run. They would, he said, "plan an entire community before the first bulldozer starts clearing the site." His brother, Bill, added: "Access to a swimming pool or a baseball diamond is as important a part of what a purchaser buys as solid walls or a strong roof, because he's not just buying a house, he's buying a way of life."

And the life had to center around a low-cost but inspiring home: the Cape Cod. Alfred stripped them down to the bare essentials: two bedrooms, a living room, a kitchen, and a bathroom. Aside from a couple of nostalgic touches—a birdhouse on each fence that matched the shutters, a relief of a candle on each banister—the homes would be models of futuristic cleanliness and ease. "There will be no need for chiffoniers or dressing tables in these little houses," Abe boasted to the press. "That furniture will all be a part of the closets, which will cover an entire wall of each bedroom and contain appropriate storage space for all clothing of all members of the household, as well as linen and blankets. There will be thirty-two closets in all. They will be shallow, and when any closet door is opened, a light will go on automatically, so that no one need rummage to find what he wants."

There would be a bookcase in the stairwell, a kitchen hutch, a metal linen closet with pink and gray wallpaper, venetian blinds. With Bill's shrewd deal-making skills, they planned to fill each home with state-of-the-art and name-brand accessories: stainless steel Tracy sinks, General Electric stove and refrigerator, a Bendix washing machine. Bill, as always, wrote up the ads like Barnum promoting the greatest show on earth. "Mrs. Kilroy Gets the Best," he penned for an ad promoting the automatic washer included in the Levittown homes. One legendary adman balked at Levitt's insistence upon doing his own ads, telling him he was violating every rule of the trade—but, he added, Levitt did write good copy. And the copy sold homes.

With Abe at the helm, there would be plenty of fruit trees and shrubs outside. "Every man has a right to flowers!" Abe declared to one reporter. In all, despite the constraints, the Levitts didn't view the homes as antiseptic 750-square-foot boxes. They were what some architects called "machines for the living," made to be modified. Each home had a stairwell leading up to an unfinished attic that could be built out. With the living room and the kitchen in the front of the house, expanding the back would be an easy bump-out project. The house was a small postage stamp on a sixty-by-hundred-foot lot, with plenty of room to build.

For Alfred, coming up with the finished product was an inspirational work-in-progress. "We don't follow a recipe," he said. "We build by taste, like a good cook." Architecture critics would marvel at his unconventional approach. "Alfred [draws] on all sorts of muses," wrote one, "from Wright to the sliding-glass windows at a White Castle hamburger stand (the spark for using double-glazed Thermopane) to the ancient Romans' diversion of hot-water springs under stone floors (which inspired the radiant heat coils embedded in Levittown's concrete slabs)." If Alfred didn't like how a house was turning out, he would tear it down and start again; the model home went up and down thirty times, at a cost of $50,000, before completion.

But it would take a machinelike process to build these machinelike homes. The production would be standardized to churn out homes like cars on an assembly line, except, in this case, the assembly line came to the product. The idea was to own and automate as much as possible, and they already had all the essentials in place. They owned a lumber mill in Blue Lake, California, that would provide the wood. The nails would come from their own factory; the cement, poured by their own mixers. To construct a home, different people with specialized skills would show up and do their task. "Teams of two or three men progressing from house to house, doing the same job on each, whether it be installing a door knob or planting a tree," as one article hyped.

And the Levitts would not be slowed down by the unions. Instead, they resolved to hire nonunion workers, whom they would pay not by the hour, but by completed projects. It was a key to what they viewed as their success in mass production: not creating a new technique, but refining one and making it more efficient. With money and patriotic zeal fueling him, Bill refused to let building codes stand in their way either. Part of Alfred's plan was to jettison basements for concrete slabs as they'd used in Norfolk. The slabs would have copper tubing for radiant heating, just like ancient Rome, as Bill reminded the skeptics. But the

history lesson didn't play with the Hempstead Town Board; code required basements, period. Without approval, the Levitts couldn't break
ground. So Bill rolled up his sleeves, sat down at his desk, and prepared
for the fight.

He knew just whom he needed to help him: the veterans of World
War II. He already had them on his side. Word had spread of the Levitts'
plan to take the vets out of the chicken coops and put them into homes.
The goal, ultimately, was to sell the homes, but for now they would be
available for rent at just $60 per month. They had no idea how many
homes they'd fill. On May 7, 1947, they announced their intention to
build two thousand rentals for veterans. For a change, they were thinking small. Half the homes were rented in two days; before long, 4,495
applicants had put down a $60 deposit for their slice of the American
Dream. But it would mean nothing if the Levitts couldn't get their slabs
approved, Bill explained in an advertisement he wrote to appeal to the
troops.

"Be at the public hearing at the town hall in Hempstead on Tuesday,
May 27th at 10:30 a.m. for the public hearing to determine whether
these houses can be built as we have designed them," Bill wrote. "The
town board has called this public hearing, and unless you and your friends
are there, it may not be approved. If you want modern, comfortable,
beautiful housing at a rental within your reach, you must be there! We're
doing our part; you must do yours!"

Bill awoke that morning not knowing who, if anyone, would show.
But one by one the men came, then in droves, in defiance. The veterans
were joined by their wives and babies, who jammed into the hall and
fought for their homes. The Hempstead Board heard the outcry and
overturned the building code. The basements were gone. Levitt had won
and was bolstered by his power to defy the law. "Very quickly breaking
all precedent, the building code was changed," he said. "A small builder
could not have brought that about." The papers agreed. A photo spread
of the hearing scene was captioned, "A Hero in the eyes of those who attended the hearing yesterday, William Levitt . . . is all but hidden, by
people crowding to shake his hand."

It was time to build. But Bill wanted one last thing: to rename the town of Island Trees, where he was building his community, after his family. His father and brother, however, didn't agree. In many loud arguments, they fought against the arrogant notion of anointing the land in their own honor. But Bill, argumentative and egotistical, won in the end, as always. When the local paper objected to the notion, Bill trumped them too—by buying the paper and becoming the publisher himself. "I wanted the new name as a kind of monument to my family," he later explained. "And, by gosh, I wasn't going to brook any interference." Good-bye, Island Trees; hello, Levittown.

The Levittown machine kicked into high gear in 1948. The home building was broken down into twenty-six assembly-line steps—from digging the footings through putting on shingles and exterior landscaping. Workers came and went like ants as newsreels filmed the progress. By July, Levitt & Sons had soared from making eighteen homes a day to thirty. It was postwar American innovation at its best.

As the first tenants moved in, images of their joyous homecomings swept America. That Levittown was just a bunch of half-built homes on muddy fields made no difference. When the veteran carried his wife across the broken path into his new home, that was all that mattered. The neighbors swapped tools, helped each other outfit their homes, brought flowers and food. Door-to-door salesmen showed up with accessories to meet their needs. "Milk wagons raced each other to the occupied house while a truck advertising a diaper service roamed hopefully up and down the streets," reported *Newsday*, the large newspaper servicing Long Island and Queens. Inside the homes, the new washing machines were happily spinning. The war after the war—the battle to house the troops—had been won.

The media anointed Bill Levitt, the face of the company, as American royalty. Though the Levitts had not invented suburbia or mass production or a variety of other innovations, they had the knack and the timing to become the ones who personified these trends. Reporters from *Time*, *Life*, *Fortune*, *Reader's Digest*, and *Newsweek* lined up to interview Bill Levitt—and that was all in just one week. LEVITT LICKS THE HOUSING

SHORTAGE trumpeted one typical headline. AN ACCOMPLISHMENT OF
HEROIC PROPORTIONS said another. *Newsday* declared it a "model community." And what the media most admired was Bill Levitt's Great American tenacity; he was a warrior of industry out to save the ordinary man.
"Any other builder at any other time would not have had the organization," *Harper's* said, "could not have bypassed union restrictions, and
could not have secured the financing. The Levitt story is a tale of how he
was relieved of some of these obstacles, got around others, and ran into
the remainder head foremost and knocked them down."

Bill Levitt had a way of making everyone play by his rules. And in his
brave new town, there were plenty to go by. To live in Levittown, residents had to follow the list of rules spelled out in the lease. "Item 17: No
fences, either fabricated or growing, upon any part of the premises . . .
Item 21: No laundry poles or lines outside of the house, except that of a
portable revolving laundry drier."

The most important rules were emphasized in all-capital letters. "THE
TENANT AGREES NOT TO RUN OR PARK OR PERMIT TO BE
RUN OR PARKED ANY MOTOR VEHICLES," and "THE TENANT
AGREES TO CUT OR CAUSE TO BE CUT THE LAWN AND RE-
MOVE OR CAUSE TO BE REMOVED TALL GROWING WEEDS
AT LEAST ONCE A WEEK BETWEEN APRIL FIFTEENTH AND
NOVEMBER FIFTEENTH. UPON THE TENANT'S FAILURE THE
LANDLORD MAY DO SO AND CHARGE THE COST THEREOF
TO THE TENANT AS ADDITIONAL RENT."

The Levitts meant it, particularly Abe. The draconian horticulturalist
would drive the muddy roads through the neighborhoods checking up
on the quality of his nascent lawns and saplings. Residents joked that
they knew he was coming when they saw a big black Cadillac slowly inch-
ing down the street without anyone, apparently, behind the wheel; that
was Abe.

When he wasn't making the rounds, he took to admonishing the Levittowners in his column, "Chats on Gardening," in the *Levittown Tribune*.
"Cultivation, cultivation, cultivation!" he once fumed in his column. ". . . I
notice in my inspections that even many of those gardeners who cultivate
do so in an inadequate measure . . . I have said so many times that the use

of a hose with metal nozzle attached should never be used in a garden that I believed the warning would spread and its use discontinued. But I see hundreds doing this very thing and then wondering why their trees and plants die."

He even took parents to task for letting their boys run wild over his precious lawns: "They ride roughshod through the group plantings in parks without thought of the destruction resulting there-from. Won't you warn your boy . . . that his bicycle will be taken from him if he rides over or through plants . . . I raised two boys myself. And I have five grandchildren who, I wager to say, would not throw a piece of paper in any place but a waste basket. It is training, training, and more training that eventually succeeds in making good citizens."

Another capitalized item in the lease would be the most restrictive of all: "THE TENANT AGREES NOT TO PERMIT THE PREMISES TO BE USED OR OCCUPIED BY ANY PERSON OTHER THAN MEMBERS OF THE CAUCASIAN RACE." This was part of the FHA standards that had regulated homogeneous communities for years. But, just as Levittown was gaining steam, it would come under attack. In 1948, the Supreme Court ruled that the clause was "unenforceable as law and contrary to public policy." Bill gave a nod to the most powerful court in the land by later removing the language from the Levitts' leases, but had no intention of changing their policy.

"The policy that has prevailed in the past is exactly the same policy that prevails today," Bill Levitt told the press after announcing the decision in 1949. "It is the same policy that all builders in this area have adopted and the elimination of the clause has changed absolutely nothing . . . Levittown has been and is now progressing as a private enterprise job, and it is entirely in the discretion and judgment of Levitt & Sons as to whom it will rent or sell." Levittown would remain whites-only.

As Levitt said, his was certainly not the only such town in America. But the price of fame was to single out Levittown as the most notable example. Outraged at Levitt's practice, groups including the NAACP, the Civil Rights Congress, and the American Labor Party tried to get the FHA to pull out its mortgage loans from the community because "Levitt is using federal aid and assistance for unconstitutional purposes."

African-American veterans would show up, only to be steered away by Levitt's salesmen. In December 1949, an African-American veteran named Eugene Burnett came to Levittown looking for a home. As he was touring the model house, he approached a salesman and said, "Pretty nice house. I'm interested. Would you give me an outline of the procedure, how do I apply? Do you have an application of some sort?" Burnett watched the salesman's face turn solemn. "It's not me," the salesman explained, "but the owners of this development have not as yet decided whether or not they're going to sell these homes to Negroes."

In another instance, the mother of a World War II veteran went to the Village Green Restaurant in Levittown, where sales agents were making deals for homes. Levitt's attorney looked at her and said, "We will not sell to a Negro veteran." As she was led outside, she found three other black veterans being denied admission to the restaurant at all. The mother and others held a sit-in at Levitt's office, protesting the policy.

Levitt met with the NAACP, but was ambivalent at best. "Give me a chance to get some people in here, because if I start out with black people, I won't get any whites," he explained. "If I get enough white people in here, then I sell to everybody, provided they're acceptable." For Bill, it was a necessary part of the plan—a way to insure his homes against what he feared would be, as he once said, their diminution in value. "We can solve the housing problem or we can solve the racial problem," he said, "but we cannot combine the two." And he had one word to describe those who questioned his ways: *Communists*. "Despite the skeptics and the professional critics and the Communists," he said, "we believe in Levittown, in its honesty and goodness. What's more, we believe most of the tenants feel as we do."

In living rooms across the community, concerned residents formed an activist group called the Committee to End Discrimination in Levittown with the purpose of integrating the town. Despite Levitt's claims that bringing in blacks would trigger white flight, the group released a poll that found 61 percent of residents in Levittown favored allowing black families into the community. Regardless of such findings, an editorial in *Newsday* backed Levitt: "Organizations which appear to be either Communist-dominated or Communist-inspired have been attempting to raise a racial issue at Levittown. The issue did not exist until it was fostered by people not immediately affected by it. Their only real motive seems to be to set race against race, and if possible, to bog down the Levitt building program, which means homes for thousands of people."

Some Levittowners also openly equated the fight for civil rights with Communism. One morning, Yale graduate student John Liell, in town doing research for a dissertation on Levittown, approached an elderly woman to fill out a survey. She eyeballed him skeptically. Is this about "getting niggers into Levittown?" she asked. "Because I don't want anything to do with that." When he told her it wasn't, she explained that "a lot of Communists" in town had that very mission in mind.

An important player in Washington lent his support to Levitt too: McCarthy. For the young senator fighting his early war against what he perceived to be the Communist breeding ground of public housing, Levittown was a model. As he presided over the U.S. Senate Joint Committee Study and Investigation of Housing in 1947 and 1948, he had a powerful partner in the brash Long Island builder, who came to testify on his behalf. "Mr. McCarthy is first a veteran," Levitt quipped, "second a U.S. senator, third a very aggressive young man typical of the type of leadership that you might expect in Washington from now on, and fourth, he exhibits a passionate interest in housing that almost amounts to a phobia. Parenthetically, I might add, he is also a Republican."

Levitt gave McCarthy a personal tour of his model town, and McCarthy posed for photos in front of the washing machines that would be included in every home. The power play paid off. As a result of McCarthy's housing bill, veterans could now get mortgages within their reach. And that was just the fuel the Levitts needed to execute the final stage of their plan: sales.

The Levitts declared that their new ranch models would be available for sale to veterans for the low price of $7,990. Bill marketed it in promotions as "the most remarkable value the United States has seen" and hyped the cutting-edge gadgets and gear they were throwing in: Two-Way Log Burning Fireplace, Thermopane Insulated Glass, Tracy All-Steel Cabinets, and, most remarkable of all, that amazing new invention everyone wanted, a television set, built right into the side of every stairwell.

Vets didn't just heed the call, they camped out. They lined up outside the Levitt sales office in lawn chairs and hammocks with tins of hot coffee, waiting for their turn to sign up the next morning. Outside the door, picketers from the NAACP protested the racial covenant, passing out literature and trying in vain for an hour to gain support. But the buyers were not dissuaded. "We've waited since the end of the war for something like this and now we've found it," said one woman.

Newspaper reporters crushed in to breathlessly report the phenomenon: "In a scene reminiscent of the storming of the gates of Versailles and the Yukon gold rush, almost a thousand veterans, wives and full retinues of kids besieged Levitt and Sons yesterday, clamoring for an audience—and a new house." Even the sales process resembled an assembly line, with rows of salespeople taking checks and handing over keys like something out of a Charlie Chaplin movie. They boasted of selling 650 homes to 1500 buyers in just five hours. "It's even bigger than we thought," Bill Levitt declared.

Business exploded. In 1949, Levitt & Sons built 4,604 homes, which they sold for $42,195,000. By November 1951, just four years after the first family moved into Levittown, the last of the 17,447 homes built on the former potato fields was occupied, and the total population had grown to nearly seventy thousand people. By 1952, the seven Village Greens around Levittown bustled with sixty-six stores—supermarkets, drugstores, barbershops, and dry cleaners. Residents filled the parks and walked to stores to get their goods. Levitt & Sons were building one out of every eight homes in the country. The dream of the model town was realized, and the fairy-tale story behind its creation was gaining traction all over the country.

The Levitts were not just the nation's biggest builders, but icons of optimism, titans on par with Walt Disney and Henry Ford—and better. "I'm not going out on a limb when I say that Levittown might very well be the model for housing projects all over the nation," one Senate committee member said during a visit. "And the Lord God said to Abraham [Levitt], 'Let there be homes! And there were," one reporter wrote. "Only in America could a boy raised in the slums of New York—Abraham Levitt—with only a few years of elementary school learning, become the largest home builder in the world," Levitt & Sons vice president Charles Biederman told the press.

Levittown honored the patriarch by ordaining Abraham Levitt Day in October 1951, and a thousand people crowded into Levittown Hall on the Parkway Village Green to celebrate. After the Levittown Opera played "Glory Road," a bronze plaque was unveiled on the Levittown Hall, depicting the guest of honor. "Levittown to me is just like a child to its parent," Abe said. "It is not just a commercial enterprise, I want the people of Levittown to be happy. Particularly do I want the children to grow up in a fine atmosphere; it's the children I am interested in." Children, he added, including his boys, William and Alfred. "The success of a parent lies in his children."

But as the Levitts' fame grew, it was Bill Levitt who clearly became the country's favorite son—much due to his own flair for self-promotion. Bill would receive the Veterans of Foreign Wars' highest honor, the Good Citizenship medal, for his suburban town. *Life* published a picture of Levitt posing in front of his ivy-covered Manhasset office with the caption "Nation's Biggest Housebuilder."

Time magazine put Levitt on its cover and had, like the rest of America, fallen head over heels for Bill's bold ways. "Levitt and Sons' President William J. Levitt describes the product simply as 'the best house in the U.S.,'" the article read. "Coming from Bill Levitt, that exaggeration is natural, and pardonable. At 43, the leader of the U.S. housing revolution is a cocky, rambunctious hustler with brown hair, cow-sad eyes, a hoarse voice (from smoking three packs of cigarettes a day), and a liking for hyperbole that causes him to describe his height (5 ft. 8 in.) as 'nearly six feet' and his company as the 'General Motors of the housing industry.' His supreme self-confidence—his competitors call it arrogance—is solidly based on the fact that he is the most potent single modernizing influence in a largely antiquated industry."

Now it was time to do even better. Flush from the success on Long Island, the Levitts announced a second development to be built in Pennsylvania, just north of Philadelphia. Ads appeared in magazines painting a picture of happy housewives with sparkling appliances, "quiet, spacious beauty . . . gently curving streets with modern lighting uncluttered by cars . . . Everywhere you look, your eyes rest on the loveliness of well-kept lawns, majestic shade trees, fruit trees and flowering shrubs." This great new mass-produced suburb would, as Bill Levitt wrote in an advertisement, be the "most perfectly planned community in America."

And whites-only.

Five

A GOOD HOME

THEY WANTED WHAT everyone else wanted: a good home in a good community. The Myerses were in their twenties and ready to begin their new life together. As long as Daisy had known Bill, he had effused about the fun and freedom of York. Frustrated with the Jim Crow South, he was more determined to return to Pennsylvania with his new wife, which he did in 1950.

But it only took a few spins around the block with the real estate agents to realize this was no model town after all. Bill had gotten a job as an engineer working on turbines at the York Corporation in town. He had saved up plenty of money to get the house of their dreams. But every time he and Daisy got into an agent's car, they found themselves driven to the poorest, and invariably black, parts of town. The homes there were falling apart with broken windows and rickety foundations. As an erudite fix-it man, Bill knew a bad deal when he saw one. But when they asked to be taken to other parts of town, the agent would just look them in the eye and say that nothing else was available.

While communities such as Levittown had explicit racial covenants in their leases, many places relied on their own means of exclusion. This is called racial steering—the practice of real estate agents refusing to show or rent homes in white neighborhoods to blacks. It infuriated the Myerses, who had broken down color lines for years. After several incidents, Daisy finally lamented the situation to one real estate agent. "You shouldn't feel bad," he explained, "my wife and I can't buy where we want to buy either."

"Why is that?" Daisy said.

"Because we're Jewish."

Unwilling to give up, the Myerses took matters into their own hands. Bill's family had been around long enough to have some connections in high places, and they found an agent to show the young couple a lovely town house at 45 East Maple Street. The brick house had three bedrooms, one and one-half baths, and plenty of room for kids. That only one other African-American family lived in the neighborhood made no difference to Bill and Daisy. This was the home they wanted, and no one could stop them.

Once they moved in, it didn't take them long to realize not everyone was happy about their plan. Late at night, they would hear their neighbors slamming doors or banging the lids of their metal garbage cans. Someone was taking a tin pail and throwing it against the ground again and again and again. Bill and Daisy lay in bed listening to the commotion, but chose not to respond. Just because they were in the North didn't mean they were safe from racial violence. Bill, the more reserved of the two, wasn't one to cause a stir. Daisy tried to ignore as best she could. "You can't think about it as such," she would say, "you have to put it in the back of your mind. Because if you think about things like that as foremost in your mind, you won't get anything done. You won't be able to function." It was best, they decided, to stay quiet.

But they couldn't ignore the couple next door for long. One morning, they heard someone pounding on their front door. "Who are my neighbors?" the person hollered.

"I am," Bill called, "Come upstairs."

The angry man opened the door and marched up the steps, but when he saw Bill, his jawed dropped. "Benny?"

The man had been Bill's high school classmate in York years before—and knew Bill as Benny from his days playing clarinet. Soon the rest of his family came over, including his sister-in-law—the woman, it turned out, who had been banging the doors and cans after the Myerses moved in. "I'm sorry," she told Daisy, "but we didn't know who was moving in here." She tried to explain to Daisy how she had grown up among black people but couldn't help feeling superior to them nonetheless. As she kept clumsily apologizing, Daisy thought, Too little too late.

For Daisy, it was getting difficult to live as she had in Richmond—compartmentalizing her feelings about racism. Though she enjoyed her life on East Maple, she couldn't believe how segregated life in this Northern town was. African-Americans had to sit upstairs away from the whites in the movie theater. As a substitute teacher, she was not allowed to teach in her neighborhood schools, which were white. After answering an ad for a low-rent-housing administrator and speaking with the company by phone, she showed up in person—and the supervisor was surprised to see that she was black.

"*You* are Mrs. Myers?" the supervisor asked.

"Surely," Daisy replied.

The woman, a former social worker, hit it off with Daisy, but she confided that she wasn't sure "whether I'm allowed to hire a Negro or not." Her bosses were conservative white men, she explained.

Daisy felt the woman was sincere. "I understand," she said.

A few days later, Daisy got the call—and, to her surprise, the job. Her responsibility was to interview low-income families to determine if they were eligible for housing loans. She would conduct her interviews in person at their homes. She couldn't believe the conditions of the black families' homes she visited: no running water, no electricity, outhouses instead of bathrooms, seven people living in two squalid rooms. With every trip, she realized how "sheltered," as she put it, she had been all her life.

One day, Daisy interviewed a white man about a possible loan and he said, "They tell me niggers gonna live side by side with white folks out there, and I ain't fillin' out no forms until I find this out." Daisy's supervisor tried to placate the man. "There are many people of different races in this world," she said, "and someday they will learn to live side by side if America is going to be the democratic country she set out to be."

As Daisy listened quietly, she thought to herself, When will people ever learn to get along with each other regardless of color? And how much better the world will be if we can get over that hump. But she wasn't about to throw herself into the fight. I'll leave that to somebody else, she thought.

Across the country, however, plenty of others were taking up the fight for civil rights. They proved that ordinary people could bring about extraordinary change. But they would often pay a price.

Despite the Supreme Court's ruling against racial covenants, terrible events in housing continued. In 1951, an African-American bus driver and veteran in Chicago named Harvey Clark wanted exactly what the Myerses wanted: a decent home. He found one in Cicero, a white suburban neighborhood. But when he showed up in his moving van, he wasn't met by welcoming neighbors. Instead he was met by the police, who told him he needed a special permit to move in. No such permit existed. Then they assaulted him until he fled. Despite eventually winning an injunction against the police, the violence against Clark continued—culminating with a mob breaking into his house and setting his furniture on fire. When a crowd of thirty-five hundred rioted on the site the next night, it took the governor's calling in the National Guard to bring the violence to an end.

Clark wasn't the only one taking a stand. Also in 1951, a battle was brewing in Daisy's home state of Virginia. Barbara Rose Johns, a sixteen-year-old African-American high school junior in the small town of Farmville, organized a student protest against the inequalities of black kids' education. She and her classmates didn't just demand desegregation, they went on strike—refusing to go to class for two weeks. Soon after, the NAACP took up their cause too, filing a case against the county school board to desegregate once and for all.

They had supporters in Topeka, Kansas. There, Oliver Brown wanted his seven-year-old daughter, Linda, to attend a perfectly good white school nearby instead of being bused to an African-American school. The NAACP sued the school board on his behalf. At the same time, another NAACP suit was pending in Clarendon County, South Carolina, where twenty black parents were challenging segregation in their own elementary schools.

The three cases were heard together by the Supreme Court on

December 9, 1952, but the first was *Brown v. Board of Education of Topeka*. Nearly a year and a half later, on May 17, 1954, the ruling finally came along: "We conclude, unanimously, that in the field of public education the doctrine of 'separate but equal' has no place," announced Chief Justice Earl Warren. "Separate educational facilities are inherently unequal." What started with the courageous actions of a few schoolkids and their parents had transformed the nation. With the *Brown* decision, the modern civil rights era had begun.

But as the Myerses and others observed, the harsh realities continued. Despite the *Brown* win, enforcement was another matter entirely. Governors in the South denounced the victory. Georgia governor Herman Talmadge called the decision "a mere scrap of paper," and Governor James F. Byrnes in South Carolina warned that "ending segregation would mark the beginning of the end of civilization in the South as we have known it." Mississippi senator James Eastland said the ruling signified the destruction of the U.S. Constitution. "You are not obliged to obey the decisions of any court which are plainly fraudulent," he advised his minions.

The small town of Money, Mississippi, soon showed how far some Americans were willing to go to fight back. One night in August 1955, Emmett Till, a fourteen-year-old boy from Chicago visiting his grandfather in town, on a dare from friends allegedly exchanged words with a white woman in a convenience store. "Bye, baby," he was thought to have said as he passed her on the way out. Three days later, Till's dead and bloated body washed up on the edge of the Tallahatchie River. A cotton-gin fastened with barbed wire hung from his neck. He had been shot in the head.

Till's death sent shock waves around the country. His mother insisted on an open casket, and a picture of the boy's mangled corpse was published for all to see. It was an indelible image and moment. For white supremacists, it galvanized them against what one editorial writer in Mississippi termed a "Communist plot" to desegregate the South. For African-Americans, it underscored the brutality lurking behind the wealth and prosperity of the postwar nation.

During the widely publicized trial, Till's aging grandfather risked his

life to testify against and identify the suspects: the husband and friends
of the white woman his grandson had passed by. In that simple gesture
of pointing at the suspects, Till's grandfather proved the power an individual could have by taking a stand. But he also showed how unjust the
outcome could be. The all-white male jury, despite the overwhelming
evidence, found the defendants not guilty. As one writer later put it, the
message was clear: "The word spread through the black community. Keep
your mouth shut." And like other Americans across the country, the Myerses heard it loud and clear.

As the Myerses began their new life in York, Daisy had enough distractions to keep her from taking a stand about anything. She and Bill were
busy turning their house into a home. Bill started fixing small appliances
and equipment in the backyard. He became known around the neighborhood for his handiness, and people would routinely bring by appliances for him to fix. But when it would rain or snow, he'd have to head
inside, where there wasn't a suitable space to do this work. One day, he
wished to Daisy, he'd have a house with a garage he could convert into
his workshop.

But they enjoyed their lives as a young couple. At night they'd stayed
up late playing music, Daisy on the piano, Bill on clarinet. They also began a family. In 1952, they had their first child, William III, and, two
years later, Stephen. As the house bustled with activity, Daisy and Bill's
love grew deep and strong. Daisy prided herself on the quality of their
relationship. She made a list of their golden rules: never go to bed angry
with each other, to listen and not just talk, to plan fun things to do with
each other, to make up after a fight, and never be afraid to say "I'm
sorry." Daisy admittedly found this last rule the most challenging of all.
While Bill tended to be amiable, Daisy was considerably more head-
strong. As she would put it, "I feel 'my way' is the right way most of the
time."

While her home life was so strong, however, her job was proving difficult for the most troubling reasons. Despite her tireless work for the
housing administration, racism prevented her advancement. She learned

this when her supervisor—the woman who had hired her and with whom she had become friends—told her she was leaving her post. Daisy was well liked and loyal, clearly the best candidate for the job. But her supervisor's boss coldly let her down. "Mrs. Myers," he said briskly, "a new lady will be in to take over the job as supervisor. I'd like you to teach her everything you know. You see, this lady has no experience in this field but has worked as an accountant."

Daisy's heart sank. When she had applied to work here in the first place, her employers had made a huge deal out of the amount of experience the job required, but now they were hiring someone with no experience. Experience was secondary, Daisy realized, because the applicant was white. Daisy had had enough. Soon after, she marched up to her boss and gave notice. The man begged and pleaded, sheepishly explaining that this wasn't his doing, it was at his boss's insistence. He offered Daisy incentives to stay, including a raise in salary. She and Bill could use extra money, she knew, but Daisy also knew that her way was the right way, and this time she wasn't going to say she was sorry. So she left.

But the cost of her decision didn't take long to arrive. Daisy and Bill had two boys for whom to provide. And just as their overhead was mounting, Bill got laid off from his job. They tried to make ends meet, with Bill picking up odd jobs and Daisy working as a substitute teacher. Their dream of a perfect home and a perfect town would have to wait. For now, they would pack their bags and go to Philadelphia, where, they hoped, more opportunity would be found.

Philadelphia proved a disappointment. They lived in a cramped two-bedroom apartment on the second floor over Walnut, a noisy street. They had both lived in homes their whole lives, and with two little boys now climbing their walls, they desperately wanted to get back into one more than ever. Daisy just wanted what anyone else wanted, she said, "to raise the children somewhere where they have green grass and a fence around it—a home with space and surroundings and good schools. The suburbs are an ideal place for everyone."

In the fall of 1955, they finally found a slice of the American Dream of their own: a two-bedroom home in a community about an hour north of Philadelphia called Bloomsdale Gardens. The houses were attached, four or five in a row, but the development had a warm and open feeling. It was fully integrated, with just as many whites and blacks. The house had green back and front yards, a walkway and a patio. Bill still didn't have his dream garage to convert into his work space, but he agreed to convert the utility room into a makeshift tool room instead.

Life in Bloomsdale Gardens began to resemble the ideal they had harbored for so long. Good neighbors. New friends. Bill found a job working at a refrigeration company in nearby Trenton, New Jersey, where he earned a $5,000 annual salary. He supplemented his income with part-time jobs, such as washing dishes at Howard Johnson's. Daisy cared for their boys and became active in political groups. Bill got voted president of Bloomsdale's Civic Association, and he and Daisy worked to register voters—just as her parents had done in Virginia long ago.

A spirit of change was around them, and they could feel it. Ever since the ruling on *Brown v. Board of Education*, a new era was sweeping the country. When the Myerses settled down after dinner one cold night, they watched the latest struggle unfolding on their black-and-white TV. It was taking place in Montgomery, Alabama. On December 1, 1955, a forty-three-year-old woman who worked as a secretary for the Montgomery NAACP boarded a bus just as on any other day. In the South, as Daisy had long experienced, the buses were segregated. In addition to having to sit in the back of the bus, African-Americans had to give up their seats in the middle section if a white person wanted one. But on this day, when the bus driver told Rosa Parks to get up and relinquish her spot, she refused. And she was arrested.

Word spread of her courageous act, and the black leaders in town quickly organized a boycott of the bus system. It was time to demand equal rights in transportation once and for all. Locals packed the churches to hatch the plan and drew up signs. PEOPLE DON'T RIDE THE BUSES TO-DAY, the signs said, DON'T RIDE IT FOR FREEDOM. Black-run taxicab companies agreed to lower their fares and only charge the equivalent of a bus ride. A group called the Montgomery Improvement Association formed and nominated a leader, a twenty-six-year-old preacher named Martin Luther King Jr.

Crowds packed in to hear the dynamic young man speak. "There

comes a time that people get tired," King intoned. "We are here this evening to say to those who have mistreated us so long that we are tired—
tired of being segregated and humiliated; tired of being kicked about by
the brutal feet of oppression . . . For many years we have shown amazing
patience. We have sometimes given our white brothers the feeling that
we like the way we were being treated. But we come here tonight to be
saved from that patience that makes us patient with anything less than
freedom and justice. One of the great glories of democracy is the right to
protest for right . . . We will not retreat one inch in our fight to secure
and hold on to our American citizenship." The crowd burst into triumphant applause.

With the Myerses and the nation following the saga in newspapers
and on TV, the Montgomery boycott dragged on for months. King
called for a strong but nonviolent protest. The supporters endured long,
tiring walks through cold, awful weather, but did not venture back onto
the buses. They refused to comply until the system was equal—and
open—for all. It would not come easy. In response to the boycott, segre-
gationists were growing in numbers and in power. A bomb went off in
the house of King and another leader. No one was injured but the stakes
were rising. Finally on November 13, 1956, nearly a year after the protest
began, the U.S. Supreme Court ruled that buses would be desegregated
once and for all.

King had become a national icon for a movement on the rise. And
while the Myerses supported his efforts with all their heart, they remained leery of getting too deep into the civil rights struggle themselves.
They had busy lives of kids, jobs, and chores. They had a home. They
weren't about to risk it all for the sake of this fight. "We'll take a back-
seat," Daisy said, "we won't be at the forefront."

But they couldn't ignore the inequalities right in their own backyard. On all sides of Bloomsdale Gardens, a strange new community
was sprouting up. Crews built it wildly fast like some cartoon assembly
line. Trucks plunged saplings into muddy fields. Rows of identical homes
popped up wall by wall from the ground. Busy men carried shiny appliances inside the finished homes. Smiling couples began filling the
houses with their children and dogs. They were young. They were happy.

They had come from miles away to live here in Levittown, Pennsylvania, the second community from the nation's biggest and most beloved builders.

And not one of them was black.

Six

PIONEERS

THEY CALLED HER Biff. The dog was a brown mutt with cute
bright eyes, and best of all, she was now a Wechsler. Little Katy
Wechsler with her dark, curly hair crouched at the end of her narrow
hallway in the Bronx and called her name—"Biff! Biff! Biff!"—for hours,
delighting in watching the swift, little pooch dart up and down the way.
Bea and Lew had given their kids the puppy on the night before they
moved out of the Bronx. Biff was part of their promise—along with an
IOU to go see Jackie Robinson play—in return for moving to the suburbs without a struggle.

By August 1953, the time had come to join what was now the greatest
internal migration the country had seen since the western expansion of
the 1800s: the flight to the suburbs. Flush with postwar money and se-
duced by assembly-line convenience, more than twenty million Americans were moving into these neighborhoods. For veterans such as Lew
eligible for the GI Bill, the iconic place offering the biggest suburban
dream for the littlest money was Levittown. Now the Wechslers were heading to the newest Levittown—being built on five thousand acres of
broccoli and spinach fields in Bucks County, Pennsylvania—to begin
again.

From its inception in 1951, there was one main distinction between
this place people were calling Levittown II and the original one on Long
Island. While the first Levittown had a degree of organization, it was
still, by the family's own admission, a seat-of-the-pants project. But the

new community would be different; in Pennsylvania, it was all about the master plan. "We bought five thousand acres, and we planned every foot of it," Bill Levitt boasted. "Every store, filling station, school, house, apartment, church, color, tree, and shrub" would be coordinated by the Levitts.

The plan started with one of the main reasons to come to the area: jobs. The second-largest steel mill on the East Coast, the Fairless Works of the United States Steel Corporation, was set to open in the Delaware Valley in 1952. The steelworkers would need homes, and housing these blue-collar veterans was the perfect challenge—and market—for the Levitts.

Even more so than the Long Island community, this Levittown, which started with "absolutely nothing," Bill said, would have to be completely built from the ground up: the roads, the sewer and water systems, the homes, and community. For Alfred Levitt, it was a delectable challenge, and he stayed up many a night deep in the Hole of his house sketching out his plan for something that was still new in America: a perfectly planned, but affordable, suburban town. There would be a variety of affordable homes, from the modern ranch Levittowner, to the more upscale Country Clubber, each complete with the built-in appliances and hideaway storage areas that the Levitts had trumpeted on Long Island.

Each neighborhood would be contained in a one-mile-square unit called a master block, with between three hundred and five hundred homes in each. There would be Little League fields, Olympic-size swimming pools, and an enormous shopping plaza that would be the biggest east of the Mississippi. Schools would be close enough, Bill promised, so that "no child will have to walk more than one-half mile to school or cross any major road." Abe Levitt insisted that each plot would have a lawn, over a dozen trees, and more than three dozen shrubs and bushes. In total, he liked to boast, there would be more than forty-eight thousand fruit trees in town—just one reason that magazines such as *House and Home* anointed him "God's gift to the nurseryman."

Each Levittown neighborhood bore an idyllic name—such as Stonybrook, Lakeside, or Birch Valley—and the streets within that area all started with the letter of the alphabet that began the block name. In

Dogwood Hollow, for example, there would be Deepgreen Lane and Daffodil and Daisy streets. The idea was that each neighborhood would assume its own identity and sense of pride. "It is hoped, tender shoots of friendship, kindness, and goodwill can push through the chaos and blight of our machine society," the *New York Times* wrote of Levittown, Pennsylvania's promise.

The Levitts eagerly promoted their new town, taking out full-page ads in the local papers to trumpet their tagline: "The most perfectly planned community in America!" On December 8, 1951, they opened the door to their showroom, a one-story building with glass walls called Houses of Levittown. Mobs of eager home buyers lined up outside waiting to crash in. Inside the showroom, crisp and dutiful sales agents took the couples through the selection of homes, detailing all the modern appliances and amenities that awaited them. Visitors were invited to inspect "all equipment and materials . . . down to the last gallon of paint." By the end of the opening weekend, a staggering thirty thousand people had come through the showroom.

Sales were unstoppable. More than sixteen hundred homes were being sold a month, with up to fifty sales being closed in the showroom at a time. With the first Levittown having already elevated the builders to icons, the second one evoked the greatest hyperbole yet. The *New York Times* called it "one of the most colossal acts of mortal creation." The *Saturday Evening Post* wrote, "Bucolic Bucks County was jarred as it had not been since that other dour December day when word got around that Washington crossed the Delaware." Observers marveled at the utopian planning. "There is no social strata in the community, and therefore no social upper crust," read a community survey. "Everyone is socially on a level with everyone else, thus forms of discrimination associated with Society are eliminated."

After the first residents, John and Philomena Dougherty, moved into the Stonybrook portion of Levittown in June 1952, Bill Levitt vowed to send the woman a bouquet of flowers—roses, carnations, and orchids—every year on the anniversary of their move-in date. "Sure there's a thrill in meeting a demand with a product no one else can," he said. "But I'm not here just to build and sell houses. To be perfectly frank, I'm looking for a little glory too. I want to build a town to be proud of."

One hot summer day, the Wechslers pulled up to the muddy fields of Levittown with Biff barking out the window. They eagerly joined the line of other veterans at the showroom. After years of renting in New York, they were thrilled at the prospect of owning their own home at such a low cost. Lew and Bea eyed the model homes in the showroom and picked out the best one they could afford, the Levittowner.

The home had everything, they marveled. A bedroom for each family member. A backyard for Biff. A fireplace open on both sides. And, best of all, thought Bea, a brand-new washing machine! So much for scrubbing clothes by hand on a board. They fawned over the community amenities—the pool, the playgrounds, the fruit trees. Even a shopping center was on its way. With Bea's sister, Florence, and her family living in Levittown too, it would be like one big happy camp, with all of them together every day, and the cousins within biking distance.

As they drove following the map to their new home, however, they realized that finding their address would be another story. Despite the glossy sales brochure, Levittown, they saw, was still very much a work in progress. Homes were half-built, lawns big muddy tracts. As they slowly rode toward the Dogwood section, they realized the roads even lacked street signs. It was like a Marx Brothers movie. They kept passing the same couples driving in circles with their maps looking for their homes. But when they finally pulled up to a tiny ranch home, second one in from the corner, marked 39 Deepgreen Lane, all they saw was paradise.

The shared experience of pioneering imbued the neighborhood with a deep sense of community. The Wechslers became fast friends with their neighbors across the street, the Wertzes. George Wertz was a hardworking Lutheran steelworker and union man. He and Lew swapped stories about union protests, which Wertz too had participated in upstate. He and his wife had two daughters, who quickly pulled Katy into their front-yard games.

The Wechslers also became close with the neighbors on the corner, thirty-five-year-old Irv and thirty-two-year-old Selma Mandel and their daughter, Ricky, who was Nick's age. Irv was a drapery salesman and supplied all the new homes in the area. Down the block were Tina and Barney Bell and their three kids. Barney was from Texas and drove a truck for Coca-Cola, but was politically liberal and always there to lend a hand.

While Lew was off at work at the DeLaval Steam Turbine Company in nearby Trenton, New Jersey, Bea enjoyed life at home with her neighbors and kids. It reminded them of the shows that were coming on television such as *Father Knows Best* and *Ozzie and Harriet*. The friendly milkman would show up in his truck and drop off ice-cold bottles, then give Bea and her kids a lift over to the swimming pool.

After the Bronx, Katy and Nick relished the outdoorsy freedom and adventure. They roamed the half-built homes and teamed up with other kids on the block to build a fort outside their house. Katy was growing into a tough young girl, just like the Wechsler women before her, and would go to great lengths to ward off the tough kids in town. When a towering bully kid gave Nick a noogie on the spot of his polio-shot bruise, Katy let him have it until he backed off for good. "He's bigger than us," she told her brother in her New York accent, "but he's a wimp!"

On weekends, they'd spend time in their yard with other families, barbecuing and playing with Biff. Lew, always handy, embraced the do-it-yourself culture of the neighborhood—fixing up his house when he could. But, despite Abe Levitt's rules and regulations, he drew the line at his lawn. Following his decades in the city, Lew just didn't have the patience to clip, edge, and mow his grass. George Frazier, a fellow Levittowner with whom he carpooled to work, kept ribbing Lew about taking care of his lawn. Once after work, George even took Lew on a tour of his own well-manicured lot. "This is what a lawn is supposed to look like," Frazier admonished Lew. It was too little too late. By the time Lew got back, his lawn had been restored to a perfect cut—courtesy of the Levitts, who left the bill for the work on his front door.

This wouldn't be the last time the Wechslers tangled with the Levitts. When the kids went to school in the fall of 1953, Bea took a job as a waitress in town. One morning a hunched older man came for lunch. It was

Abe Levitt. He had an entourage of salespeople with him attending to his every need and request. To Bea's terror, he sat at one of her tables. When she approached him, he reached into his coat and handed her his pocket watch. "Give this to the cook!" he demanded. "Tell him I want a three-minute egg! Not two minutes! Not four minutes! A three-minute egg." Bea took the watch back to the cook and told him the story. The cook smiled and said, "Fuck him."

Even the Wechsler kids felt the sting of the town's rules. One morning Katy and Nick ran out to see their newly constructed fort. It had been a work of passion, cobbled together from old lumber and roomy enough to house them, Biff, and even the neighborhood bully, who, since his smackdown by Katy, had become their friend. As they dashed out the door, however, they found the fort had been destroyed, torn down by construction crews to make way for more new homes coming in.

"We should do something so that we always remember this," the bully said, "so that we'll always be in this club together." Good idea, they agreed. They set the fallen fort on fire and watched it burn.

No matter how much they enjoyed being pioneers in Levittown, the reality of Levitt's plan could not escape them: Levittown was whites-only. Or close to it anyway. While Bea and Lew noticed a few families of color—Indian and Mexican—there were no blacks at all.

In 1952, the *Nation* magazine sent a writer to Levittown, Pennsylvania, to investigate. "There's something I want to ask you about that's very important to me," he said to a sales agent, who "lifted a reassuring hand" and replied, "You mean the talk of colored people living here? Listen, this is the point of the sale—just between you and me—we sell to whites only, mister."

In Levittown, New York, residents who fought against the policy quickly felt the wrath of the nation's largest builder. After a family there, the Rosses, hosted an interracial playgroup for kids in both Levittown and the surrounding communities in 1950, Bill Levitt informed them that their lease would not be renewed. Once again, integrationists took up the fight. The NAACP defended the tenants, and the American

Jewish Congress filed a brief asking the courts to consider "the dangers to our democratic way of life arising from residential segregation."

In June 1951, a crowd packed an auditorium at Hofstra College for a "Conference to End Discrimination in Levittown." William Cotter, the African-American chair of the Committee to End Discrimination in Levittown, which organized the event, wrote a letter appealing to attendees. "The Constitution says 'yes' . . . The Supreme Court says 'yes' . . . But William Levitt and Sons says 'no,'" he wrote. "By openly refusing to rent or sell homes to Negroes, the Levitt organization has run counter to American democratic thought, and has condemned Levittown in the eyes of all thinking Americans who believe that now, as never before, the fullest expression of democracy is mandatory." Cotter concluded, "Help us realize Levittown's boast as 'the Veterans' paradise—for all.'"

But it was to no avail. The Nassau County Supreme Court ruled that Levitt had the right to refuse renewal of the Rosses' lease. He could throw out the parents, Adolph and Lillian Ross, and their two young children. On February 18, 1952, the night before the eviction, the Wechsler's hero, Jackie Robinson, joined protesters organized by the National Coalition of Christians and Jews to rally in support of the Levittown families. "Our world is changing," Robinson told the crowd, "and today qualified persons of all colors and creeds are being given opportunities as never before in the business, professional, and sports worlds." When asked if he supported the Rosses' cause, Robinson said he was "wholeheartedly in favor of the actions of any group to blot out discriminatory practices." And he added, "If Mr. Levitt and other organizations would stop and think whom they are hurting, perhaps things would be different."

Adolph Ross stood firm and said he would not leave until the Levitts agreed to "end this un-American discrimination against Negro people." The next day, four hundred supporters stood defiantly in front of the Rosses' house to ward off the evictors. They carried boxes of cake and placards of protest with phrases such as END DISCRIMINATION IN LEVITTOWN and PHONE LEVITT. Faced with such opposition, Levitt finally bowed, and the family was reluctantly allowed to remain. But the battles would continue.

Soon after, an African-American family named the Cotters sublet a home from a white family in Levittown, New York. The resident was none other than William Cotter, the chairperson of the Committee to End Discrimination in Levittown and a past president of the Great Neck chapter of the NAACP. Cotter had tried to buy a home for his family in Levittown only to be told by the Levittown management company he was "undesirable." But he managed to sublet a home instead. When word got out, Bill Levitt closed in again for an eviction.

Cotter went to court, claming racial discrimination. While Levittown's management company said Cotter had simply stayed in the home after his lease had run out, the comments were racially charged nonetheless. "If we don't like the color of your necktie," said the Levittown attorney, "then we don't have to rent to you." This time, Levitt would not back down. The judge ruled in favor of Levitt, and Levittown's attorney accused Cotter of unnecessarily stirring up racial issues. In December 1953, the Cotters were forced to leave. As volunteers from the Committee to End Discrimination carried signs saying KEEP BROTHERHOOD IN LEVITTOWN and sang "Go Down Moses" and "God Bless America," marshals carried Cotter, and his furniture, outside in the rain for good.

Three days later, a white Levittown family offered to sell the Cotters a house, and they accepted. They remained there without incident, and two other black families would move into the community as well without a problem. But Bill Levitt refused to change his policy. "It was not a matter of prejudice, but one of business," he insisted. "As a Jew, I have no room in my mind or heart for racial prejudice. But, by various means, I have come to know that if we sell one house to a Negro family, then ninety to ninety-five percent of our white customers will not buy into this community."

But towns near Levitt's defied any such easy prediction. Ronek Park, a community near Levittown, Long Island, was a postwar development that was open to all potential buyers from the day sales began in 1950. The builder, Thomas Romano, promised the homes would be available to anyone "regardless of race, creed, or color." When it opened, *Newsday* observed that most of the buyers were black. Not far from Levittown, Pennsylvania, the community of Concord Park, built by Quakers, was diverse and thriving. The town's motto: "Under Quaker Leadership, Democracy in Housing."

Bea and Lew took Concord Park's success to heart. They weren't alone. The *Saturday Evening Post* and other publications became publicly critical of Levittown's stance. Letters came in supporting integration. Opponents voiced their outrage too. "A large majority of people moved to Levittown because there are no Negroes," wrote one. The *Trenton Evening Times* called for action. "The eyes of the world are upon [Levittown]," the paper read. "For what happens here may help bring American democracy raised to new and greater heights. Or it may establish an evil pattern that could tend to destroy the freedom on which this country is based."

The Bucks County area had a long history of integrationist activity, mainly exercised by the local Quakers. As far back as the 1700s, Quakers had fought to free slaves in the area. In fact, they and other activists had been working on civil rights issues under the auspices of the Bucks County Interracial Committee for years before Levitt and his exclusionary community arrived. In 1952, the activists formed a civil rights organization called the Human Relations Council.

Bea and Lew were delighted to discover that the spokesperson of the group and leader of the area's Interracial Committee was an old college buddy of Lew's named Paul Blanshard Jr. He was joined by other notable community leaders, such as Sam Snipes, a bow-tied Quaker lawyer whose ancestors had lead the emancipation struggle almost two hundred years before. And they were not about to back down now, no matter how powerful the Levitts had become. As Blanshard promised in the *Saturday Evening Post*, "The day will come when a Negro family will move into Levittown."

The Human Relations Council along with a Quaker group called the Friends Service Association made the integration of Levittown a top priority. As Blanshard put it, the goal was "bringing moral pressure upon leaders in housing and industry who foster discrimination." They called for meetings with Bill Levitt, but he turned them down. With enough persistence, however, they finally got a sit-down and brought along a celebrity, the Bucks County writer Pearl Buck, for good measure. When

Bill stood firm against their proposal to integrate, however, even Buck couldn't take it, and she stormed out of the room.

The Human Relations Council organized workshops and meetings against Levittown's racist plan. Residents went to a meeting at a church on the topic of integration, and Ralph Abernathy, one of Martin Luther King's close friends and colleagues, was the speaker. At one point during the impassioned gathering, an African-American from Concord Park stood up and said that she lived in an integrated community, why couldn't Levittown be that way? What did Abernathy think? "Well," Abernathy said, "if Martin were here and heard this question, he'd say, 'Things are looking up in heaven!'" The first step to change, in other words, was questioning the situation.

On January 15, 1955, the groups threw their support behind the NAACP when it sued the federal mortgage agencies that helped finance the Levittown houses in Pennsylvania. The lawsuit came to pass after six black veterans claimed to have been denied the right to buy homes in Levittown because of their race. "Levitt's bias policy has not gone unnoticed," wrote a director of the NAACP in Bucks County in a letter to the editor. "We do state firmly that the NAACP resolves to use the courts, legislation, and public opinion to crack the iron curtain of bias housing policies and to keep campaigning until we bring to an end such painful disparity between American principles and American practices."

In a statement, the Human Relations Council said it "deplores such discrimination, especially at this hour when the fate of man may hang on the realization of proper rights by the colored people of the earth. It seems more important than ever in America to live by the principles we teach. There will be some who judge this statement as a condemnation of a single building firm. This is but a fraction of its intent."

Representing the veterans, Thurgood Marshall, the NAACP chief counsel and famed lawyer from *Brown v. Board of Education*, tried to get an injunction placed against Levitt "as long as he uses the credit, guarantees, insurance approval and assistance of the Federal government," Marshall said. However, the Philadelphia district court dismissed the suit, ruling that while the FHA and Veterans Administration did provide loans, they were not congressionally charged to prevent housing discrimination. Levitt had skirted the law once again.

As the sad reality of Levittown's racist policy lingered, Bea and Lew struggled with more disillusionment of their own. On February 25, 1956, Nikita Khrushchev, first secretary of the Communist Party of the Soviet Union, gave what became known as the "Secret Speech" or "Khrushchev Report," detailing the atrocities practiced under the preceding Stalin regime. Bea and Lew, after a lifetime of political action, couldn't believe their ears. "They were murdering Jews," Bea said. "How could socialists do this?"

Lew felt "shattered" by the report, he said. But some of their friends in the movement were more than shattered. Some had nervous breakdowns. "This is the end," Bea said. "If this is what socialism can bring, then I don't want it. I'm not a Communist anymore. I'm finished." It was a devastating thing to say, after a lifetime supporting the cause. And it wouldn't be so easy to move on. Despite McCarthy's having been censured in 1954, red-baiting continued as the country waged the Cold War. To make matters worse, the Wechslers knew they would forever bear the brand of their affiliation, and the threat of retaliation, from lost jobs to lost lives, was still as real as ever—especially in Levittown.

Levitt had, after all, built his communities on the promise of keeping out both blacks and Communists. Now Communists were under fire. In Levittown, New York, a battle had been waged over a song called "Lonesome Train." Penned by a folk artist who had written many union songs, "Lonesome Train" was a tribute to Abraham Lincoln and the freeing of the slaves. The song had been played for schoolchildren as a tribute to President Lincoln.

But a Catholic magazine declared the song "so patently loaded with Communist propaganda that even a tyro in Communist lore could detect it." And a battle had broken out in Levittown, New York, as members of the Board of Education wanted it banned. The community formed groups to explore what tolerance meant in a newly blazed community. With the approval of the Board of Education, the Anti-Defamation League of B'nai B'rith planned a "Workshop on Human Relations" to discuss such issues

in a high school in Levittown. But the approval didn't come without objections. "I don't like the title 'Human Relations,'" said one member of
the Board of Education. "I'd like to ask them if they'll let their daughter
marry a colored fellow and see what they'll say." The song was never
banned, but the fires had been stoked against the integrationists and others who wanted to meddle with the "human relations" in town.

The legacy of Joe McCarthy, the senator who had once walked the
streets of Levittown with Bill Levitt and who died in disgrace on May 2,
1957, still loomed large. Now the supporters of the fight against exclud-
ing African-Americans from Levittown, Pennsylvania, were fanning the
Communist fears. Pearl Buck saw Levittown's racial covenant and uniformity as ominous reminders of Communist China. "When I walked
through Levittown one day and saw hundreds of houses being built, all
for white families and not one for Negroes," she wrote, "I saw a straight
line of connection between those houses and the fact that Communism
won China away from us, that it threatens at this moment in Indo-
China, that because of it thousands of American boys lie dead in Korean
soil." Local author James Michener agreed. "Any evidence of racial discrimination in the United States is carefully searched out by Communists and transmitted to Asiatic newspapers for widespread publicity," he
said at a meeting of the Human Relations Council in the area.

As Bea and Lew busied themselves with their daily lives, the raising of
their kids, their jobs, their home, they grieved for the cause they were
leaving behind. Lew wasn't getting far with the unions in town, which
were considerably more conservative than he had been accustomed to in
the past. It began to seem as if the promise the Wechslers had believed in
for so long—the promise of a new world, a new home, a new life—was
fading. Even the Human Relations Council's efforts to integrate Levittown seemed hopeless.

Every so often, an African-American family would make contact with
the group and they would all meet at the local William Penn Center, a
community gathering place, to discuss if and how the family might move
into the town. But it wouldn't take long for the sense of futility to
spread. "Where will the house come from?" someone would say. "Where
will they buy?" another would want to know. "Who will the neighbors

be? How will they react?" With so many obstacles being thrown up by the group, invariably the prospective buyer would back away.

One night after such a discussion deteriorated again, Lew finally spoke up in frustration. If they were going to change the town, they had to start somewhere, he said. "I don't see that it should be such a problem," Lew said. "Levittown houses are being sold every day. Any one of us could buy the house next door, move into it, and sell our house to the family. This would be aboveboard and would avoid two negatives: the deception of the 'straw buyer'; and the sense of a 'spite sale' in which the white seller disappears into another all-white community." Lew looked around the room and waited to see if someone would volunteer to step up, to take action, to put into place a plan that would tear down Levitt's wall once and for all.

No one did—not even the Wechslers. They had real violence to fear. As one member of the group wrote in a newsletter, "We must be realistic and recognize, good friends, that the more effective we are, at least in the first instance, the more opposition may arise. Our existence thus far has been fairly serene perhaps because our accomplishments are so few. No one of us can say how well we will be able to stand up when the heat is on." Even in America's most famous suburb, Levittown, there was no telling what their neighbors were capable of doing.

Seven

NEIGHBORS

IF YOUR CAR breaks down in Levittown, residents liked to boast, you don't have to look far for a neighbor to help. And if you lived on Timber Lane, the neighbor to ask was George Capps. A twenty-two-year-old Korean war veteran and worker at a Trenton wire-manufacturing company, Capps was an amiable handyman about town who lived with his twenty-one-year-old pregnant wife. Like most Levittowners, they were young and eager to start a new life.

Capps had been living in Virginia and traveling up the coast in a carnival when his troupe arrived at Levittown to put on a fair at a local church. Capps, however, hurt himself during the event and was hospitalized—forced to remain after his colleagues pulled out of town. Hearing of the story, a Levittowner named Betty Peart organized the local Girl Scouts to send get-well cards to Capps in his room.

But, they discovered, Capps couldn't read the cards. He was illiterate. This moved Peart, who dispatched Girl Scouts to the hospital to read the cards to him in person. Capps decided to stay in Levittown for good, buying a little house just down the block from the Pearts'. The neighbors took to him and his wife and discovered Capps was good with machines. He became known as the guy who could fix anything that broke.

One night that winter, on Friday, January 22, 1954, Capps headed down his street for a walk. A car had broken down in front of the house of his neighbors, the Gibbonses, and he was going to lend a hand. But no one was home at the Gibbonses' house that night. Mr. and Mrs. Gibbons were spending the night in Philadelphia, where Mrs. Gibbons was hospitalized with a heart condition. Their daughter Marta, a fifteen-year-old high school sophomore, and her seven-year-old half sister, Sue, were babysitting at their neighbors' across the street. When Capps called earlier to ask if he could help with their dad's broken-down car, Marta told him her parents were away and he'd have to do it later.

At about ten P.M. that night after Marta came home and her half sister went to bed, Capps phoned again about the car. Then he came over. Capps then either forced or talked Marta into leaving her sister and taking a drive in his 1937 Ford. They went to the frozen Curtis Lake, near the intersection of two busy highways, Route 1 and Route 13. On a cold night like this, the lake and surrounding woods were empty. There alone on the edge of Levittown, Capps raped the girl twice. When he was through, he said, "Suppose I get you pregnant like I did my wife?" Marta vomited and burst into tears. She told Capps she was going to tell her stepfather what he had done to her. Bolting from the car, crying and hysterical, she ran from the lake. Capps leapt after her, striking her down. Then he ran back to his car to get his gun.

He only chased her for a few feet before squeezing the trigger of his .32-caliber pistol, firing a bullet into the back of her head. Marta hit the ground. Capps, in a panic, decided to get rid of the body. He grabbed the dead girl's legs and dragged her two hundred feet into a ditch. As he sped off into the night, he tossed her clothes from the window and disappeared back into Levittown's winding streets.

It was two days before the police found Marta's green sweater hanging from the branch of a tree. Before long, they had traced the evidence back to Capps, who confessed. News of the sensational crime shocked the community. Neighbors barred their doors. Parents refused to let their daughters babysit. It was a defining moment for Levittown, an eruption of evil in their perfectly planned world. "It could have happened anywhere in the world," the local paper wrote, "but IT HAPPENED HERE!" Betty Peart, stunned that a man she had helped had done this, sank into despair— unable even to change her baby's diapers.

In May, a jury sentenced Capps to death. The district attorney summed up the murder by comparing Capps to a rabid dog, "a beast of

prey . . . stalking your child as its victim." Marta's grief-stricken stepfather said, "I thought he was a good neighbor."

It was September 24, 1955, and the Levittowners needed a reason to celebrate. They had one: Walt Disney was coming to town. The iconic en-
tertainer stepped off a train in nearby Tullytown, climbed into a black
limousine, and headed for their community. He wasn't just there to
honor this world-famous suburb, he was giving his name to the community by dedicating the first-ever school to bear his name: Walt Disney
Elementary.

Disney had reason to be interested in the utopian plan. As early as
1948, he had started talking about his distaste for urban chaos, traffic,
and noise—and the promise of life in a supportive, planned garden community. He quoted from books such as *Garden Cities of Tomorrow* and
Out of a Fair, a City, which mapped out ideas for new kinds of living
centers. Like Alfred Levitt, he saw the promise fulfilled in the dreams of
science fiction writers such as his friend Ray Bradbury. One time when
Bradbury suggested Disney run for mayor of Los Angeles, Disney replied,
with Bill Levitt–style bombast, "Why should I run for mayor when I am
already king?"

As Disney pulled into Levittown, enthusiastic fans crowded to greet
him with homemade signs. DISNEY DAY IN LEVITTOWN read one banner.
LEVITTOWN WELCOMES WALT DISNEY read another, alongside a drawing
of Mickey Mouse. After introductions by fifth- and sixth-grade students,
Disney took the stage in his gray suit and dark tie to inaugurate the school
and set down the symbolic cornerstone. A camera perched atop a car
filmed the news. As the newly formed Walt Disney School Band played,
and the Girl Scouts Brownie Troop #184 stood by Uncle Walt's side, the
crowd watched as the American flag was raised over the school.

Behind the scenes, however, the Levitt's fantasy world was beginning
to crack. While the nation still had a love affair with the veteran-friendly
suburbs, artists and critics began taking the towns to task. The science
fiction film *Invasion of the Body Snatchers*, which chronicled a town of
people taken over by an alien virus, played up the soul-sucking uniformity

of the cookie-cutter existence. *Rebel Without a Cause*, the movie starring
James Dean, dramatized the frustration teenagers felt with stifling 1950s
conformity.

Books such as *The Lonely Crowd* and *The Man in the Gray Flannel Suit*
depicted the hollow lives of uniform suburban men. "The typical postwar development operator was a man who figured how many houses he
could possibly cram onto a piece of land and have the local zoning board
hold still for it," read a typical line from John Keats's novelistic critique,
The Crack in the Picture Window.

Women began complaining about feelings of isolation, lamenting how
the independence they had experienced during the war years been traded
for a life of appliances. They were, as one writer put it, "feminine . . .
ghettos in which husbands and fathers were reduced to harried visitors
who turned over their paychecks to becurled, complaining, coffee-klatching
wives and materialistic whining children, whereas wives and mothers were
reduced to neurotic, child-driven chauffeurs and the generic term for this
social milieu had become 'Levittown.' "

Critic Lewis Mumford was especially derisive of Levittown. "It is a
one-class community on a great scale, too congested for effective variety
and too spread out for social relationships . . . Mechanically, it is ad-
mirably done. Socially, the design is backward." Levitt, he argued, used
"new-fashioned methods to compound old-fashioned mistakes. It's a
suburb, and suburbs are just an expansion of mistaken policy to build
without industry. We have to build complete, well-integrated 'new towns,'
not monotonous suburbs with great picture windows that look out onto
clotheslines."

With his huge but vulnerable ego, Bill Levitt shot back at such criticisms: "What would you call the places our homeowners left to move out
here? We give them something better." He had as much to say to his
brother, Alfred, whenever Alfred brought up the criticisms of their town.
"We're not selling to Mumford," Bill would snap.

When a local paper in Bucks County, Pennsylvania, brought up the
exclusion of blacks in his latest town, Levitt shot back again: "The plain
fact is that most whites prefer not to live in mixed communities. This attitude may be wrong morally, and someday it may change. I hope it will.

But as matters now stand, it is unfair to charge an individual for creating this attitude or saddle him with the sole responsibility for correcting it. The responsibility is society's. So far society has not been willing to cope with it. Until it does, it is not reasonable to expect that any one builder should or could undertake to absorb the entire risk and burden of conducting such a vast social experiment."

Despite the controversies and criticisms, nothing could get Bill Levitt down. In fact, Levittown's front man only became more famous—and beloved—with every passing day. With his dapper clothes, plucky sound bites, and Barnumesque panache, Levitt made great copy. He was an underdog turned hero, a metahero, in a sense, the man who'd saved the veterans after they'd saved America. The press portrayed Levitt as the swashbuckling, if not eccentric, superstar.

"Strangely enough, the biggest house builder in the U.S. has built no house for himself," marveled *Time*. "In winter he lives with his pretty wife Rhoda and their two sons . . . in a twelve-room Fifth Avenue apartment, which he rents for $4,900 a year. Summers they spend at Great Neck, L.I., in an English Tudor mansion (which Levitt rents for $7,500 a season) which has both a swimming pool and a private bathing beach on Long Island Sound. On summer weekends Bill sometimes plays golf (low 90s) with wife Rhoda (low 80s) but is not disturbed by his constant defeats. Says he: 'I hate all forms of exercise.' "

However, as Bill took on critics and pumped up his own image, it exacted a cost: He alienated himself from his brother, Alfred. The press had begun to pick up on the disparities between the two boys. While Bill cruised the muddy streets in his Cadillac, Alfred drove a Ford. Bill would be described dressed in "royal blue sports coat, light slacks and fawn-colored oxfords," while one writer noted that Alfred "didn't give a whoop" how he appeared. While Bill was on the cover of *Time*, Alfred's mug could only be seen in engineering-magazine ads shilling nails. " 'ES-nails really work,' Alfred S. Levitt says," read one ad. " 'Now we can use gypsum or insulation for sheathing purposes instead of boarding.' "

With Bill hogging the spotlight, Alfred found his own ideas increasingly overshadowed. He lamented how, despite fighting "tooth and nail" against the inclusion of ugly carports in his homes, he gave in to his brother's desires. Alfred was still stinging from the cancellation of his own dream project, called Landia. Compared to Levittown, Landia would be tiny. The 675-acre Jericho, Long Island, residential development was to embody all his community ideas: parks, a town center, a train station, and shopping mall. The Levitts bought the land in 1951, but the project stalled when a freeze in building hit during the Korean War.

Though Alfred incorporated some of the ideas into Levittown, Pennsylvania, there was no doubt about who was taking—and seeking—the credit: his big brother. If either brother would be remembered for Levittown, it would be Bill. Part of this was by design. Bill had the right skills and personality to run the show, and when they divvied up the shares, Alfred agreed to give him the reins. Bill owned 50 percent of Levitt & Sons, while Alfred had 49 percent, and Abe, the last 1 percent. And there was no question who was boss.

To make matters more difficult, their aging father had pulled himself out of the company's day-to-day operations to ease into retirement. That meant Alfred was now left to defend himself against Bill. And he had other matters weighing on him too: a divorce. In 1953, he left his wife, Sylvia, for a nineteen-year-old model he met in Paris. Though he was financially solvent, he faced having to pay a high enough sum to Sylvia that he needed more cash.

So he considered his options and made his decision: he would sell his shares in the company to Bill. He had other projects he wanted to build, new dreams to pursue. In 1954, he left Levitt & Sons for good. From now on, any battle in Levittown would be his brother's to fight alone.

Eight

AN EXTRA BEDROOM AND A GARAGE

O NE DAY IN the spring of 1957, Daisy Myers rushed across her living room to her husband, Bill. What's so urgent? he wanted to know. She took his hand and placed it gently on her round belly. He tried to speak again, but Daisy shushed him as he felt a kick from the baby inside. To their delight, the Myers family was growing. And that meant one thing: They needed more house.

At their home in Bloomsdale Gardens, sons William III, four, and Stephen, three, were already sharing a room. With their next child due in July, Daisy and Bill wanted a three-bedroom home—particularly if they had a little girl, who would need her own space. But, on their modest salaries their options were limited. Then a friend suggested they look in the one neighborhood they hadn't even considered, Levittown.

The idea surfaced one night during a social gathering held at one of the Levittown homes. This was not the first time the Myerses had ventured across the road from Bloomsdale Gardens into Levittown. Daisy had been shopping in the town's Shop-O-Rama stores since they'd moved into the area and never thought twice about it. She had also been taking classes at Temple University in Philadelphia, and some of the women in her car pool lived in Levittown.

Daisy had become active in local affairs. As the recreation supervisor for the Bloomsdale Gardens school board, she was in charge of a local playground where black and white children from both communities played. She went door-to-door in Levittown collecting money for charities, including the Red Cross and the Levittown Library. Just as her parents had been active in local politics in Richmond, Daisy joined the Levittown League of Women Voters, often attending local discussion groups, sponsored by the William Penn Center, such as this one tonight.

Topics ranged from local politics to community affairs, and despite being the only black members of the group, the Myerses felt welcomed. What they didn't know was that some in the crowd were hatching a plan. Over coffee and cookies after the discussion, a member of the group approached Bill and said, "Do you know a nice Negro couple that would like to move to Levittown?"

Bill, well aware of Levittown's whites-only policy, was taken aback. It hadn't, after all, been long since the NAACP had lost its lawsuit to integrate the town. Despite his family's involvement in the town, Bill couldn't imagine a black family moving in. He and Daisy were passionate about their causes, but Bill had no desire to cast themselves as protagonists in a civil rights battle. He'd seen news reports of lynchings and shootings down South. He'd watched the violence that had erupted over the Montgomery bus boycott that followed in 1955 after Rosa Parks had refused to give up her seat. The last thing he wanted was to put his wife and children at risk. "No," Bill told the man, "I don't know any Negroes who would want to buy a home in Levittown."

When he told Daisy the story on the drive home to Bloomsdale, however, she surprised him by saying, "How about us?" She was only half-kidding. Her motivation wasn't political, it was personal. The baby was coming. They needed a bigger home. They had failed to find an adequate house in surrounding areas and were now facing the prospect of moving back to a crowded apartment in a rough neighborhood of Philadelphia. If moving into Levittown meant getting a good house in a good school system, then maybe that alone was worth exploring the idea for real.

During the next meeting of the discussion group, Bill approached the man who had posed the question from before. "Suppose we wanted to move?" Bill said.

A special meeting was called by members of the discussion group to explore the matter further. Daisy thought it should be called the "Levittown Committee to Discuss the Successful Move-in of a Negro Family." To

Bill and Daisy's dismay, however, the discussion seemed to become an interrogation. They were questioned for hours about their background and intentions. Daisy began to feel that these people were more interested in the idea of transforming Levittown than in the reality of the family's desires and situation.

"We're just ordinary people," she said, "we never cause a stir or get into trouble." They just wanted what any family would: an affordable home in a nice community where they could live their lives. They weren't looking for a fight. The group shared their concerns. Tensions had been building in Levittown. On the heels of the discussions, yellow pamphlets had appeared in favor of exclusion with forged names of Jewish families—a ploy, some believed, to stoke the fires of anti-Semitism and keep the activists at bay. Levittown seemed like a peaceful suburb of backyard barbecues and baseball games, but none knew what their neighbors were capable of doing if an African-American family actually moved in.

Over three more meetings, the group met to talk in greater depth with the Myerses about the possibility of their moving into town. Because Levittown sprawled over four municipalities, some suggested that the problem would be particular to the neighborhood in which the Myerses might buy a house. What if, someone suggested, they simply went door-to-door to poll residents on how they felt about having a black family as neighbors? Then, with this information, they could decide how to proceed.

Daisy recoiled. "Negroes have too long been expected to ask for permission for what they deserve," she said. Plus what was the point of tipping off racists, who could then have time to organize their resistance? If the Myerses were going to move in, then they should just move in. No questions asked.

All they needed was the right house. With a garage, Bill said.

Forty-three Deepgreen Lane, the house next door to the Wechslers', was empty. Their neighbor Irv Mandel had suffered a heart attack in 1955. Unable to work in his family's drapery business, Mandel and his wife had moved in with her family in Philadelphia and put their home on the market. The small ranch Levittowner like the Wechslers' had three bedrooms and was painted a cheery shade of pink. The carport had been converted into a garage.

The house had been on the market for close to two years. A recession had hit Bucks County and the market for homes had stalled. With Levittown now housing over sixty thousand people, demand had largely been met. Unhealthy and unemployed, Mandel was desperate. One afternoon in the spring of 1957, he knocked on the Wechslers' door. Lew had never seen his neighbor looking so forlorn. Mandel needed to unload the house before he went broke. Despite all his and his Realtor's efforts, there had been no progress. They needed to show the home to more people. Just imagine all the black families out there who would love a home like this one, Mandel told Lew, if only they could get in. He hesitated. "Do you have any objections if I let a Negro Realtor show the home? If you do object, I won't offer the house to them."

Bea and Lew knew exactly what Mandel was suggesting: selling his house to an African-American family. If a black family moved in next door, it would almost certainly impact them—in ways no one could predict. But they had an additional concern—and secret. With red-baiting still alive and well in America, they had no idea what would happen if their Communist past came out. If this happened in consort with an integration battle, well, there was no telling what might happen. However, they had never backed down from a fight, and the opportunity to integrate the most iconic suburb in America was too great to resist.

"Would you meet with other couples to see if they could find a black family to move in?" Mandel asked. The Wechslers agreed. But they had no idea if they could find a family strong enough to take such a personal risk.

A few nights later, they met in a Levittown home with a small group of couples they had known from the Human Relations Council and the Friends Service Association. It was genial crowd, and hot coffee and cookies were on the table. Chief among the people gathered was Snipes, the Quaker attorney. Then the Wechslers met the only black couple in the room, a tall, handsome man with a pencil-thin mustache, Bill Myers, and his pregnant wife, Daisy.

The Wechslers and others listened attentively as the Myerses explained their housing predicament and the style of home they were seeking. Daisy, who'd grown up in a three-story house, longed for a ranch home so that the family could be on one floor. Bill expressed his desire for an enclosed garage that he could use as a workshop. As Lew heard them speak, he almost jumped from his seat. The Myerses were describing Mandel's home to a T. "The house next door to us is on the market," Lew said, "and the owner would sell to a Negro family."

On a subsequent afternoon in April 1957, Bill and Daisy drove a mile from their house in Bloomsdale Gardens to meet Lew at his home on Deepgreen Lane. When they followed him over to the little pink house next door, they couldn't believe their eyes. It had everything they needed and more. There were three bedrooms, central air-conditioning, even a new washing machine and dryer. The kids had plenty of space to run around on the lawn; and Bill and Daisy had room to garden and barbecue.

Daisy fell in love with its being a ranch, and that everything was on one convenient floor—no hiking up and down the steps with her kids anymore. With his heart pounding, Bill headed giddily past the kitchen and threw open the door to see his lifelong fantasy come true: a garage. It felt meant to be. The house was even just around the corner from a street named Daisy Lane. And at $12,150 it was the right price; the Mandels would make just $150 on the price they had paid in 1953, but they were ready to make a deal. As a veteran, Bill would be eligible for a GI Bill loan, and the Myerses would just have to come up with a $2,000 down payment.

As badly as they wanted the house, Bill and Daisy went back to their home in Bloomsdale Gardens to weigh the pros and cons. They were well aware of the gravity of their decision. While they always had, as Daisy put it, "a faith that 'right' would triumph," they considered the potential consequences. Every night after the boys were asleep, they would sit on the edge of the bed and ask themselves, "How much can we take? How much can the children take?"

They weren't just putting themselves into the fray, after all, they were including their children too. As young parents they had to face the most awful possibility of outcomes. "Would we be able to live in the home once we bought it?" Daisy wondered. "To what extent would our neighbors object? Would the developer, by some maneuvering, try to get us out? Could we live a normal, happy life in Levittown? Could we protect our children?"

At times like this, Bill fell silent. He was, as Daisy put it, a "deep thinker." "Well," he said, "I don't know if it would be worth it." They were both well aware of the potential price with the civil rights struggle brewing around the country. At the same time, they felt the support of friends and neighbors and had read letters and editorials in local papers discussing the need for integration. Maybe we are crossing too many bridges before we get to them, they concluded.

The next day they picked up the phone and called the Wechslers with their decision.

Lew looked out his window one morning to see his Levittown carpooler, George Frazier, waiting in his car out front to drive them to work. As Lew stepped outside to greet him, Frazier, as usual, good-naturedly teased Lew about his unkempt lawn. Frazier pointed at Lew's patches of weeds and brush, then motioned to his own immaculate green swath. "You really got to do something about that lawn, Lew," he said, as Lew smiled and nodded his head. But Lew had other things on his mind.

Since getting the word from the Myerses that they wanted to buy the house next door, Bea and Lew had spent the early summer quietly helping them prepare for the move. Everyone agreed to respect Daisy's desire to keep the move quiet. Lew only told one person, his neighbor Barney Bell, the Texan truck driver, of the plan. Bell was supportive and reassuring. "What can happen?" Bell said. "We live north of the Mason-Dixon Line."

The Myerses were anxious to get into the house in time for their oldest boy, William, to go to school in September. Lew accompanied Bill to various banks in an effort to secure a loan for the $2,000 down payment. But they had difficulty obtaining one. Bill was even turned down at a black-owned bank in Philadelphia. Through the grapevine, however, Bea and Lew heard of a wealthy philanthropist in New York City who might be of help.

One day, Bea, Lew, Daisy, and Bill went up to the city to meet with the woman in her vast apartment in Manhattan. She agreed to loan the Myerses the down payment with no interest. But she was concerned. "I can lend you the money," she told them, "but I would have a very guilty feeling if anything happened to you." This was the North, they replied, racial violence only happened in the South. Don't worry, they assured her, everyone will be fine.

While they agreed not to announce or publicize the move, the general topic was on people's minds anyway. On July 9 at the Faith Reformed Church in Levittown, a public meeting was coincidentally held to discuss "Fair Housing in Bucks County—A Panel Discussion Held in Levittown, Pa., on the General Subject of Open Occupancy Housing," under the auspices of the Lower Bucks County Council of Churches. Though the organizers were not aware of the plans to move the Myerses into town, their meeting explicitly addressed the issue head-on.

A local real estate appraiser told the crowd that, despite Levitt's fears of a loss in housing values, his industry's studies of trends in Philadelphia proved otherwise. "There is no depreciation in values when colored families move into a neighborhood," he said. "As a matter of fact, in some areas, there actually has been an increase in prices because of the pressure which the demand of colored buyers has put on existing housing because of their shelter needs."

A local Levittown minister, the first clergyman to come to the town in 1952, appealed directly to the group. "Suppose, for example," he said, "that a Negro family were to move into Levittown tomorrow, or next week, or next month, or next year. What would be the reaction of the people of this community? What would be your reaction to this Negro family? Would it be based upon hearsay, rumor, emotional panic, irresponsibility, mob violence? Would it be based upon reason, faith, love, and human understanding? This is a question which we had better decide in our community, and we had better decide it now. For whether a Negro family moves in tomorrow or next year, that day will arrive when will find one or two or more Negro families moving into Levittown."

Four days after the meeting, Daisy gave birth to a baby girl they named Lynda. Bill was "tickled pink," as Daisy said, about finally having a daughter. Brothers Stephen and William awed over their little sister's tiny fingers and toes. With two big brothers to contend with around the house, Lynda would make good use of the extra bedroom waiting for her on Deepgreen Lane.

It was moving time.

Nine

43 DEEPGREEN LANE

AUGUST WAS ALWAYS a tense month in Levittown. Kids climbed the walls at home. Fathers idled around off work. And mothers tried in vain to keep everything in order. But the unseasonably hot and dry August of 1957 spiked tensions even higher. Bucks County baked in the worst drought in Pennsylvania history. Rain had not fallen since April, and the one-hundred-plus-degree days without precipitation had cost local farmers more than five million dollars. Pennsylvania governor George Leader asked President Eisenhower to declare Bucks County a disaster area.

Attorney Sam Snipes feared tensions would grow even worse on Tuesday, August 13, 1957, the 110th day of the drought. That was the day, as he and a handful of others secretly knew, that the Myerses were arriving in Levittown. Three days before, Snipes had settled the closing between the Mandels and the Myerses. Though Snipes's Quaker ancestors had been involved in civil rights struggles for years, he knew that the fight for Levittown was historic, and risky. On the advice of a Realtor friend who had experience with helping blacks move into white neighborhoods in Philadelphia, Snipes had decided to write a letter of notification to Bristol Township police chief John R. Stewart of the Myerses impending arrival so the authorities could best prepare:

"I will appreciate your Police Force giving careful place on or about the premises of Mr. and Mrs. William E. Myers, Jr., at 43 Deepgreen

Lane. Mr. and Mrs. Myers are, I believe, the first Negro family to move into Levittown, and come very highly recommend as citizens who will be an asset to the community."

Snipes sealed two copies of the letter—one to the police chief, and one to the Myerses on Deepgreen Lane—and put them in the mail.

The next morning, Bill and Daisy packed the last of their belongings into the moving van. They delicately wrapped their sherbet glasses in a separate box, which they put in the back of their baby-blue-and-white Ford Mercury. They stood on the curb, with one-month-old daughter Lynda and the boys, outside their Bloomsdale Gardens home.

One by one, neighbors came up to say good-bye. Bill and Daisy had purposefully not told too many of their specific plans, for fear of inciting a crowd at Levittown before their arrival. Bill hadn't told his parents either, because he didn't want them to worry. In a sad twist of fate, Daisy didn't have the chance to make such a choice. Both her stepparents had died within a month of each other just a few months earlier. Daisy took comfort in knowing that they wouldn't have to bear the worries about her move. However, she knew they'd be proud of her courage and her commitment to starting a new life.

By ten thirty A.M., they were on the road. Daisy and Bill had spent the past two days at 43 Deepgreen Lane preparing the new house for their arrival. Scrubbing floors. Painting. Putting the final touches on the children's rooms. The neighbors who saw them coming and going were, in fact, quite happy; they assumed the black man and woman were workers and that if the family moving in could afford such help, they would surely make fine additions to the town.

After driving less than a mile from Bloomsdale Gardens, the Myerses pulled into Levittown. It was a sweltering morning, with just a few kids playing outside. Abe Levitt's precious emerald-green lawns had turned an awful brown from the drought. Clothes hung out back on the Levitt-approved clotheslines, not one dish towel in sight—as the regulations required. Any trepidation Daisy and Bill felt quickly vanished into the tumult of moving into a new home with three young kids. As Bill pointed the movers to the appropriate spots in the house, Daisy changed Lynda's diaper and Stephen and William darted around, exploring their new house. Though they wanted to play outside, Daisy urged them to stay indoors because of the stifling heat.

When a knock came on the front door two hours later at one P.M., Daisy barely noticed it in the rush of activity. She opened it to find the mailman, a surprise since hardly anyone knew they were there. "Can I speak with the owner of the house?" he asked.

"I am the owner," she replied.

The mailman blanched. "You? You're the owner?"

"That's right."

In a daze, the mailman handed her a letter and left.

"Did you see how he looked?" Daisy said to Bill. "He looked ill." Daisy opened the letter to find it was from Snipes, a copy of the notification he had sent the police chief alerting him of their arrival. Daisy and Bill couldn't understand why the mailman had come to their door at all, since the letter wasn't registered. Why hadn't he just slipped into their mailbox? they wondered.

It didn't take long to find out. The mailman had wanted to see for himself who this black couple was inside the home. Now he was going door-to-door down the street alerting the neighbors. "It happened!" he told them. "Niggers have moved into Levittown!"

When the afternoon edition of the Levittown newspaper landed on doorsteps that day, it had the usual mix of homespun stories. A voter drive for the fall elections would be held at the William Penn Fire House. Two cars collided the pervious night on the Levittown Parkway. The Science Explorer Post of the Boy Scouts was looking for new members.

Tucked in the bottom, left-hand corner of page two was a small three-paragraph item. FIRST NEGRO FAMILY MOVES INTO LEVITTOWN the headline read. "The first Negro family to buy a Levittown house moved into the Dogwood Hollow Section this morning. Mr. and Mrs. William Myers, Jr., moved here with their three children, William III, 4, Stephen, 3, and Linda [*sic*], one month. Formerly residents of Bloomsdale Gardens, the couple moved to the area two and a half years ago from York, Pa.

Mr. Myers, who is an engineer, is employed by C.V. Hill and Co., in Trenton, N.J., in the refrigerator testing laboratory. He is a World War II veteran."

One by one the Dogwood Hollow neighbors began making their way outside. Just fifteen minutes after the mailman had been at their home, Daisy and Bill began to see small clusters of people gathering on the brown lawn of the Wertzes home across the street. As Bill and Daisy watched the crowd form, their telephone rang. Daisy answered.

"Hello?"

"I will not let my children drink chocolate milk again as long as I live!" said a hysterical woman on the other end, who then hung up.

Daisy's heart raced. "Do you think there will be any trouble?" she asked Bill. Outside the window, the neighbors across the street craned. Bill put his arm around her shoulder and forced a reassuring smile. "Oh, they just came for curiosity," he said. "It's nothing to worry about."

The Myerses returned to their chores. When the doorbell rang again later, Daisy opened it cautiously. This time the warm faces of their discussion-group friends were there to greet them with a lunch of sand-wiches and cake. As they sat around eating, Daisy and Bill told their friends about what had happened with the mailman and the onlookers outside. When their friends handed the Myerses the afternoon paper, it all made sense. The mailman had spread the word. The truth was out. Now they would just have to see how this would all unfold.

They weren't the only ones. Next door, Katy Wechsler was home alone babysitting her brother, Nick, while her parents worked. The Wechslers knew the Myerses would be moving in that day and planned on getting together with them once they all got home. In the morning, Katy had gone next door to greet Bill and Daisy and invited them over to the house for some cold lemonade. The children played together happily. Once the My-erses had gone home, however, Katy began to get an ominous feeling.

Across the street at the Wertzes, small clusters of people began to linger again. By two thirty, a procession of cars began slowly driving down the block. The traffic built until, ninety minutes later, it was at a crawl. Katy grabbed the phone and dialed Bea, who was working now as a book-keeper in nearby Bristol at a fuel-delivery company.

"There's a riot going on," Katy told her mother.

"What do you mean?" Bea said.

"There are cars going by one after another! It's been weird; they slow down, stare into the house next door, then go around the block and do it again." Katy peeked out her window at the gathering crowd of people on the Wertzes' lawn. Bea said she'd be right there. As she drove home, she knew there was trouble when she hit the strange jam of traffic leading into the Dogwood Hollow community. Some of the cars had Confederate flags in the windows.

By the time Lew came home from work, he found about fifty people milling around as the cars continued their procession up the street. Lew was surprised to see the groups of people at the Wertzes. George Wertz, after years of being neighborly, was showing his true colors. Lew watched George milling with the mob across the street as the cars with Confederate flags rolled slowly down the road dividing them.

By seven thirty P.M., reporters began showing up among the crowd, taking pictures and interviewing onlookers. One of them came to the door and asked Bill Myers why he'd moved to Levittown in the first place. Bill lit a cigarette. "I only wanted to buy a nice home and provide well for my family, as every American, who is able, likes to do," he said. "We will be good neighbors, and I know, or at least hope, that those around us will be the same. We are churchgoing, respectable people. We just want a nice neighborhood in which to raise our family and enjoy life."

But, as the reporter walked away, Bill's fear began to set in. Because of the heat, the windows were open and the family could hear the curses being spewed nearby. Daisy, who had pulled her boys inside from playing in the backyard, tried in vain to establish some sense of normalcy. The Wechslers had come over with Nick and Katy, and the children played. Now Daisy was struggling to get her children to settle down to sleep. But there was no peace to be had. A drunken man had pushed his way up to their front door, where he was now talking with Bill, who could smell liquor on his breath.

"All I want to know is who sold this house to you people?" the man slurred. "How much did you pay for it? What right do you have to come? I just want to find the people who sold it. Just tell me what their names are. When did you make settlement?"

Bill looked him squarely in the face and replied, "It's all part of the public record. Check it." When the man stumbled back to the others in the mob to share the news, Bill and Daisy heard a commotion. "Something is going to happen!" they heard someone shout. "I'm sticking around to see it!"

Inside the Wechslers' home, Bea and Lew decided it was time to take action before violence broke out. Lew and his friend Peter Von Blum, a Quaker who had been part of the discussions preceding the Myerses' move and had come over when he heard of the mob, said they'd go outside and try to reason with the growing crowd. Bea's throat constricted. She had marched in the streets in the Bronx as a teenager, been thrown down the steps during a housing fight. But she had never felt so under siege. "Don't be a hero," she implored her husband. "Be careful, Lew."

Lew wasn't concerned. He had faced plenty of opposition in his years as a social activist, and he wasn't going to fold now. He reassured her gently that everything would be okay. As soon as he stepped outside into the night, he found a scene unlike any he'd experienced before. Women stood cursing and spitting. Men grumbled about "niggers." Many of them made it clear that they had come to Levittown because Bill Levitt had promoted it as whites-only. "Levitt promised!" shouted one man near Lew. "He should get them out even if he has to buy them out!"

"The NAACP bought the house for the nigger as a test case," shouted another.

"No one wants them here," remarked a third. "Let's drive them out!"

Lew stepped right up to him. "The Myerses have the same right to buy a house as I do, or he does," Lew insisted, referring to an onlooker nearby.

A towering man with a scowling face came over. It was the father of the neighborhood bully who had helped Nick and Katy build their fort after Katy had beaten him in a fight. "You should be ashamed of yourself!" he told Lew. "Our houses are worth only half of what they were yesterday."

"I doubt there are many black families in Philadelphia who are anxious to move into Levittown now," Lew scoffed wryly.

Inside the pink house behind them, Daisy and Bill pleaded for help from the police. "This situation is being taken care of," the cop on the phone assured them. But with a glance outside at the growing mob in the darkness, they knew the truth was otherwise. Calls to the state police were no more helpful. "It's up to the local police to handle this," they were told. Bill and Daisy stood by the phone as their children cried in the background. Suddenly, two drunken men stumbled up outside their picture window clenching beer cans.

"Let's blast them to bits!" they heard one yell.

"Yeah," the other replied, "let's do it! We just need some dynamite!"

Before the men could act, the lawn was flooded with flashing blue and red lights. The Myerses and Wechslers breathed a sigh of relief as the police cars pulled up outside. But then something strange happened. The police made no move to disperse the crowd. They just ticketed some of the cars out front while the mob lingered. The police, many of whom also lived in Levittown, were letting the chaos ensue. Whose side were they on? the Myerses wondered. And, they decided, they had had enough—they were not going to remain here one minute longer. Bill asked for a police escort. With heads ducked, Bill and Daisy held their kids firmly and made their way to their blue-and-white Mercury outside. Reporters barked questions. Flashbulbs popped. Mob members jeered.

As the Myerses pulled away in their car, they could barely make their way through the crush of people. Daisy held baby Lynda in her arms as they drove slowly out of Dogwood Hollow back to the home in Bloomsdale Gardens they thought they had left behind.

Standing on the lawn outside, Lew watched the Myerses go with sadness. Then suddenly he found himself and his friend Von Blum left there in the dark alone with the mob. A lone streetlight glowed over the corner mailbox. There stood the hulking flattop-haired man who had, in just a few hours, distinguished himself as the leader of the group. He was

James E. Newell Jr., a thirty-year-old electrician from Durham, North Carolina, who lived around the corner on Daffodil Lane.

Beside Newell was a sidekick, an unemployed forty-eight-year-old named Eldred Williams, who had emerged from behind the wheel of his gray Pontiac station wagon. Williams was thin and short, with sharp features and a cigarette dangling from his thin lips. A crowd had formed around them as Newell stood sermonizing at the mailbox. What had started as a debate about the Myerses had begun to shift to threats of violence. Von Blum heard people talking of beating up the sympathizers. The mob eyed him and Lew. One of the people was a reporter from the local newspaper, the *Levittown Times*.

Suddenly, Lew felt a hand on his shoulder. He turned around to find his friend Barney Bell, the Texan truck driver with whom his family had become so close. "Lew," Bell drawled in his Southern accent, "you'd better go back into your house. It could get rough here." Lew eyed Bell, who was standing there with another mutual friend, who nodded. The message was clear: It was time for Lew to go back before he got hurt, and his buddies would watch his back.

Once inside, he and Bea saw out their window as Newell continued ranting and inciting the crowd, which had now grown to over 250 people since the police had left with the Myerses. At ten P.M., they saw a familiar man emerge from the shadows in a bow tie and suit: Sam Snipes. The Myerses' diminutive lawyer had received a call that evening telling him of the disturbance on Deepgreen Lane, and he wanted to do anything he could to help. Snipes eyeballed the agitated crowd, until he heard someone say, "Let's get the house!" Snipes wasn't a big man, but he was fast, having set records in the quarter mile in college, and knew he could get away in no time if need be. So he put himself in between the mob and the home in defiance, suggesting to them in vain that plainclothes cops were in the crowd.

"Thirty pieces of silver!" someone shouted, in reference to Judas' pawning of Jesus to the Romans, and another picked up the refrain: "Thirty pieces of silver!" Snipes did his best to ward them off, but they kept chanting the refrain. From out of the crowd came a cherry-red cigarette butt, which hit Snipes in the chest. More cigarette butts followed. Snipes tried to scan the faces, to imprint some record of these Levittowners in his mind. He caught a glimpse of Newell, hulking and flattopped. But that was all. Suddenly from out of the mob, a pack of teenagers stormed up to the Myers home and began hurling rocks. Six stones rained down on the home. Two of them crashed through panes in the Myerses' picture window, littering their new home with broken glass.

Cutting through the night came six police cars. Fifteen policemen poured onto the lawn carrying clubs. Feeling overwhelmed by the situation, Police Chief John Stewart had called the county sheriff, C. Leroy Murray, to come help. It was the first time in twenty-nine years a sheriff had been called in to restore order. But order wouldn't come easily. As the police were putting forty-five-year-old Howard Bentcliff and his forty-four-year-old wife, Agnes, in the car, the woman began to rave, "Come on, let's everybody get arrested! Let's make a big thing out of this!"

Three teenage boys, age fourteen to seventeen, also refused to leave. "Here is where the nigger lovers live," one shouted, pointing to the Wechslers' house.

"These niggers must have good lawyers to have the cops protect them," said another.

"These cops are all nigger lovers!" screamed the third, as the police finally dragged the teenagers away to arrest them for disorderly conduct.

Sheriff Murray grabbed his bullhorn and read the crowd the riot act, forbidding more than three people from gathering outside the Myerses' home. But the leaders of the mob had already hatched a plan to keep the family out of their suburb for good. They would call on the hero who had made their community whites-only in the first place: Bill Levitt.

Ten

THE SECRET CASTLE

INSIDE THE FORTY-THOUSAND-SQUARE-FOOT headquarters of Levitt & Sons near Levittown, Pennsylvania, Bill Levitt had a large oak desk with a telephone and an ashtray for his ever-present Camel cigarette. But when the *Bristol Daily Courier* reporter called on Wednesday morning, August 14, he didn't reach the boss. Instead, a Levitt spokesperson fielded the inquiry about the sale of the home on 43 Deepgreen Lane: Had Bill Levitt, the famed builder who had refused to sell homes to African-Americans, finally relented?

The Levitt & Sons representative assured the reporter that the sale was a "private transaction" that had no connection to the company. As far as the spokesperson knew, "there had been no cancellations of new home sales in Levittown." The Levitt exhibit center was packed, as always, he noted, and open for business. The press weren't the only ones having trouble getting Bill Levitt on the line. Representatives from the mob tried in vain to get ahold of the man they perceived to be their sympathetic leader. Bill Levitt was out of town, they were told.

Levitt had reason to duck the spotlight. Word of the riot had lured reporters and news cameras from around the nation. Organizations in the area publicly decried the violence he had allowed to ensue. "The right to live where one chooses is a basic American tradition," wrote the Bucks County Americans for Democratic Action in a statement. "Anyone who participates in mob rule in violence to oust a man and his family from his home is acting in an unlawful manner and against the democratic process.

We believe there is a place in the community for the Myers family and that they should be treated as any other new resident of Levittown."

For years, Levitt's party line had been that selling homes to African-Americans would cause the whites to move out, just as his family had done when a black district attorney had moved next door to them in Brooklyn. He failed to say why this would matter: Even if blacks replaced some whites, after all, the homes would still be filled. Why did he care about color?

The Concord Park Civic Association, from the low-cost, integrated community of 139 homes near Levittown, challenged Levitt on this point. A Concord Park spokesperson said, "We live in homes much like those in Levittown . . . It is a fact that the value of our homes has not decreased but improvements by white and Negro homeowners have added to the value. The Bucks County Realty Board has established the value at one thousand dollars higher than when the homes were built."

But as he ducked the spotlight in the wake of the Myerses' move, Bill Levitt remained firmly committed to his plan. As far as he was concerned, he had been standing up to opposition for decades about his whites-only policy; he had defied the orders of the Supreme Court, and he had become the country's biggest builder. And he wasn't going to mess with success now. In his mind, he was just giving the people what they wanted. In fact, at the same time that the Myerses were moving in, he was further expanding his exclusionary empire.

With his domineering father, Abraham, and his meddlesome brother, Alfred, out of the company—and his son William Levitt Jr. and nephew Roy Sheldon now on board instead—Levitt focused on his plan to build more whites-only communities across America. He set his sights on Willingboro, New Jersey, just ten miles south of Levittown, Pennsylvania, across the Delaware River. By now, he had acquired more than 90 percent of the township. More than fifteen thousand homes could be squeezed on the tracts, he estimated. He also had his eye on purchasing the 2,230-acre, eighteenth-century plantation of the Belair Estate in Bowie, Maryland, just fifteen miles from Washington, D.C. The plan: to construct six thousand homes there. The estimated profit, as one paper reported: six million dollars.

For Levitt, the combination of fortune and fame, the glory of having risen from nothing to become an iconic American tycoon, ballooned his enormous ego more than ever—and having just turned fifty, he obliterated any midlife crisis by living more lavishly and brazenly every day. He bragged that he despised exercise besides golf and relegated himself to reading only newspapers and magazines. He leased a sprawling apartment on Fifth Avenue in Manhattan and, in his bow ties and pin-striped coats, became a fixture around New York City. He rode in a chauffeur-driven limousine, spending long nights drinking Rob Roys with society leaders at nightclubs such as El Morocco. He had his own table at the ritzy Colony restaurant. He would be the first one to tell everyone where to sit, then order himself a juicy steak and tell everyone else what he or she should be eating.

He owned a mansion on Long Island where he indulged his every whim. A fan of fresh corn, he had a corn patch planted in his backyard. His butler would bring a hot, steaming ear of fresh corn out on a plate whenever it was in season. Long a supporter of Jewish causes, he and his wife, Rhoda, were known for their philanthropy in community groups around Long Island. Rhoda spent so much time at the local golf clubs that she became a leading player, with a 44 on the front nines.

While Rhoda was busy leading a fund-raising tournament at the Glen Oaks Club, Bill would get into a private plane and head off for work or play. On one occasion, he flew a bunch of buddies down to Havana to party at the Yacht Club. On the way back in his corporate jet, he told the pilot they were making a pit stop in Nassau, Bahamas. With eighty dollars from his friends, he marched up to the craps table and kept playing until he had won twenty-five hundred dollars—enough to pay for an extended week's vacation on the island for him and his group.

Stateside, he'd jet down to Bucks County and head for Levittown, Pennsylvania, in the back of his limousine. The car would wind through the curvilinear streets, past the houses, and the stores at the Shop-O-Rama, past the Walt Disney School, and up into the sections of streets all beginning with letter *R*—River, Rustleleaf, and, finally, Red Cedar. In the midst of the ranch homes, the car would cut left up a hill into the woods on a private lane tucked away on three rolling acres. On the right rose ten-foot walls and a medieval-looking watchtower. The car stopped at a wide wooden gate, like a drawbridge and a moat. Behind the gate was a five-bedroom mansion and a kidney-shaped swimming pool. It was Levitt's secret castle, the hub of his secret life.

While his wife and two boys, William and James, lived in New York, Levitt had a second life here in Levittown, Pennsylvania, with a mistress: his secretary from Levittown, New York, Alice Kenny. The affair had gone on secretly for years, and the home, which he had bought while building Levittown around it, was just as secure. No one could see what was going on behind the towering walls. Few Levittowners knew their founder lived nearby upon a hill, just one mile north of the Myerses' home on Deepgreen Lane.

As Daisy, Bill Myers, and their kids drove slowly into Dogwood Hollow in their blue-and-white Mercury the morning after the incident at their new home, the neighborhood seemed eerily quiet. It felt almost as if the events of the previous day had not happened. The family felt weary, having been up late the night before in their old home in Bloomsdale, replaying the scene. Daisy lay in bed awake asking herself questions she couldn't yet answer.

She wondered, "What toll would this take on Bill? Would he be able to hold on to his job? Are we different from the average family that moved to Levittown? Are we immune to the yearning for a little suburban home with green grass and flowers all around? Do we love our children less than they do? Are we sick and tired of ghettos? Do we have the right to choose a neighborhood or do the neighbors have a right to choose us? Have they come to tell us where we shall or shall not live? Aren't we human? What hope could we have that their distorted values would change? And, was it our responsibility to bring about the conversion? . . . Will this be the children's first memory of their new home?"

As they pulled into the driveway of their new home, evidence from the prior night's mob was impossible to ignore. Trash and cigarette butts littered the lawn, and the beautiful picture window at the front had jagged holes. Fear and anger shot through the Myerses when they saw the shattered window. What had they done to deserve this? Daisy thought, Why had this been done to an average American family? We are average, despite the fact that our skin is black.

Someone had tried to repair the front window, but the damage had been done. When Daisy and Bill opened the door, they saw a rock in the middle of the living room, surrounded by more glass. Daisy recalled a passage from the Bible: "Let him who is without sin among you be the first to throw a stone at her." Looking at the stone on her floor, she couldn't believe how something so small could be so foreboding. "The rock, weighing less than an ounce," as Daisy put it, "carried tons of hatred with it."

But they were determined not to let the hatred wear them down. While Bill kept the children away from the broken glass, Daisy began to sweep up the floor. Bill and the kids tended to the painting in the back, slapping fresh coats of paint on the walls. Daisy cooked up a hot breakfast, and they sat down to eat. But no sooner had they started to eat when the phone began to ring. They heard from family and friends and strangers, who were now getting word of the riot through the news and radio reports.

"I'm ashamed of my race," said a woman calling from across the state. Daisy thanked her for her support and hung up. Then the phone rang again. This time, it was man from Yuma, Arizona. "You may be sure that many of us are with you in your struggle against ignorant prejudice," he said. "Stick this out as long as you can, for it is brave people like you who are showing the world that all men are created equal."

The Myerses even got a call from a man at the local oil company, who pledged to help get them whatever they needed and bemoaned that the few hundred people in the mob had sullied the reputation of Levittown.

The moment Daisy hung up the phone, the doorbell rang. Bill approached the door cautiously. When he opened it, he was relieved to see his neighbors: the Wechslers. They had come with representatives of the Friends Service Association, who were there to help them throughout the day. And they quickly needed all the help they could get. Reporters began to call and show up wanting statements. Scared for their lives, the Myerses had been sleeping in their old home in Bloomsdale, and everyone wanted to know when they would be staying at their new home in Levittown. "My hot water and heating system isn't hooked up yet," Bill told a reporter, and he also said he had an oil tank that needed to be repaired. "As soon as that's complete I expect to move in," for good, Bill said. But he included a caveat: "If I feel there is some danger involved, I may have to reconsider."

Lew lent his support. "They have a right to live the same as any other Americans," he told a reporter from the *New York Times*. "The violence last night was horrible. I hope it ends." Just as the Myerses were feeling themselves drawn into the center of action, Bea and Lew now felt themselves in the midst of a struggle again. But this was different from their years fighting for causes in the shadow of McCarthyism. They were on the front lines themselves.

That day, Nick and Katy played with Stephen and William Myers in their backyard, trying to have a normal summer afternoon. Suddenly, they saw the strangest sight. Someone was throwing pears, one after another, at them from his lawn: The big fat bully who had helped them build their fort had now declared his standing on the side of the mob.

As the Myerses and Wechslers hurried the kids inside, they watched in horror as the mob outside began to grow again despite orders from the police not to congregate. Even the Circus Days event at the Shop-O-Rama and the dance for "subteeners" at the Levittown Indian Creek Pool couldn't keep the crowds away: teenage girls with long, white legs in dark blue shorts and plaid, sleeveless shirts. Teenage boys in cuffed blue jeans with greased-back dark hair. Pregnant women. Women with babies. Stoic men with crossed arms. They all surveyed the scene.

The stream of motorcycles and cars, many of which now brandished Confederate flags, was constant. By three thirty P.M., more than a thousand cars had come by 43 Deepgreen Lane to gawk. The Bristol Township policemen tried in vain to hold them back. They dispatched two police officers to block off each of the three points of entry to the neighborhood to anyone but residents. But they were no match for the crowd.

By seven P.M., the cars with Confederate flags were back caravanning around the homes. The Myerses had had enough. One-half hour later,

Daisy and Bill gathered up the children and headed for their car, accompanied by a police escort. As they left the house, the rowdy crowd fell quiet. When faced with the Myerses directly, this real family, these real people, not just some abstract entities, the crowd's demeanor changed. They were weak. Without a sound, they watched the Mercury drive away.

Once the Myerses were gone, however, a newfound energy emboldened the crowd. With twenty police officers now watching, the mob headed up to the Myerses' lawn. "We spent a lot of money on our homes," yelled one man. "They'll be worth nothing!"

"This is why I moved out of Philadelphia," another concurred.

People's minds raced with conspiracy theories, that the Myerses had been set up by the NAACP. "Whoever persuaded them to move here naturally picked a model Negro family," one woman said. "It's the families that will follow that worry me."

The police threatened to give parking tickets to anyone out front and would direct the crowd off the lawn—only to see them come back on as soon as the officers backed away. Before long, they gave up the cat-and-mouse game for good. The Wechslers watched out their window with horror as the police, who were supposedly there to protect them, let the crowd form unabated. To their astonishment, near nine P.M., the bulk of the police officers got into their cars and drove away.

One mile away at the Bristol Township Building in Levittown, the weekly commissioners' meeting was under way. Among the group was Hal Lefcourt, an early Levittowner, one of the first to move in, so original that he had earned the nickname Mr. Levittown. Few burst with town pride more than him. Raised poor in Newark, New Jersey, Lefcourt was thrown out of the marines for his severe stutter, but scraped enough money together to be one of the first five families to move into the community.

Lefcourt often recalled being greeted by William and Alfred Levitt upon his arrival with the first settlers in town. "We're happy you're here," they told him, "you're going to love it here." He relished those early days. He became active in politics, getting elected as a commissioner. He was known as the voice of the community, the PR guy for the town.

"There has never been an American Dream in America but Levittown," he would say.

As a member of the Bristol Township Board of Commissioners, he met with the group every week. But this was no ordinary meeting night. At ten P.M., the door burst open. Lefcourt looked out in shock on the angry faces of the mob. He had never seen anything like it in town before. They jammed into the room, dozens of them, hooting and hollering and demanding that the commission take action against the Myerses' move. "Do something!" they shouted. "Do something!"

One man came forward and decried the police's efforts to force people from protesting around the Myerses' home on Deepgreen Lane. "Disturbing the peace is one thing," he said angrily, "and talking is something else. Remember there's freedom of speech here!" The mob hollered behind him in support. "My wife is foreign-born," the man continued, "and she says the police here are worse than the Nazis in Germany!" The crowd shouted again in support.

"Last night was not an example of America!" replied the township manager bitterly.

The town solicitor tried to reason with the group: "You know as well as I do that the state constitution or the federal Constitution contain no words that mark out people for black or white . . . The federal courts have ruled in this matter. This question is not in the scope of the legal limitations of the commissioners."

Lefcourt agreed, "Let's end it here and now. We are a duly elected body. Our responsibility is to defend to the best of our ability the protection of property regardless of race, religion, or creed."

But the mob wasn't having any of it. "There's no law in this land that says we have to live alongside of them," said the mob's spokesman. "The family that moved into Dogwood Hollow caused the riot, not us."

"I abhor mob rule," Lefcourt replied, "and my advice to you people is to go back to your homes and try to work this out peacefully."

But the shouts continued. Minutes later, another group poured in, filling the room beyond capacity, with more than one hundred people. In the front row, Lefcourt saw the pinched face of a Levittown woman. "You tell that black cocksucking son of a bitch to get the hell out of here!" she shouted. "We're coming after her and we want her out of here!"

Lefcourt stared at her for a second, then glanced over to his lawyer for approval. They exchanged nods; whatever Lefcourt was going to say was fine by him. Lefcourt burst out, "You punk! Get out of here! Every one of ya, get outta here! You want her out, go get her out!" Lefcourt began to cry as he said the words, as he realized that this town, this great place he had taken so much pride in, was crumbling. "She lives in America where I live," he cried, "and she has a right to live wherever she wishes!"

There was a call for order and a slam of the gavel. But there was no way they could continue their regular meeting, and at eleven P.M., it was adjourned.

Lefcourt went home, shaken. What was happening to his Levittown? How had this nightmare replaced the dream? His telephone rang. "Lefcourt?" said a man with a thick Southern accent on the other end. It was James Newell, the flattopped leader of the mob who had been riling up the crowd at the mailbox on Deepgreen Lane on the night the Myerses moved in. Lefcourt knew Newell well. Newell was a Democratic committeeman, but also, Lefcourt thought privately, "a no-good, bigoted son of a bitch." And now he was inflamed that his group couldn't convene. "They won't let us meet," Newell said.

"Put a flag on top of your house then," Lefcourt screamed into his phone, "and go meet!"

The next day, an emergency meeting of the Human Relations Council, along with members of the local clergy, took place at the William Penn Center, the building where their plan was first hatched. Forty-five people from town organizations including synagogues, the women's league, and the Levittown Civic Association were in attendance. Because this was August, many clergymen were away on vacation, but their colleagues put out the urgent word to get back to Levittown immediately to help quell the crisis. Together they drew up a statement:

"We regret the violence, mob gatherings, and other unfortunate actions directed as a protest against the arrival of the William Myers family to our community. We know that many other residents feel as we do that the maintenance of human decency, law and order, and religious morality are of primary importance to the well being of our community. The events of the past few days have thrust our Levittown into such prominence that we now find ourselves responsible to our state, our nation, and to the world at large for the achievement of a solution worthy of us as Americans. Demonstrations of racial and religious bigotry have no place in our community, and we know that future developments in Levittown will keep faith with the wholesome democratic traditions of our nation."

They weren't the only ones pleading for help. That afternoon, Pennsylvania governor George Leader had been heading from his office in Harrisburg to his home when his secretary handed him a telegram from Levittown's chief of police. "The citizens of Levittown are out of control," the wire read. "The police have done all they can to quell the violence in which the Negro's home was stoned and two picture windows broken." As a result, the Levittown police urgently needed help from the state police so that the situation can be "quelled without bloodshed," Leader was told.

The telegram had come to the right man. Leader, a dapper forty-year-old with round glasses, was riding a crest of popularity. After winning election in an upset as the second-youngest governor in U.S. history and second Democrat to win the post in Pennsylvania in fifty years, he was featured on the cover of *Time* magazine, interlocking his hands victoriously over his head. He was also a native of York, Bill Myers's hometown.

Horrified by the events at Levittown, Leader condemned the disturbances during a county meeting with one hundred party leaders. "I am ashamed that this occurred in Pennsylvania," he told them. "The stoning of the home of the first Negro family in Levittown is completely alien to the historic principles on which Pennsylvania was built. Any family has the right to live where it can obtain the right of legal possession—on any street, road, or highway in the Commonwealth. Pennsylvania was founded by Quakers as a haven to all oppressed peoples."

While just a few dozen people showed up to support the Myerses, the mob had no problem outsizing them. Six hundred protesters gathered in the parking lot outside the John Billington VFW Post on Haines Road, just one mile from the Myerses' home. Cars crawled, and people were coming and going. The police lingered outside directing traffic, but little more. People from throughout the crowd took to the stage to denounce the Myerses. Some had come from as far as Philadelphia, they said, to make their voices heard. But the crowd considered this a town affair and resoundingly booed any outsiders. Finally their leader, Newell, took the stage to applause.

As the former commander of the post and the county's VFW, Newell had rented the post this night for one dollar. Dressed in dark slacks and a white shirt, the hulking man towered onstage over the crowd. Newell had trouble speaking over them, and he and his peers onstage tried in vain to quiet the boisterous crowd. One by one he fielded questions and comments from the crowd. It was said that the Myerses were being served by a local oil company, whom Newell suggested they boycott in protest. When some said boycotts were illegal, Newell said they should just cancel their contracts instead. The crowd cheered.

Five clergymen from throughout the community had shown up to talk sense in the group, but found only simmering hatred. One man in the mob even tried to pick a fight with one of the clergy, then announced that he was the chairman of the group they called the Levittown Betterment Committee. The purpose: "to protect betterment of our homes, community, family and investment and to organize interested active citizens in a legal and peaceful manner." Volunteers were picked, two from each of four major sections of Levittown—Area One, Area Two, Area Three, and Area Four—to go door-to-door soliciting members who would help them drive the Myerses from their home.

When they announced that they needed a volunteer in the Appletree Hill section, a hand shot up from the crowd. It belonged to John Bentley, a Democratic committeeman in town and onetime zoning officer for Bristol Township. He was not the only civic leader in the mob; he was also joined by the tax collector for Falls Township, who became the head of Area One, as well as a candidate for commissioner. Bentley was also a charter member and incorporator of the Levittown Fire Company Number 2.

He, like the others, felt the Levittown Civic Association was not taking enough action against the Myerses' moving in. He stepped to the stage and was asked if he would pledge membership to the group. "Yes," he said, "I would." Anyone who wanted to join the group could do so for the membership fee of one dollar.

One of the men elected as an area chief, John Piechowski, spoke up. He held an article from *Collier's* magazine that recounted William Levitt's reasons for not selling to blacks. " 'The Negroes were trying to do in six years what the Jews had not been able to completely do in six thousand,' " Piechowski quoted Levitt as saying, " 'and, being a Jew myself, I have no racial prejudice whatsoever, but if I sold to Negroes, ninety percent of the white people now buying homes would not buy.' According to Levitt's statement, the Betterment Committee must represent ninety to ninety-five percent of the people in Levittown." Piechowski concluded by saying, "The Prohibition was passed by Congress, and was repealed, so why can't the Civil Rights Bill also be repealed?"

As the crowd roared in approval, Newell spoke up again. "We will do everything within legal and peaceful means to get the Myers family out of the community," he explained in his Southern accent, looking down on the sea of the white faces. White men in horn-rimmed glasses. White women with wavy, dark hair. White teenagers in jeans. "But if it doesn't work, then we will have to do something else."

Others in the crowd weren't so subtle. There were only two ways to get the Myerses out, one man said, "We can vote them out, or we can force them out." The crowd had already made up its mind. One person replied, "Voting won't do any good." Others suggested alternatives. One man shouted, "Burn them out!"

Into the night, the angry crowd of hundreds marched down the lanes. What was once the model community didn't look like Levitt's sketches anymore. The hateful mob filed past the ranch homes like something out of a *Frankenstein* movie, as fearful faces peered out picture windows. When the mob arrived at Deepgreen Lane, however, they met resistance. A foot detail of twenty-one Pennsylvania state troopers stood outside with their clubs to greet them. They were led by Captain Alfred Verbecken, a veteran of the police for thirty-four years. They would stay, as ordered, for twenty-four hours, then with order restored they would leave.

This night, the Myerses were not there. They had driven up to York to get away from the insanity and visit Bill's parents. But as the Wechslers and their friends could see, the presence of the state police was not breaking up the crowd. The Levittowners were ripping a page from Bill Levitt's book and defying the law despite the orders. Lew jokingly called them the "Levittown Bitterment Committee." Drawing from union techniques, they formed a giant picket line, marching in pairs of two side by side, teenagers and parents, mothers with babies in strollers, clapping their hands in rhythm. They started in front of the Myers and Wechsler homes and circled around the block.

Down the street, Barney Bell, the Wechslers' truck-driving Texan neighbor, decided he had had enough. If the police weren't going to stop the violence, then he would. He stormed outside, jumped into his car, flipped the ignition, and floored it right over his perfectly mowed lawn toward the mob of racists—slamming on the brakes just a few feet away from them. The mob scurried from his lawn, but, as Bell told a reporter, he was the one aghast.

"This don't make any sense," he said. "This won't accomplish anything. These people don't have any right to do this." The mob was defying the Myerses' right to live where they wanted to live, he added, "and my right to sleep." Across the street, the mob closed in again on the Myerses' home. Someone hurled a rock the size of a baseball through the air, smashing it into the side of the house.

Before long the damage and chaos were spreading outside the neighborhood. Late that night, a police officer was driving near the Walt Disney Elementary School. Just two years before, Disney had come to inaugurate the school and its special role in this town. But now, under the dark skies, something else rose up in the place of that promise: an eight-foot-high bamboo cross wrapped in turpentine-soaked rags. And it was burning.

Eleven

THE BABY WON'T KNOW

THE BABY WAS fussing again. Daisy held Lynda, the month-old child bundled in white, in her arms as the blue-and-white Mercury hit a bump in the highway. Bill was behind the wheel, jazz music on the radio. Stephen and William, the boys, were fidgeting and playing in the back. It was Thursday morning, August 15, two days after the riots had started in Levittown, and they were escaping to York, back to the hometown they had left behind.

Though it only took two hours to get there, York felt like a world away. As Daisy looked out the window at the old familiar buildings, her mind reeled. Not long before, she had felt so alien here, so disappointed over the racism in the town that Bill had described with such great promise. They had left to seek a freer life near Philadelphia, away from the neighbor who was banging their door when the Myerses moved in. Daisy had always imagined that her life would have some kind of upward arc, that things would get better, for herself, her husband, her kids. But now, as they escaped the chaos of Levittown, York took on a new light, a beacon, a place to rest. And it was a place, they had decided, to leave the boys temporarily behind. They didn't want Stephen and William to have to endure the troubles in Levittown and had arranged to leave them with Bill's parents until things settled down. But no sooner had they walked into Bill's parents' house then came a knock at the door. Bill's father opened it to find a sea of reporters, cameras flashing, notebooks flapping in the air.

"Now let's have the Levittown story!" the reporters said.

Daisy and Bill eyed each other. Daisy's heart sank, as she instinctively held Lynda tight. There was no escape at all. What had happened to the Myers family I knew last week? Daisy wondered, feeling empty and confused.

Bill squeezed her hand as the reporters came in, shouting questions. While Bill had been quiet for so long, always wanting to stay out of the fray, there was no lying low anymore. "Nothing whatever will prevent me from living in the house," he told the newspeople. "I bought the home and I intend to live there." The photographers began snapping photos of the family on the couch. Bill propped Stephen, dressed in a crisp white shirt and striped pants, up on his leg, while Daisy held baby Lynda awkwardly aloft. The baby was crying as the bulb flashed, freezing them there, Bill's and Daisy's eyes on the baby, little Stephen reaching his arm toward her to help.

After a fitful night's sleep, Bill called upon their contacts within York to seek some kind of intervention in Levittown. A family friend knew someone in the House of Representatives who had just the guy for them to meet. The next morning, Daisy and Bill left the children and drove to the state capitol in Harrisburg to meet with Attorney General Thomas McBride. Daisy and Bill warmed to the tall, handsome man from the start. McBride's ancestors, like the Quakers, had come from a long line of people who fought for their civil rights. After emigrating from Ireland, he told them, his grandfather pulled a shotgun to ward off rioters from the Know-Nothing Party who had come to burn down a Catholic church that had just been built.

McBride told them how, when he was a young man in the National Guard in the 1920s, racists had several times burned crosses on his lawn because of his fights on behalf of blacks. It wouldn't be the last time. His wife, a schoolteacher in Bensalem, had once told her students that the Ku Klux Klan were cowards. News spread, and she came to school one morning to find a cross burning on the lawn.

Now they were facing the specter of such violence in the suburb of Levittown. Just that morning, a telegram had come to the governor's office from the Citizens Committee of Levittown warning that "violence is a probability," and that they needed help.

McBride listened attentively, then looked at Daisy and Bill. "I have one question. Do you want to stay in Levittown?"

Daisy and Bill replied, "Yes."

That was all McBride needed to hear. The state police had already gone once to Levittown to try to quell the uprising and left, but now he would send them back. "The state police will be there when you return and will remain there as long as necessary," he said.

While Daisy and Bill sought help in Harrisburg, Bea and Lew hunkered inside their home for the fight of their lives in Levittown. After years of protesting and leading union battles, they called on all their organizational skills. The house was a bustle of activity as the mob jeered and hollered outside. Reporters and TV crews poured into their home. Katy and Nick were busy making ice-cold lemonade and serving the glasses to their guests.

The director of civil rights for the AFL-CIO sat at their kitchen table, working the phones to supporters from Philadelphia to New York. "Our committee works as the human rights arm of the labor movement," he told a reporter. "All people regardless of race, creed, or color are entitled to the decencies of human life. The right to a good home is one of these rights, and we propose to do everything possible to help the Myers family enjoy these rights."

Lew came over and chimed in saying that he was "shocked" at the treatment the Myerses had received and blamed the police. "If the police had done a more efficient job," he said, things would not have "gone this way."

For Bea and Lew, this was not just the fight of the town, this was a fight for the country, and for their neighbors. "Mrs. Myers is a wonderful woman," Bea told the reporter. "She has been a teacher in Bristol Township's Recreation Department. It is a shame that this has happened, but I still believe that we will live in peace." The reporter scribbled in her notebook. Bea had one more bit to add: "Please say how proud I am of my daughter, Katy, because although I wasn't home when the Myerses moved in, my little girl brought them over here to get a cold drink and a chance to rest. I am proud of her because she acted in an American manner."

Outside the Wechslers' window, the mob forming in plain view of the police told a different story of America. Ordinarily, the Levittowners would be home tonight watching *Dragnet* or *The Lone Ranger*. This evening, James Newell and his cronies at the Levittown Betterment Committee had called another meeting at six P.M., but it wouldn't be at the VFW. After the negative attention, the commander of the Department of Pennsylvania VFW announced that they were investigating the matter. "I personally and officially denounced association of our organization's name with this matter, regret its occurrence, and forbid any such meetings at the Levittown post, or at any other VFW post," he said.

Undeterred, Newell led the mob to the backyard of a home just around the corner from the Myerses' on Dogwood Drive. Hundreds of his followers marched down the street—so many that it became difficult for attendees to park. One gray-haired man asked a resident man named Snyder not attending the rally if he could park on his lot. "If you come in peace, all right," the resident replied, "but any violence, and I'm going to call the police."

The gray-haired man snarled, "Do you mean to tell me you are denying me the right to park here?"

Snyder eyeballed him defiantly. "You understand what I told you."

The gray-haired man turned to the mob. "Gang! Here is a goddamn nigger lover!"

"Where?" someone yelled.

"Where is the son of a bitch?" another cried.

Snyder's wife heard the commotion from inside her home and came running outside over the lawn. "I defy you to harm one hair on my husband's head!" she shouted.

"Let's get rid of the big son of a bitch of a nigger lover!" the gray-haired man shouted. A group of teenage boys drove slowly up in a 1949 car. They had knives and guns, they said, and they'd be happy to help the mob. Eventually, the mob retreated, but then the Snyders' phone rang. "Look here," said the voice on the other end of the line, "if you know what is good for you, you want to watch your step because I am telling you we have crosses to burn on sympathizers' lawns."

Mrs. Snyder hung up and called the police urgently for help. "What can we do to protect ourselves?"

"Within your rights," she was told by the police, "if anyone tries to harm you bodily, you can kill. But try not to go that far."

By now, over six hundred people filled the Levittown streets outside. The Betterment Committee had been working the crowd, passing around a petition to recruit members. "Protest from the citizens of the _____ section of Levittown, Pennsylvania," it read. "We, the citizens and home owners of Levittown, Pennsylvania, protest the mixing of Negroes in our previously all-white community. As moral, religious and law-abiding citizens, we feel that we are unprejudiced and undiscriminating in our wish to keep our community a closed community. In as much as having equal rights, the Negroes have an equal opportunity to build their own community of equal value and beauty without intermingling in our community. We therefore feel that we must keep our community closed to protect our own interests."

Dressed in dark slacks and a white, button-up shirt, with the sleeves rolled up his thick triceps, Newell got onstage. He was flanked by a crewcut man in a long-sleeved, plaid shirt. Eldred Williams, the thin, scrawny sidekick with a cigarette dangling from his lips, lurked nearby. Men with crossed arms looked up, and a little girl sat on her father's shoulders. Newell informed the crowd that they needed to get 51 percent of the Levittowners to sign the petition to get the Myerses out. The crowd cheered. But he urged them to not descend into "mob violence. We have to settle this by peaceful means."

Bentley, the former township zoning officer, urged the crowd "not to panic. Don't put your house up for sale because of this. That is what they want." The crowd burst into applause.

Ruth Rolen, a black female reporter from the *New Jersey Afro American*, was trying in vain to interview the protesters. She roamed the lawn in a long dress clutching a notebook as a dog began to bark. Nearby, a

The Levitts, from left, William, Abraham, and Alfred. (*Courtesy Levittown Public Library*)

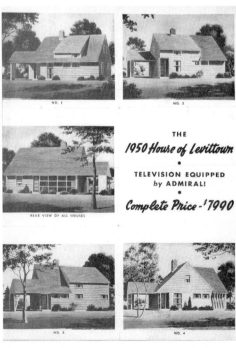

THE
1950 House of Levittown
•
TELEVISION EQUIPPED
by ADMIRAL!
•
Complete Price - $7990

A Levitt ad. (*Courtesy Levittown Public Library*)

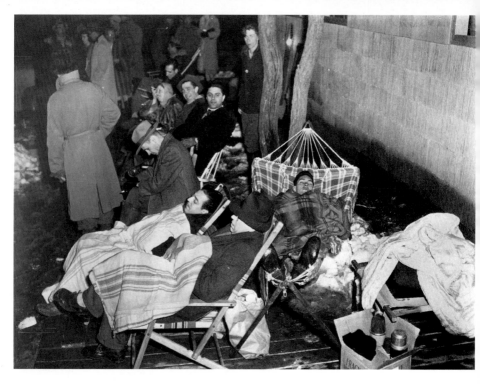

Camping out for Levittown homes.
(Courtesy Levittown Public Library)

Taking orders for
Levittown houses.
*(Courtesy Levittown
Public Library)*

The Myers family, from left, Bill, William III, Lynda, Daisy, and Stephen. (*Courtesy Charlotte Brooks*)

The Wechsler family, from left, Bea, Nick, Lew, and Katy. (*Courtesy Wechsler family*)

A crowd forms outside the Myers home on Deepgreen Lane. (*Courtesy Temple University Urban Archives*)

Broken windows from stones thrown at the Myers home. (*Courtesy Temple University Urban Archives*)

Daisy Myers holds baby Lynda as they look at the mob outside their kitchen window. (*Courtesy Charlotte Brooks*)

James Newell of the Levittown Betterment Committee addresses a crowd.
(*Courtesy Temple University Urban Archives*)

A mob surrounds a police car near the Myers home.
(*Courtesy Temple University Urban Archives*)

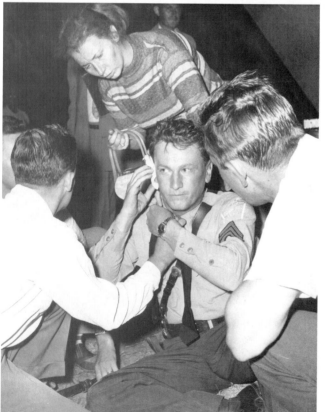

Bill Myers, left, and Lew Wechsler work together in the Myers home. *(Courtesy Charlotte Brooks)*

A Levittown police sergeant injured by a rock thrown during the Myers protest. *(Courtesy Temple University Urban Archives)*

Lew Wechsler with the KKK letters painted on the side of his home. (*Courtesy Queens Borough Public Library, Long Island Division, New York Herald Tribune Photograph Morgue*)

Bill Myers, left, and Lew Wechsler on Deepgreen Lane. (*Courtesy Charlotte Brooks*)

The Myers family, with baby Barry, pose for a picture outside their home on Deepgreen Lane after winning their battle in Levittown. (*Courtesy Myers family*)

William Levitt found hard times in the years following the Levittown riot. (*Courtesy Temple University Urban Archives*)

disheveled man in an orange shirt said with a devilish smile, "Even dogs don't like niggers, they can smell them too." As an Associated Press photographer aimed his camera at the scene, the man in the orange shirt protested, "Don't take our pictures with those niggers!"

Observing the fracas, Newell spoke up again, urging the crowd for "no mob violence." A few applauded, but one man barked back, "You sound like you are on the niggers' side!"

Newell stood firm, urging them not use the word *nigger*. He began to joke about the threats on his life that he had allegedly endured since taking his stand. "I was supposed to be dead tonight," he said, eliciting laughs. But with just a bit of encouragement, he slipped back into his diatribe: "Why did Mr. Myers pick out our area? Is he a fool or does he think he's better than any other colored person?" The crowd cheered as Newell became more invigorated. "We will try our best to give Mr. Myers consideration, but are we to allow our happy community to go to pot?"

More cheers, and cries of "No" met him back.

"We must settle by law this situation in which one man did not have the decency and common courtesy to respect the rights of other men," Newell said.

As his speech came to a close, reporter Rolen pursued the mob as they made their way through the night to the Myerses' neighborhood. They clapped and jeered as they cut through the streets. Some broke off toward Newell's house, which became a makeshift headquarters, teeming with acolytes. As Rolen and her colleague tried to get inside, one of Newell's followers shouted, "Don't let them come in here!" But then, from the shadows, Newell emerged to usher them inside.

Leaning back against the wall with his beefy arms crossed over his chest, Newell tried to explain himself. He had nothing against the Myers family personally, he said, and added that his mother lived next to a black family in Durham.

"So why do you object to colored residents living here?" the reporter asked.

Newell cracked a grin. "Would you like me to live in your neighborhood?"

"Yes,"she replied.

At that, Newell stammered, "Well, I can't express myself very well I guess."

From behind him, a supporter chimed in on Newell's behalf: "He doesn't want them living here because of all the crime and violence that happens where colored people live."

"But isn't the movement you're leading here against colored people a type of resistance that encourages lawlessness?" Rolen said.

Newell stared down at her and replied, "This is different." Then he went back to join the crowd outside. Down the block by the Myerses' home, he found the state troopers waiting. The troopers did not interfere with the protest, despite that they admitted to a reporter that the crowd was unlawfully assembling after being read the riot act. As Captain Verbecken explained, they were willing to look the other way: "As long as it stays orderly, there is little we will do about keeping them away."

As Newell worked his way through the crowd, Verbecken beckoned him into his car and asked, "Are you the spokesperson for this organization?"

"We are all spokesmen," Newell said, "but I was asked by neighbors to speak for them, and they are all my friends, so I took over the job."

"Well, what's the purpose of this congregation?"

"Protesting the moving of this colored family into this neighborhood."

"Well, don't you think you are barking up the wrong tree? If you have any complaint, report it to the police, and don't take the law in your own hands."

"We always tell people we don't want any violence."

Verbecken eyed him, as the crowd noisily milled outside the car windows. "How can you control violence when you have got a group of persons with an ax to grind as large as this?" he said dubiously. "Did you tell them this the other night when the windows were broken?"

"We always tell them we don't want any violence," Newell repeated, then left.

Outside, the jingling bell of an ice cream truck cut through the night. With so much action, the driver had filled his truck with treats. As his truck came down the block, the mob lined up to buy Popsicles and chocolate-dipped cones, kids clamoring for money from their parents. A cop rushed over to break up the crowd. It was against a township ordinance, he said, to sound the ice-cream-truck bell after eight P.M.

"This is America!" the crowd began to angrily chant. "This is America! This is America!"

The ice cream truck's jingle was turned off. But the ice cream continued to sell. That night, the ice cream man said, his business was a "landslide." Soon, the marching mob resumed its course, circling around and around the Myerses' home. The person leading the march was a seven-year-old boy.

At six P.M. on Saturday, August 17, the Wechslers could see a crowd forming again down the road on Dogwood Drive—just down from the Myerses, who were still away. Now someone put a park bench on a lawn, so the mob could have somewhere to sit as they jeered. A rumor had swelled that the Myerses were moving in that night. Newell made the rounds with Eldred Williams at his side.

Despite the police order not to congregate, the mob felt they could be as defiant as Levitt and insisted they would stand their ground. More than three hundred people—men in shorts, women with strollers, teenagers on bikes—crowded behind the house, spilling out onto a nearby field, waiting for the meeting to begin. It was being delayed, however, Newell told them, until they had one more necessary ingredient: an American flag. A half hour later, someone showed up with the flag, which was hung on the side of the house.

Newell lowered his head in prayer as he said, "Our Father, who art in heaven, hallowed be thy name. Thy kingdom come. Thy will be done, on earth as it is in heaven. Give us this day our daily bread. And forgive us our trespasses, as we forgive those who trespass against us. And lead us not into temptation, but deliver us from evil. For thine is the kingdom, and the power, and the glory, for ever and ever."

The crowd replied, "Amen!"

One by one speakers took the stage, which had now been outfitted with a microphone. One man began by making overtures to the Myerses, showing faint signs of sympathy. But the crowd booed and jeered, inspiring Newell to take the stage. Newell beamed from the attention. He had put on a suit jacket and one of his favorite ties, an extrawide number doodled with putting greens and golf clubs. Newell called for order. There was no need for violence against the Myerses, he said, the crowd were dedicated instead to finding "peaceful and legal means" of getting them to leave. Negroes wouldn't be happy in Levittown, he added. They were just trying to help them by not having them here.

The crowd cheered, but then Newell caught something in the corner of his eye: the sheriff's car approaching, along with a dozen police. Sheriff Murray took the stage amid catcalls and boos as he read a statement: "Mob rule has never succeeded in attaining any goal. Use good judgment and return to your homes peacefully before serious consequences result."

As the crowd booed, Newell grabbed the microphone and read the first amendment: "Congress shall make no law respecting an establishment of religion, or prohibiting the free exercise thereof; or abridging the freedom of speech, or of the press; or the right of the people peaceably to assemble, and to petition the Government for a redress of grievances."

Before long, six hundred mob members gathered back at the Myerses' house, and the police moved in to get them. When one man resisted, a policeman charged, grabbing him in a headlock as a state trooper rushed in and struck the man with his club. As chaos broke out, a photographer closed in to capture the moment, but a police club smashed him in the face.

Every Saturday, the *Levittown Times* ran a column by the thirty-two-year-old Reverend Ray Linford Harwick of the Evangelical and Reformed Church of the Reformation in Levittown, Pennsylvania. Harwick was one of the first clergy in the community and was an upstanding husband and father, and his column, called "The Pastor Speaks," was well read. Sam Snipes, the Quaker attorney who had helped the Myerses early on, described Harwick as leading "a very fine liberal church that stands up for every good cause."

On Saturday, August 17, Harwick's column exhibited his usual blend of folksy and earnest style. He wrote that he sympathized with those who found the Bible's language stilted and daunting and comforted them by allaying the pressure to master more than that which they were able. "As a sailor can learn to sail the ocean without knowing all its mysteries," he wrote, "so you and I can learn enough truth to live well without knowing all there is to know about God."

Back in his home in Levittown, however, Harwick had spent the week learning truths of his own. On the morning of the fifteenth, just after coming home from vacation with his family, Harwick got a call from the president of the Lower Bucks County Council of Churches about the Myers incident. Harwick was stunned. As liberal as he had been, he had never preached about civil rights or had to consider such outcomes in his community or parish. The first thing he did was to get down on his knees and pray. Then he went over to the Myerses' house to help.

Harwick hurried between the Myerses' home and the meetings of the Betterment Committee, trying to bridge the chasm—but to no avail. And he saw things beyond his imagination. The preaching of hate by the mob. The defiance of Newell and Williams. The assertion that they would throw out the Myerses using "peaceful and legal" means. At one meeting, Harwick and a few other clergy appealed to the mob, only to see the angry, scowling faces rush at them and threaten one clergyman with violence.

Harwick volunteered to become chairperson of the newly formed Citizens Committee for Levittown—a group designed to keep the Levittown Betterment Committee at bay. The town was dividing, and he knew which side he was on. When a local reporter asked him to make his first statement for the group, Harwick said, "Many people and many additional religious and civic organizations share our feeling against violence. The Citizens Committee for Levittown has formed so that all decent and law-abiding citizens and groups may make themselves heard in their community and around the world." Harwick told another reporter, "This is no longer a local situation. The eyes of the world are on us."

Other religious groups throughout Levittown joined the cause. The Lower Bucks County Council of Churches released a "Statement Concerning Fair Housing Practices" urging each resident to "do his utmost to welcome all new people into our area and do everything in his power to make all newcomers feel accepted." The Jewish Community Council of Lower Bucks County issued its own stand, "knowing that an upright man is a blessing to his community and that the color of a vessel gives us no clue to its contents."

The same group, along with the Council of Churches, the William Penn Center, and Levittown Civic Association, and the Friends Service Association put out their own opposition in a "Declaration of Conscience," which read, "We regret the violence, mob gatherings, and other unfortunate actions directed as a protest against the arrival of the William Myers family to our community. We know that many Levittown residents feel as we do that the maintenance of human decency, law and order and religious morality are of primary importance to the well-being of our community. The events of the past few days have thrust our Levittown into such prominence that we now find ourselves responsible to our state, our nation, and to our world at large for the achievement of a solution worthy of us Americans. Demonstrations of racial and religious bigotry have no place in our community, and we know that further developments in Levittown will keep faith with the wholesome democratic traditions of our lives."

One paper praised the "admirable and Christian sentiment" expressed by the Myerses' next-door neighbors, who said, "They have a right to live the same as other Americans." Lew Wechsler couldn't help but laugh: "I, a Jew, have expressed these 'Christian' sentiments!"

On Sunday morning, August 18, after the weekend of riots, Harwick and his fellow clergy across Levittown took to their pulpits to urge peace. At the Hope Lutheran Church, one reverend devoted his entire sermon to the conflict. "I regret exceedingly that a group of Levittown citizens have used violence in an attempt to settle the dispute over the William Myers family's residence in Levittown," he said. "It constitutes a violation of God's will and cannot call forth his blessing upon our community." Others urged members to "become a center of calmness and peace in your own neighborhood . . . and indicate by your words and actions, at any mention of violence to property or person, that this is not the way."

But the message was lost on the Betterment Committee. That morning Newell issued a statement of his own that read, "The Levittown Betterment Committee . . . has gained strength and intends to stand upon its constitutional right and the right to free and peaceful assembly. We denounce the action of C. Leroy Murray, sheriff. We wish to announce openly to Sheriff Murray that we are calling another meeting this week. We want all Levittowners to join us in decrying the only real violence today: the brutal clubbing of one of the citizens of Levittown by the Pennsylvania State Police. Another protest meeting is planned. We want a peaceful, orderly and uninterrupted meeting. The purpose of the organization is that of restoring our entire white community."

It didn't take long for Harwick to discover the price that came with speaking out. That night after his church service, his phone rang at home. Harwick's wife answered. "This is the KKK calling," the person said, then hung up.

The phone rang again. "This is the white citizens council calling," this one explained, and hung up.

The next call came: "Nigger lovers!" The line went dead.

Harwick did his best to engage those who would remain on the line. They spoke of their fear of losing the value of their homes, the ones they had worked so hard to buy and maintain. Harwick strained to convince them otherwise, but it was to no avail. The minute he hung up, the phone would ring again.

"Hello?"

"How many children did you say you had, Reverend? Is it three?" Then the line went dead.

Less than a mile away, Daisy and Bill sat on the edge of their bed at their old home in Bloomsdale Gardens. They had driven back from their trip to Harrisburg and York and left their boys temporarily with Bill's parents, taking only baby Lynda and their necessary belongings with them. Nothing was left in this old home of theirs but their bed and a few boxes. Despite the presence of the state troopers, they knew that the tensions in Levittown were escalating. They couldn't help but fear what might happen when they stayed at Deepgreen Lane for good. "Do you think it's safe to sleep there now?" Bill said.

There were no guarantees, they knew, but at the same time they felt a new strength emerging—a refusal to be run out of their home by the mob. They would have to take a stand. "Well," Daisy replied, "we have to make it our first night sooner or later, so we might as well start now." In the bassinet, they heard Lynda fussing again. "If we're killed in that house," Daisy told Bill, "the baby will be too young to know. At least we'll have the boys to carry on."

Twelve

THE MISSING THUMB

AUGUST 1957 WAS supposed to be a month of celebrations for Bill Levitt. Levittown, New York, was getting ready to honor its tenth anniversary with a communitywide bash in October. There would be a beauty contest and a festive ball. Fashionable townies would dance to all the year's biggest hits—such as "That'll Be the Day" by Buddy Holly and the Crickets—late into the night. Levittowners flooded the mom-and-pop stores along the town's communal parks, the village greens. They would even have a float chugging down the main road to honor the town's fairy-tale rise from the potato fields, like a beanstalk from a magic garden, after the war ended not long ago.

While the Levitt legacy was being honored, Bill and his brother, Alfred, were busy building their next ventures. Bill now had enough land to build his next Levittown—Levittown, New Jersey, which was on track to open the following year. Alfred, now on his own, was building an apartment complex on Long Island. The two brothers were still congenial, even though they no longer worked together. Abe, happily retired, tended to his own gardens and joked that both his sons were constructing communities near mental institutions. "All is all right," he said, "the boys are building close to insane asylums."

But despite the growth and honors, it was becoming painfully clear that Bill's new reign as the sole Levitt of Levitt & Sons was jeopardizing the company's brand name. While he sat in the back of his chauffeured limousine getting whisked from restaurant to nightclubs in New York or between his family in the city, and his life in the secret castle in Pennsylvania, it was difficult to escape the scandal exploding around Deepgreen Lane. The fairy tale was in danger of being overshadowed by reality.

In the past, Bill Levitt had found creative ways to maintain control of his own story. He wrote his own press releases, conducted his own press conferences, and the reporters eagerly regurgitated the heroic story of the builder who saved America. When there had been outrage over his desire to change the name of Island Trees to Levittown in New York, Levitt responded by buying and becoming the publisher of the local paper—and silencing his critics. The national press had, meanwhile, focused largely on spreading the fairy-tale version of the Levittown story and was still slow to cover the emerging civil rights movement in depth. The *Levittown Times* in Pennsylvania supported Levitt by refusing to publish an editorial denouncing the riot against the Myerses.

Other local publications, however, began to take aim at America's most famous builder. BILL LEVITT THE CULPRIT was the headline on a damning editorial in the *Philadelphia Evening Bulletin*: "Levittown was conceived and built as an all-white community by William Levitt without any concern of the social implication involved. From the beginning all Negro applicants were turned down on the sole basis of color. The builder let it be known that he would not under any circumstances sell a single house to any Negro, regardless of his character or financial status. It is reasonable to assume that Mr. Levitt used racial prejudice against Negroes as one of his chief selling points . . . Thoughtful citizens pointed out to Levitt the unfairness of his enterprise and disastrous results which would naturally follow from the establishment of such a town in the Commonwealth of Pennsylvania. But he was not interested in the valiant struggle being made in this State by public officials and civic-minded citizens to improve the relationship between white and colored citizens. His only concern was to make money."

For Levitt, the moneygrubbing accusations fed on the worst stereotypes. In fact, he was a generous philanthropist, particularly in support of Jewish causes. During the war, Levitt had led his local chapter of the United Jewish Appeal for Refugees and Overseas Needs to fund Jews facing persecution in Eastern Europe. Since then, he had made many donations to the state of Israel.

But his stance on civil rights was tarnishing his image. Meanwhile, the Wechslers provided a different Jewish response to the struggles of African-Americans: not divisiveness, but solidarity. Levitt's refusal to take such a stand led critics to hold him accountable for the ugliest of crimes. "Of course," the *Philadelphia Evening Bulletin* editorial concluded, "the hoodlums who stoned the home of the Myers' family this week are not blameless and deserve the scorn of all decent people, but the real culprit is Bill Levitt, the architect and builder of this cess-pool of hate."

For the ambitious tycoon, the Levittown fantasy was being torn down before his eyes. "Levittown is a disgrace to America!" wrote the *Philadelphia Tribune*. "The people responsible for this Jim Crow town in the Commonwealth of Pennsylvania are as prejudiced as the most anti-Negro bigot in the Deep South." In nearby Trenton, New Jersey, LEVITTOWN'S SHAME was the title of an editorial in the *Trenton Evening Times*. "Levittown is a new and attractive community which so far in its brief history has had a creditable record of good neighborly relations and orderly behavior by its residents," the item read. "It is in many respects a model town . . . [but] this demonstration of racial antagonism reveals an unseemly and repulsive aspect of life in a community whose people enjoy many superior advantages. Something better in the way of tolerance was to be expected of them . . . It is not conceivable that this demonstration of mob violence is representative of the spirit of Levittown as a whole."

The battle was, in fact, not just bringing out the ugly side of Levittown; it was also bringing out the inspirational. Every day, legions of supporters turned out to join the Myerses' and Wechslers' stands. Lew's United Steelworkers Union asked members in an editorial printed on the front page of the union newspaper "not to participate in any un-American acts of bigotry" and to "unite with the law enforcement bodies and the many good people of Levittown to help stop these acts of bigotry."

The working people in the Bucks County area began to line up against Levitt too. The Joint Council representing thirty thousand members of the Amalgamated Meatcutters and Butcher Workmen condemned "the disgraceful incidents following purchase by a Negro family of a home in Levittown." The president of the group said, "It is shocking that within the area enshrining Independence Hall, the cradle of our liberty, and in a state founded by men and women fleeing from authoritarian restriction of their civil rights, we should witness a racist outbreak hitherto thought possible only in our notoriously more backward communities." Philadelphia mayor Richardson Dilworth agreed: "I know that the Southern advocates of segregation must be sitting back and getting a horse laugh out of what is happening in Levittown."

The very people of Levittown considered the standoff as nothing less than the fight for the soul of new suburbia. "You look toward the pink house with the white trim and you wonder too about the young people inside who are colored," wrote one Levittowner in a Philadelphia newspaper. "Do they love their children less than you love yours? Do they thrill less at the sight of the first crocus in the spring? Do they fret less when the crabgrass begins to gnaw into a neatly trimmed lawn? Are they immune to the yearning for a little suburban home with green grass all around?"

On Monday morning, August 19, Bill and Daisy Myers had one last breakfast in their Bloomsdale Gardens home. It was sadly quiet without the boys. Lynda napped soundly. Steam rose from the coffee Daisy poured in Bill's cup and mingled with the smoke from his cigarette. The six long days of this ordeal had exacted a toll on Bill. He was having trouble sleeping from all the anxiety. Daisy urged him to see a doctor, who told him it was nervous tension. But now it only felt worse.

Today was the day they would move to Levittown once and for all. But to make matters more difficult, the two-week vacation Bill had taken from work was over and he had to return to his job. When Daisy hugged him good-bye, she felt at war with herself—frozen numb on the outside, but with a storm of fear underneath. As the door shut behind her husband, she had never felt more alone.

Before long the doorbell rang. It was a friend from Levittown there to accompany Daisy and Lynda to 43 Deepgreen Lane. Daisy took one last look at the Bloomsdale Gardens house she was leaving behind and hit the road. As they cut through the curvilinear Levittown streets at eleven A.M., remorse consumed her. She feared how much they could take, and what might happen to them in the end. African-Americans were being hung and killed in the South, and who was to say what their fate would be here? Suburbia looked different, but the presence of evil was the same.

As she came up Deepgreen Lane, her heart sank even deeper. What had happened to the once beautiful pink and white-trimmed home with which she had fallen in love? As she looked at the ranch with its boxy windows and tiny garage, other words flashed in her mind: Dull. Unattractive. Insignificant. Unworthy. It was, she resolved, "the house of doubt," and her family's fate was on the line.

This feeling was underscored by the four police officers she saw guarding the front of her home as she arrived. With the two white friends who drove her carrying her small suitcases and towels, Daisy took Lynda in her arms and walked steadily to the door. Daisy's head swam with doubts about their future, and their safety. The voices of the neighbors talking about blowing up her house with dynamite echoed in her head.

As she approached, however, she couldn't believe her eyes. Friends and strangers had come to clean up the mess. Their lawn was mowed. Their curtains hung. Their broken window, replaced. She was touched by the outpouring of love amid such overwhelming hate. Maybe things would turn around after all. But when she unlocked her door and pushed to open it, the door wouldn't budge. Daisy's heart pounded again. She checked the window to see if, somehow, another stone had been hurled through and was now blocking the door from opening.

With another shove, she finally got through—and was stunned to see what was blocking the way: an enormous pile of mail that had been slipped through the door's mail slot. In just the few days since they'd been away, letters had arrived from all over the world, from Australia to their neighbors right down the street in Levittown. Daisy opened one, hesitantly, and began to read. What hateful words awaited her? she wondered.

"You're not alone," it read. She quickly opened another. "We're with you," it read. And another. "Stick with it," this one reassured, "don't let these prejudiced, ignorant people drive you out of your home." One by one, Daisy opened each letter to find words of support—not one had a word of hate. The more she read, the more she felt something inside herself shift. For months, she and Bill had reassured themselves—and others—that all they wanted was a good home. They didn't want a fight. But this wasn't just about Levittown and her family anymore, this was about the civil rights of all people. This house was more than a home. It was becoming a symbol. And she felt herself changing too. She was part of a community that reached far beyond Levittown. It was the community of every American who sought equal rights. Realizing this, she had never felt so strong.

Less than an hour after she came in, a small crowd began forming across the street again. All the while, the cops just stood by. Soon the men and women in the cars were honking too, making as much noise as they could—clapping, singing, shouting. They were getting used to this. Now instead of just milling about, they would sit on the benches on the lawn across the street and accost the Myerses in comfort. Throughout the afternoon, the ice cream truck would come by, selling desserts to the onlookers. Daisy saw the Confederate flags in the windows of the cars going by. There were plenty of flags to go around; they were selling them at the Levittown Shopping Center next to the barbecue and lawn supplies. As one housewife told a reporter, "It's just like a fad, everyone's buying them."

By the time Bill returned from work, the mob and reporters had gathered again. Bill could barely make it to the front door without being besieged. Once inside, tired from work and the attention, he pulled his wife aside. She had drawn the drapes to keep the chaos out of view. "Oh, Daisy," he said, "let's give up. I'm ready to call it quits."

Daisy took him by the hand. "Come here, I want to show you something." She brought him into the kitchen where a couple of friends were helping her sort through the enormous pile of support letters. Bill sat down and began to read, holding back tears. There was even a letter of support from baseball legend Jackie Robinson, urging them to remain strong. Though the press had been playing up the violence, he saw, their experience was as much about people coming together. It was not just about evil, but about good, the power of neighbors, and the enormity of what they could accomplish together. As he read, he saw their supporters around them lending hands. One showed up with a bassinet for Lynda. Others came carrying bags of groceries.

Bill and Daisy would remain quiet no more. At six thirty P.M., he and Daisy invited the reporters into their home for an interview. But Daisy turned the questions back on them: "Why don't you newspapermen write about the good things happening to us? One hundred and fifty Levittown people have written us letters. Others have mowed our lawn, hung our curtains, presented us with a fine oil painting, brought cakes and fruit, and kept us busy receiving well-wishers."

A photographer directed them into domestic poses, including one shot of Daisy filling Bill's coffee cup as he looked up at her from the table. The jeers and boos of the mob could be heard coming from outside, making the moment feel even more staged and surreal. Advisers from the various support groups stood by him. One urged Bill and Daisy to quote from the Bible to the reporters, but they declined, feeling this was too stereotypical of a response. Even their supporters were asking them to behave in what they thought were appropriately African-American ways.

Why would the family move to Levittown? one reporter asked. Why not move into Concord Park nearby where other Negroes lived? Bill explained that Concord Park was farther away from his work and would have increased his commute. But beyond that, he said, he had as much right as anyone to be here: "I am a veteran, and I feel that I have a right to live where I choose. I selected my Levittown home because it fits my family's needs."

"Would you sell the house for a profit if you could now?" another reporter asked.

"No."

"Are you afraid of the mob?" another wanted to know.

"I'm sure the police will offer protection as long as I need it," Bill said. "I'm certain this will all subside, and the people will go home soon. I know the crowds outside are not indicative of the feeling of most people in Levittown. It has been a great strain on us. I hope all this will quiet down, and I'll be able to live a normal life."

Did he anticipate such a reaction?

"I knew all the reaction wouldn't be favorable. I expected some trouble, but I never thought it would be so bad . . . All I want is to be a good neighbor, and I hope others do the same. I don't believe the demonstrations that have been held present a true picture of the feelings of the people of Levittown. All people are good of heart." And he added, "I believe that when this is over, all of us will have been enlightened and there will be no resentment."

Finally, the ultimate question came: "Will you give up?"

Outside the drawn drapes the mob hollered and jeered. Bill looked the reporter in the eye and replied, "I intend to stay in Levittown unless there are unforeseen developments. All I want is a chance to be a good neighbor. I bought this house so that my family could have a nice place to live—and all this shouting won't prevent it."

Bill's courageous words would not allay the mob outside, however. If anything, the crowd grew more restless with each passing hour. As the sun set, more than 250 people gathered in the street, defying the orders of the previous week. "I realize you have a problem and I respect it," implored an officer. "However, we too have a problem and we ask you to respect it. If not, I shall have to direct my men accordingly." They didn't listen.

"What protection do we have from this minority group?" one man shouted in reply.

"You have to take that up with the district," the officer said. "You may not take the law into your own hands."

By now, the neighbors had to find ways of coping with the riot on Deepgreen Lane. With so many people coming and going, some feared the mob would mistake their homes for the Myerses' and attack them by mistake. Families were divided, with some husbands urging their wives to take the children and leave town. Others resorted to their own suburban version of defensive tactics. One family across the street, tired of the crowd hollering and littering their lawn with cigarette butts, turned on their sprinklers, sending the mob scattering into the street. They would leave the sprinklers on all night.

But there was no deterring the rebellion. A boy threw a firecracker to taunt the cops. Then near nine P.M. someone hurled rocks from the crowd, striking a police officer and photojournalist. The police shined their flashlights over the mob, but couldn't find the culprit. "I give you ten minutes to move," the trooper announced on the loudspeaker. "One of my men and a newsman have been hit, and there must be no further violence."

As some of the mob began to back off, they hurled insults at the cops. But more than half of them remained. After the designated time passed, the trooper took to his bullhorn once again. "Your time is up," he announced, then ordered his troops, "Get them out of here!"

"Move! Move! Move!" The police shouted, as they burst into the crowd wielding their clubs. Reporters watched them hitting women in the backsides with their clubs. One man hurled insults as they moved in and was struck by officers too. They pulled him away as his head bled down his tan jacket, and his wife pleaded with them to release him.

"Brutes!" cried one person.

"Dictators!" shouted another.

"Gestapo!" cried one woman with a foreign accent. "This is America! I came here to be free. Now I have to live with Negroes! This is America!"

As the cops dragged the protesters away, others in the mob broke into song. "America!" they sang. "America! God shed His grace on thee." Daisy could hear them outside her window as she put her baby to sleep and sang her a lullaby over the noise.

The next morning, a honk came outside the Wechslers' home. Lew poked his head through the drapes and saw a car idling. It was Frazier, there to take him to work as usual. But this time when Lew came out and climbed into the car, he felt tension. Whereas Frazier had once ribbed Lew about his overgrown lawn, now they drove in silence. Finally, Frazier spoke, telling Lew that the situation on Deepgreen Lane had grown too dangerous, and his wife didn't want him carpooling with Lew anymore. This would be their last ride.

Lew couldn't tell which side of the battle Frazier fell upon, but expressed his understanding nonetheless. Once they pulled into the DeLaval Steam Turbine Company and went to their rounds, Lew saw that the tensions were seeping into his workplace too. For years, blacks had been relegated to working as maintenance men and janitors at his company. But on this day a black man came on and was given a post at the biggest, most expensive machine. Angry white faces leered around him. "The niggers get all the breaks, while we pay the taxes and get none," muttered one man near Lew. "Look at the unemployment insurance lines and who gets on relief."

Lew looked up from his machine and noticed that this man was tan from the summer. Lew piped in with characteristic humor, "You don't have to suffer, your skin is dark enough that you could pass. Why don't you just say that you're a Negro, then you can get all those breaks."

Frazier and Lew drove back to Deepgreen Lane that afternoon, but this time the charade would finally come to an end. Katy, who had been playing with the Wertzs' kids for years, came home and told her parents that the Wertz girls said they weren't allowed to play with her anymore. The battle lines had been drawn. And Bea and Lew were feeling it.

They weren't just on the periphery of a struggle anymore, they—and their children—were in the middle. For once, all their strength couldn't keep them from feeling frightfully under siege. For years, their political activities had infiltrated into their personal lives. FBI investigators showed up at their door. Lew lost jobs. But throughout it all, their children had never really felt any sort of retribution. Only now, in this civil rights struggle, had that vengefulness crossed into the world of Katy and Nick. And it terrified Bea and Lew.

The Wechslers' phone was now ringing at all hours of the day and night, with people hurling racists epithets such as "nigger-loving Jewish motherfuckers," before hanging up. Kids refused to play with Katy and Nick at their parents' behest. One night, Nick looked out the window to see one of his friends' mother screaming, "Nigger lovers," on his lawn. Another day, Lew had taken Nick to swim at the local Levittown pool, where a group of families with their children muttered something about "nigger-loving Jews."

Hateful letters poured in as well. "Mr. Lewis (I love Niggers) Wechsler," read a typical one. "If you lived here (Newark) you wouldn't let your wife and children walk the streets at night. The niggers will always be an uncivilized race regardless of how nice they may seem . . . I only hope as long as you like them, someday the nigger Mr. Myers son falls in love with your daughter and she has a nigger baby then you can be one happy family."

But the more under fire Bea and Lew felt, the closer they and the Myerses came to be. Every day, the Wechslers would go over to be with them—and their friendship was a great source of strength. While the kids played, the adults drank coffee, commiserated, and strategized. With the drapes drawn to the circus outside, Bill smoked a cigarette as he and Lew talked about their service in the war. Daisy and Bea chatted, and Nick and Katy fawned over baby Lynda. It almost seemed like a normal suburban evening. But it was constantly underscored by the sound of jeers and honking outside. The two families were from such different backgrounds, but found commonalities as they were cast together now. As Lew said, they felt as if they were under siege, and they were bonding together to survive.

Supporters form the Friends and Human Relations Council milled in and out of the house. This sense of community was a stark contrast to the hateful mob outside the window. As Bea and Lew said to the Myerses, the town was being divided into two factions: the Baddies, and the Goodies. And while the Baddies got all the press, the Goodies were showing what a true model town was all about. At one point, Daisy looked down to see a well-dressed white woman scrubbing her floor; the woman was the wife of a prominent doctor in town, and she wanted to help any way she could.

And as the mob began to grow again outside on Tuesday, August 20— a week after the Myerses moved in—they needed all the strength they could muster. With Bill's nervous tension rising and his knees constantly bobbing up and down as he sat, he and Daisy decided they would not submit to the reporters' questions anymore. Instead, they prepared a statement, which their supporters delivered outside:

"Mr. and Mrs. Myers wish to express their deep appreciation of the fair and sympathetic understanding demonstrated by the press, radio, and TV. They hope that all of these will appreciate their feeling that the sooner they can return to normal privacy the better for all concerned.

They feel that neither their new neighbors nor the police may appreciate their doing anything that may contribute to the circus atmosphere here on Deepgreen Lane."

The Myerses would give no more interviews, they concluded, until if and when they had anything else to say. And any further statements would come through their spokesperson, the Reverend Mr. Harwick of the Citizens Committee for Levittown.

To ward off the crowd, the police tried to forbid anyone other than residents from driving into the Dogwood Hollow section. They placed No Parking signs around the streets. But while the cops were able to keep out the cars, the mob began to slowly filter onto the lawns across the street, about five hundred feet away. As the police stood guard, the protesters began hollering insults at the officers. "Gestapo!" they jeered. "Wife beaters! This is Russia!"

Bristol Township police chief Stewart, the officer whom attorney Sam Snipes had initially notified of the Myerses' move-in, surveyed the mob from his car. Known around town by the nickname John R., Stewart was considered a local hero. He had battled gunslingers on horseback and climbed up a rope on the side of a ship in the Delaware River during Prohibition to foil armed rumrunners.

But tonight the suburban crowd was rallying against him. Slowly, they began to surround the black-and-white police car, staring it down. There were children and adults, defiant men and women with arms crossed, dressed in shorts and casual slacks. Finally, one man in the crowd took Stewart to task for the clubbing of the Levittowners the other night. "What are you," the man asked, "a nigger lover?"

Stewart recalled how years before, while working as a state police officer, he had once been chasing an African-American man thought to have raped a white girl. When Stewart confronted him, the man shot him twice—in the head and in the hand. Stewart still had the scar as his proof, and he would brandish it now in his defense. Now, Stewart eyed the man who called him a "nigger lover" and held his maimed hand aloft. "See that?" Stewart pointed to his thumb, a mangled stump of flesh missing a joint. "A nigger shot that off."

With each passing hour, the crowd grew and grew, forming a thick human wall five people deep and fifty yards long down the lawns across the lane from the Wechslers' and Myerses'. Many teenagers and young children were in the crowd. One young boy wore a football helmet to protect himself, he told an officer, in case violence broke out. As the mob reached four hundred people, the police officers could do little more than stare them down.

By nine thirty, the mob began to break off, one by one, darting for the Myerses' house. On cue, the cops grabbed their batons and charged forward to push them back. But no sooner had they moved than someone threw a huge rock. It flew through the air, over the angry faces, slicing the glare of the streetlight, and crashed down on a young police sergeant's head. His eyes shut as he crashed back on the ground, arms stretched on either side, his upturned hat beside him. The sergeant was a father of four, and a Levittown resident. Now he lay there perfectly still. The blood ran from the side of his head into the dry, brown lawn.

Thirteen

BATTLE LINES

ONE MORNING IN Levittown, New York, Nassau County judge
Paul J. Widlitz stepped up to the stage of the Levittown Theater
and looked out into a sea of smiling white faces. The occasion was a
fund-raiser for the upcoming Tenth Anniversary Celebration honoring a
decade since the first three hundred residents, including Widlitz and his
family, moved in. Widlitz was about to unveil a bronze plaque dedicating the theater to the town's lifeblood: the veterans.

"In addition to introducing a new concept of community building,"
he said, "the Levitt family's objective was a community of homes with
ball fields and trees where the harassed GI might take hold of life once
more. One decade has seen not only the transformation of potato fields
into a teeming, bustling community of seventy thousand people, but
also the transition of the harried, uncertain war veteran into a mature
husband, father, and responsible resident."

Despite the mounting tensions in Levittown, Pennsylvania, the residents in this sister city did their best to celebrate—and defend—the reputation of Bill Levitt and the suburb known as the "most perfectly planned
community in America." Levitt, the master marketer, had established for
years how to spin the story. He had billed his community from day one
as a dream come true, and himself as the Disney-like dream-maker.
Whether naming his town after himself or defying the Supreme Court's
stance against racial covenants, he stood unfailingly behind his product.

Now as he sat on the sidelines of the race riot on Deepgreen Lane, his followers came to his defense. With their tenth anniversary approaching, the original Levittowners went out of their way to show that—despite the critics predictions—the town was something to be proud of. They showed how, despite the assertions that they lived in ticky-tacky boxes, the community in fact valued and cultivated diversity—at least in the design of the homes.

In fact, Alfred Levitt's innovative designs were now paying off. The young, self-taught architect had specifically created these affordable homes to be modified and expanded as the owners' needs changed. He had set houses back off the roads at different angles specifically to accommodate growth. As one writer marveled, "The houses of Levittown appear to have been exactly what their owners needed—a start. Most of the early Levittowners were short on money and long on energy and ingenuity."

The buzzword around town was *remodeling*. In Levittown, New York, a magazine called *Thousand Lanes: Ideas for the Levitt Home* was dedicated to showing all the ways that residents were making over their homes. As one reporter observed, "The sound of the hammer and the electric saw goes on incessantly in Levittown." Kitchens were being squared off. Living rooms extended. Carports enclosed. Attics finished. At the adult education program in town, "How to Finish an Attic" was the second most popular class behind "Fine Arts." "It is hard in Levittown today to find a house with an unaltered exterior— and rare to find two in a row with the same alterations," the article said.

This sense of great American gumption, of the inventiveness of veterans, the ability to pull themselves up after living in chicken coops, created an incredible sense of vindication and pride. While Levitt's creation of Levittown was long deemed heroic, it was the residents who confirmed the promise in the popular imagination. "The degree to which these predictions have been refuted is probably the most remarkable aspect of the community," effused the *New York Times*. "Far from deteriorating, the property values have increased." Without irony, the national media proclaimed Levittown a truly diverse place. "And if there is one out-standing common trait among Levittowners," the *Times* concluded, "it appears the urge to be different."

With this uplifting story making the rounds despite the events on Deepgreen Lane, it was easy for Bill Levitt to continue to com-partmentalize—or deny—the divisiveness of his whites-only towns. As a result, he gladly steamrolled ahead with his plan to construct more ex-clusive communities across the land. After eyeing the Belair Estate in Bowie, Maryland, Levitt outbid rivals with a $1,750,000 offer. He would now commence building six thousand homes there, he said. As for the three-story, prerevolutionary mansion on the property, he would turn it over to local citizens to turn into a library dedicated to the legendary racehorse that once grazed on the site.

Meanwhile over in Willingboro Township, New Jersey, Levitt was busy making way for his next brand-name community. With his father out of the picture, he had no problem bulldozing the peach orchards that lined the land. He promised fifteen thousand affordable homes for vet-erans, as well as the world's largest shopping center and an adminis-tration building said to be "the last word" in modern construction. And it would now bear his name: Levittown, New Jersey.

Though Levitt wasn't speaking out on the events in Pennsylvania, the Myerses and Wechslers suspected he was playing his hand behind the scenes. On August 21, the day after the young officer was stoned outside their home, the doorbell rang at 43 Deepgreen Lane. Bill Myers opened the door to find a well-dressed white man in a suit. Bill's guard was up. Just days before, he had found the words NIGGER GO HOME scrawled on a wall of the building where he worked. The man in the suit introduced himself as a Levittown attorney and Bucks County dis-trict attorney. He was also the Republican nominee for district attor-ney in the coming election in November. "How can I help you?" Bill asked.

The attorney said he represented two buyers, whom he could not name. But they wanted to offer the Myerses $15,000 for the home. Bill considered the man. That was a lot of money, $2,850 more than the

Myerses had paid just weeks ago. Bill had a hunch about whom the man really represented: William Levitt.

Sorry, Bill said, the home was not for sale. "I am here to stay."

While the Levittowners struggled to reclaim their reputation, the situation in Pennsylvania was only growing more grim. With the stoning of the second cop, who was rushed to the hospital and found to have a concussion, America's model town was even further being torn apart.

After a fifteen-year-old boy, who claimed innocence, was arrested for the assault, James Newell, the mob's de facto leader, placed himself above the violence. "I am disgusted with what happened up there last night," he told reporters the day after the stoning of the officer. "It was unjustified and uncalled for. I have always advocated complete cooperation with the police." But the power was clearly going to his head. A meeting would be held, he promised, so that he could "tell my followers what I intend to do."

The police responded by setting a nine P.M. curfew in town for children under sixteen years of age who were not accompanied by their parents. Though the riot act had been read—and not enforced—before, the police now reiterated that crowds gathering on Deepgreen Lane would be arrested. But despite their warnings, they could not contain the violence. That night at 10:10 P.M., a second cross was found burning in Levittown—this time at the Penn Valley School in town. The wooden cross had been jammed into a backstop on the school baseball field.

Newell's minions expanded their campaign across the manicured lawns of Levittown, staging witch hunts on the slightest provocation. When a black man was seen leaving another house, Newell's crew confronted the owner, who they feared was selling to another African-American family; the man proved to be merely a worker.

But Newell was undeterred. He took the cause of the Betterment Committee to the local radio airwaves, where he espoused his racist views under the banner of free speech. Listeners took heed. Factions were increasingly convinced that Jews, Communists, and the NAACP were plotting an African-American takeover of Levittown. When word of another black family moving into town spread, opponents wasted no time—spilling trash on the lawn and vandalizing the home at a cost of several hundred dollars. The rumor, once again, proved false.

While the police were making more of an effort to keep people away from Deepgreen Lane, Newell and the Levittown Betterment Committee were secretly meeting—and the stakes were rising. One night at the home of one of Newell's right-hand men, a dozen key members—husbands and wives—met to discuss the state of affairs. While Newell glommed on to power, however, it was the pit bull of the group, Eldred Williams, the unemployed man who drove the gray station wagon, who took command.

"I've been contacted by someone," Williams told the others, "someone representing the KKK who's interested in our problem." The group decided to take a vote on whether to pursue the Klan's offer to help. Who was in favor? Williams's hand shot straight up, and one by one he was joined by others in the group—a total of eight votes for the Klan. Who was against? Just five people, including John Bentley, the former township zoning officer, and Newell. Williams stared Newell down bitterly. Williams would follow up with the Klan and report back at the next meeting.

When they gathered again the following week, Williams and his supporters were ready to move forward with the Klan. But Bentley, who had joined the Betterment Committee because he thought the Levittown Civic Association was not militant enough, feared that Williams and the others were going too far in the other extreme. "I make a motion," Bentley said, "that we have nothing to do with the KKK." This time, people agreed—and all but two backed the plan to keep the Klan away. Only Williams and one of his friends dissented. So it would be done—the group would proceed without the KKK. And when they asked if Williams had anything to report from the Klan over the previous week, he said, "Nothing to report."

But Williams could not be restrained. On the heels of the police order not to gather on Deepgreen Lane, the Betterment Committee had been trying in vain to find public places to meet. Meetings were called, only to be canceled when the proprietors of the venues discovered the purpose. On Friday, August 30, Williams defied Newell's rule and took it upon himself to act as a spokesperson for the group. He told the local papers that the Betterment Committee would convene after all: "It will be held someplace in Levittown, sometime tomorrow evening, weather permitting. The time and place will be announced later."

The next day, Williams hastily organized a meeting in the most public place of all: the baseball diamond behind the Levittown Shopping Center. More than three hundred people crowded the field as the police looked on, refusing to intervene. After the meeting, Newell ordered Williams thrown out of the group. But it was not to be. Williams had his followers too, and he would remain. During the Betterment's next private gathering, Williams was told his contact from the KKK was on the phone at his house. Newell, Bentley, and the others followed him over to Williams's house. No sooner had they stepped inside than they saw a stack of papers on a table.

"What's this?" Newell asked Williams.

"Applications for the KKK," Williams replied.

"Let's get the hell out of here," Newell told his crew, and they left.

The telephone rang at two A.M. in the home of Sam Snipes, the Quaker attorney who'd represented the Myerses in their purchase of their home. Snipes was a soft-spoken man who, like others, found himself cast into this unexpected war.

"Sam Snipes?" the voice snapped on the other end of the line.

"Yes?" Snipes said calmly.

"Are you a nigger-loving motherfucker?"

Snipes considered the question for a moment. "Yes."

As infighting gripped the mob against the Myerses and Wechslers, the supporters of the nascent civil rights struggle were facing retribution. When the Myerses needed allergy medicine, a local druggist put the house on his delivery rounds. But he could barely make it to the front door without being branded a "nigger lover." His business partner heard of the incident and insisted they stop servicing the Myerses, or lose their business. After repeated threats, the druggist suffered a nervous breakdown.

After delivering bread to the Myerses one day, the local baker returned to work the next morning to find his truck vandalized. He didn't return to their home. The milkman never came to the Myerses' home at all, despite sending them their weekly bill. When the local oil company truck was spotted at the Myerses' home, one of Newell's followers urged the others to boycott the company; thirty families followed suit. But when it was discovered that the man who'd suggested the boycott didn't comply, the others meekly rejoined.

Soon, the police themselves began drawing lines within their own ranks. One day, a reporter passed three state troopers near the Myerses' home. "Look at that house," one of the troopers said skeptically. "Myers is at work. But how about that woman and the children? What if something happens? Who is she going to ask for help? Suppose the house catches fire?"

The trooper added that some people had vowed to shoot Bill Myers on sight. They questioned why someone would remain under such conditions. The implication was clear: While some police officers respected their role in this conflict, others on the force would do only so much to protect the family.

The tensions were forming divisions between the Myerses' supporters too. Questions burned throughout the community about how—and why—the family had moved in. Leading the investigation was Ray Harwick, the young pastor who was heading the Citizens Committee on the Myerses' behalf. After taking his post, Harwick began researching the events that led up to the Myerses' move-in. This included reviewing and interviewing the actions and members of the Human Relations Council and Friends Service Association.

The more he looked, the more suspicious he became of the Myerses' primary backers: the Wechslers. Rumors were spreading within the factions that they had Communist ties. One day, Harwick showed up at Bea and Lew's home urging them to come clean "for the sake of the Myerses." Bea and Lew had received a similar visit from two Levittown rabbis who were on the Citizens Committee. The Wechslers bristled at the suggestion and refused. Politics were not the issue here, they said. "The issue is that we have publicly befriended the Myers family and publicly supported their right to live next door to us," Lew said.

But Harwick didn't back down—much to the Myerses' dismay. Though the Myerses were not familiar with the Wechslers' political background, Daisy bristled at how Harwick and his supporters were blaming Communism for the problems in town. Harwick, Daisy felt, had been "shoved" into his position of leadership simply because he was white and Christian—qualifications that didn't necessarily make him the right person for the job. By his own admission, Harwick had no experience with the civil rights movement. "I knew Negroes were out there," he said, "somewhere out there, but I was never affected."

The Wechslers and Myerses saw right through this. Daisy, who on the advice of Pearl Buck had begun keeping a journal of her experience, wrote, "A man may have all the [seemingly right] classifications and still be a failure as a leader. A leader must be genuine, have the cause at heart; he must be fully experienced with the situation and know for what he stands. He must possess the fundamental knowledge necessary. Here was an honest man who said he did not know what civil rights meant. He had never preached a sermon on brotherhood in his years of ministry. Yet he was leading the people along these paths. How could a man with his leadership ability be so unaware of the pressing problems of his day?"

The Myerses and Wechslers bristled at Harwick's red-baiting investigations in this light. Daisy was stunned when he showed up at her doorstep to tell her that she and Bill were cleared of any suspicious background. "You are clean as whistles," Harwick told them.

"What are you talking about?" Daisy said.

"I had you and Bill investigated, and as far back as they could trace, they could find no wrong."

Daisy couldn't believe his gall. But Harwick, in the name of their civil rights, continued on his mission. On August 21, he agreed to a public discussion with Newell at a local inn, sponsored by the Levittown Kiwanis Club. Newell had put on a coat and tie, and Harwick, dressed in a coat over his pastor's apparel, smiled with him for newspaper photos. Harwick reported the findings of his inquiry into the lives of the Myerses, as if anyone deserved to be investigated simply for choosing a home. Once again he said he had "completely investigated the financial background of [Bill] Myers and the financial background of his parents and in-laws" and had found Myers "clean as a whistle." He also said that he found "absolutely no evidence that the Myers move here was sponsored by the Friends, by the NAACP, or any other group."

Not everyone agreed. Joseph Segal, the head of the Levittown Civic Association, said there "seems to be a void in Reverend Harwick's information about the Negro family moving here." But Harwick was quick to make peace. To the shock of the Wechslers and other supporters, Harwick, speaking for the group, broke away from the very people who had devoted their lives to breaking Levittown's whites-only grip. The Citizens Committee, he declared, "has adopted a completely neutral stand on integration." The Myerses, he suggested, were pawns in the hands of the town's integrationists. "I don't like what has been done to bring the man here," he said, and characterized Bill Myers as having spoken with people who had given him "irresponsible advice."

However well-intentioned he might have been, Harwick could not escape the consequence of his actions. At home, his phone was now ringing throughout the day and night with harassing calls. It was shaking him and his family. On Saturday, August 24, at three fifteen A.M., the phone rang, and he answered it only to hear, "Nigger lover!" and veiled threats to his family. He turned to his wife. "Go home to your parents," he said, "and take the children."

The next morning, he watched his family leave. As soon as they walked out the door, the phone rang again. And it continued all through the night. Harwick began to grow increasingly scared and paranoid and began to search his house for signs of an intruder. Desperate for help, he called the operator and said, "Is there any way you can possibly trace these calls?"

"No, sir, there's none," the operator replied.

"I have got to get some means!" Harwick snapped.

With Harwick and others under mounting pressure, the Wechslers and Myerses felt increasingly under siege as well. Days and nights passed without their leaving their homes. Dinner dates were canceled. Ordinary activities—shopping and movies—were cut back. They never knew what they would find when they opened the door.

One day when the Wechslers' bell rang, it was their neighbor and friend David Matza, a sociology professor at Temple University. Matza and his wife and young child lived directly behind the Myerses' and Wechslers' houses on 30 Darkleaf Lane. Matza was crying and distraught. He had been offered a job to teach at the University of California at Berkeley, he explained, and would be leaving Levittown in the midst of the conflagration. It pained him to think that the media might portray his move as white flight, which was anything but the case. Bea and Lew reassured him but, inside, had concerns of their own. With the Matzas gone, the crucial balance of the neighborhood was about to change.

Lew grabbed a sheet of paper and sat down at his kitchen table sketching a map of Deepgreen Lane. Bea and the Myerses gathered around him. Lew made tiny boxes representing each of the eleven houses in the area. This was a war now, and it was time to assess the sides. When he was through, they surveyed the battle map: three friendly families, four neutrals, and two hostiles. But, as Lew circled one of the friendly houses, the Matzas', the delicate balance was about to change. The house on 30 Darkleaf Lane was diagonally behind the Myerses', and directly behind the Wechslers'. If a hostile family moved into such a strategically positioned house, Lew fretted, the circumstances could grow even more grim. All they could do was wait.

The owner of the house, William Hughes, wasn't having an easy time leasing the home. A family with three small children had agreed to take over the lease beginning September 2, but then the crisis with the Myers family had made them fear for the safety of their kids, and they abruptly backed out. One night at the end of August, just as he was fearing he would never lease the home, Hughes got a call from a woman who asked if he'd be interested in leasing the home to her. "I would," he said; the price was ninety dollars per month.

"I'll be over right away," she replied. Thirty minutes later, she showed up—but she wasn't alone. Fifteen or sixteen people accompanied her as they made their way inside.

Hughes was dubious. "What's your purpose in leasing this home?"

"We, the taxpayers and property owners of the Dogwood section of Levittown, have no place to meet," she replied, "and we would like to go there and meet and talk over this situation about the Myerses' moving into Levittown."

"Who's going to be responsible for cutting the grass and looking after the property in general?" Hughes asked. "Because the people who had lived there before left it in a very poor condition. The house was very dirty, the grounds were very unkempt, the flower beds were all shook up." They all knew the rules of Levittown, after all, and how much the Levitt family wanted the lawns nice and neat. Hughes didn't want to have Levitt drive by in his big black Cadillac one day and stick him with a bill for a lawn-mowing service. "Who's going to take care of the property?" Hughes said again.

A thin, short man stepped up from behind the woman: Eldred Williams. "I live in the next block over, I'll take care of the grounds."

Hughes agreed. Then he handed Williams the keys.

Fourteen

BACK TO SCHOOL

Now's THE TIME to think about new clothing, shoes and school supplies of all kinds," read the cover of the Levittown newspaper, "pens, pencils, books, typewriters, luggage and leather goods, jewelry, cameras, toilet goods, sporting goods, bikes, and student-room furniture and projects." September had come, and Levittown, like the rest of America, was going back to school.

But this would be no ordinary return. As the harried and happy parents filed through the Shop-O-Rama to stock up on goods, their whispers revealed that they had more on their minds than No. 2 pencils. Levittown was about to get its first African-American teacher ever. Donald Theodore Burton, a twenty-six-year-old educator from Philadelphia, had been hired by the Bristol Township School Board to teach fifth-grade classes at the new twenty-eight-room James Buchanan Elementary School, which was opening as soon as construction was complete on September 16. A small item in the local paper noted that the school would serve several sections in Levittown including the residents of Dogwood Hollow.

This would be the school that Nick Wechsler would attend, and where, he still hoped, his parents would let him fulfill his dream of being a crossing guard. Nick had been working for the past year to become a crossing guard and had just learned that he'd got the position. Now he would get to wear the coveted uniform on the first day of school. Given the standoff over the Myerses, though, Bea and Lew, no matter how strong they had been in the past, couldn't bear the thought of little Nick standing there like a target. And, though it broke their hearts, they urged him to give up the post. But Nick, who possessed the streak of Wechsler strength, said no. This is what he wanted to do, and, he assured them, he would be all right.

A news bulletin from Little Rock, Arkansas, on the opening day of schools nationwide, however, suggested what violence might await. Since the Supreme Court had ruled to integrate schools in the landmark *Brown v. Board of Education* decision in 1954, Arkansas, like many states that were slowly preparing for the transition, had been simmering in anticipation. But Arkansas governor Orval Faubus had been battling to keep segregation intact—despite the orders of the courts. On September 3, the day before the first nine African-American students were to attend Little Rock Central High School, Faubus went on statewide television and said, "Blood will run in the streets if Negro people should attempt to enter Central High School." And he was dispatching the National Guard to prevent them.

The next morning as the nation watched on television, the first of the African-American children, fifteen-year-old Elizabeth Eckford, arrived in a new white dress and sunglasses. Two hundred and fifty armed National Guardsmen stood on the sidewalks surrounding the school to greet her. As Eckford clutched her notebook, a mob of angry men and women trailed behind her shouting, "Lynch her! Lynch her!" Eckford was escorted safely away and the integration of the school was thwarted. Like the events surrounding Emmett Till and Rosa Parks, the scene burned indelibly into the hearts and minds of the world. The battle of the Little Rock Nine, as the children were dubbed, had begun.

Back in Levittown, the Myerses and Wechslers received clippings of the Little Rock standoff in the mail—with racial epithets scrawled in the margins. The events in Arkansas ignited a new sense of hatred in the calls they received.

"Hello," Daisy said, picking up the receiver one day.

"Governor Faubus is just the type of man we need in Levittown," the caller snapped, then hung up.

The message was clear: The world was watching Levittown too. Though overshadowed by Little Rock, the saga of Deepgreen Lane had become an international event. Papers from Moscow to London covered the standoff in what had long been viewed as America's quintessential suburban dreamland. *Life* magazine had just run a long spread on the story that week, including dramatic photos of the Myerses and Wechslers under siege in their homes. The two families now had the state police at their homes on twenty-four-hour guard.

The Wechslers hoped the day of September 5 would at least offer a little reprieve. This was the date of two special occasions for the family: Bea's thirty-eighth birthday, and her and Lew's seventeenth wedding anniversary. The two joyous events were always a big deal in the house, and Lew liked to commemorate them by making their favorite meal: a big pan of garlicky paella. One night they had invited Daisy and Bill over to sample the meal and had a good laugh when Bill, a finicky eater, good-naturedly asked if they had some hot dogs instead.

But this year there wouldn't be anything to celebrate. At 5:05 A.M., Daisy was at her stove making breakfast for the family when she smelled something burning outside. She looked out the window into the darkness and fog and didn't see anything.

Next door, a pounding came on the Wechslers' door. The family was still sleeping, and Lew stumbled for the door and opened it to find his friend Barney Bell, the Texan truck driver who had not long before driven his car at the mob congregating on his lawn. Bell was covered in soot. "They burned a cross on your lawn!" he said.

Lew ran outside and saw the smoldering remains of the cross, which Bell had kicked over. It was five feet long and made out of tree branches, which had been bound by rags and held together with thick tape. It had been wired to the air vent of the oil heater on their front lawn. A broken jar of kerosene was lying on the driveway next to the mess.

Lew called the police to report the crime. How had this happened, he demanded to know, when the state police were supposed to be watching his house twenty-four hours a day? They had no answer.

Though there was no evidence, it seemed more and more clear that an invisible neighbor had come to their cookie-cutter town: the Ku Klux

Klan. Four milk bottles filled with gasoline and taped with cotton-wad fuses were found down the block from the Wechslers' home. Meanwhile, eleven hundred miles away that same morning, the mayor of Little Rock, Arkansas, had a cross burning on his lawn too. A reporter misquoted Lew dismissing the cross burning as the work of prankish kids. Other rumors spread that the Wechslers had burned the cross themselves to gain sympathy and implicate the Levittown Betterment Committee. Such intimations infuriated Bea and Lew, who suspected it had to be Newell and Williams's cronies.

An anonymous letter sent to their house after the cross burning said as much. The cross was "put there," the letter read, "to let you know that, although the crowds have diminished, the feelings against you have not, nor will ever be. We are members of an organization that was born in the south. It is legal and it is chartered. Need I say more? We are not an organization of terror as is commonly stated, but rather one with ideals which we believe are just and right. We are American citizens, not 'Commies' or 'riff-raff' and we are fighting and will continue to fight for what we believe to be our constitutional right . . . Think long—and think carefully—Mr. W. pull out while you can." It was signed "a citizen born in the U.S.A. Member of a legal charted organization. R.E./The south."

As word of the cross burning spread through the Myerses' supporters, so did the fear. One morning, Bea was outside when her neighbor and early Levittown friend Marcia Kasman came running up the driveway crying. Kasman fell into Bea's arms, sobbing in terror. The Kasmans like others had been supporting the Wechslers and Myerses for weeks now, but the attacks of the mob were wearing them down. She told Bea how she feared for the safety of her children. As Bea comforted her, the two appreciated how, amid all the chaos, their children were exhibiting amazing strength.

The Kasman children, Howard and Sandy, had been friendly with both Nick and Katy and the Myers boys, William and Stephen (whom Bill and Daisy had brought back from York to stay with them in Levittown). Howard was turning nine, and he wanted to invite the young brothers to his birthday party so that they would feel included too. A story in the *New York Post* headlined TWO LONELY LITTLE BOYS IN LEVIT-

TOWN described their plight, pushing tricycles and wagons alone. "William is big for his age, with large, dark sparkling eyes," the reporter wrote. "He and Stephen look like their mother. They joke with their father, painting the garage. 'They're too young to know what's going on,' the father says." But Bill Myers also admitted that the pressure was getting to them. "We've had some weak moments," he said, this was "a war of nerves."

No matter how young and innocent they were, the children were not immune to the same sort of abuse brought against their parents. When Howard Kasman's two best friends found out he'd invited the Myers boys, they told him sadly that their parents wouldn't let them attend. Howard didn't know what to do. "This is your party," his mother told him, "and this is a tough decision, but you are the only who can make it."

Howard didn't back down, but his friends' parents wouldn't either. William and Stephen came to the party, but Howard's two friends didn't. When the party was through, Howard brought two plates of birthday cake to his friends. As Lew later noted, "That superb nine-year-old diplomat had arranged the Myers boys' first Levittown social function, and retained his two best friends, despite their parents' backward views."

The Myers and Wechsler children were as heroic as their pals. Monday, September 9, was Katy Wechsler's fourteenth birthday, and she had asked friends over to her house after school that afternoon to celebrate. There had already been good news. That day Congress passed the first civil rights act since Reconstruction, paving the way for the Civil Rights Commission and the Civil Rights Division of the Department of Justice.

But on Deepgreen Lane, justice still seemed far away. As the children played birthday games outside that afternoon, a car slowly rolled up the street until it came to a stop. Katy looked up to see a mountainous man with a flattop sneering out the window: James Newell. "You bunch of nigger lovers!" he yelled at the teens, then drove off.

On the heels of this incident and the brewing storm at Little Rock Central High, Bea and Lew were more concerned than ever about Nick's plan to work as a crossing guard on the first day of school. Even more, they discovered that Nick had been assigned as a pupil in the class of none other than Donald Burton—the first African-American teacher in town. Reporters from the *New York Times*, the *New York Post*, and other media had come to observe opening day to see if a Little Rock–like riot would occur.

On the morning of September 16, Nick proudly strapped on his crossing-guard badge and said good-bye to his parents. Then, on his own accord, he walked over to the Myerses' home and knocked on the door. He told them he would gladly escort William to school. Together, the two boys walked through the street, making their way down Deepgreen Lane. They heard the voices of parents and children taunting them as they made it down the road past the reporters and patrolling police cars.

There were no riots that day at school after all. "I expected some antagonism," Burton told a reporter, "but there wasn't any. I'm a sensitive person and I would have felt it if it were there." African-American children from Bloomsdale Gardens played hand in hand with white Levittown kids in the playground. On the way home, however, the taunts came again. When Bea and Lew heard Nick's story, they asked Katy if anyone was messing with her at junior high school. Katy replied, "They wouldn't dare!" This was the same tough girl, after all, who had beaten up the bully when he'd tried to hurt her little brother. And she wasn't going to back down now.

Neither were the Myers boys. One day at kindergarten, William was sitting quietly in his seat as a white boy leaned over to taunt him: "You're black! You're black!"

William eyed him calmly. "I'm not black, I'm brown, don't you know the difference?" He then reached into his drawer and took out two crayons—one black, one brown. Slowly, he drew a brown line down the page, then a black one next to it. Then he handed the paper to the white boy, who stared at it blankly.

With the pressure mounting, Bea and Lew decided it was time for a break. They took up their friends' offer of a night out at a special restaurant in Camden, New Jersey, called the Pub. The waiter brought them a rum-and-fruit drink in a half pineapple shell called a Missionary's Revenge. They ate delicious food from a charcoal-heated cart and talked late into the night, smoking the complimentary cigars that came at the end of the meal. Life, for this night, felt normal again.

Shortly thereafter, they got a call from other close friends in Schenectady, New York, who urged them to take a break from the standoff for their sake and the kids'. "You just have to get away for a few days," the friends said. "All of you come here for a long weekend." Bea and Lew agreed and left on September 20 for a therapeutic weekend relaxing and eating a sumptuous dinner.

But reality greeted them the moment they came home to Levittown on Sunday afternoon, September 22. The phone was ringing as they opened the front door. When they picked it up, their friend and neighbor Peter Von Blum was on the line, frantic. That morning at four A.M., Von Blum said, he and his wife, Selma, were sleeping when they heard explosions outside their home. They raced outside to find a cross burning in their front yard. The makeshift wood cross, like the one that had been found on the Wechslers' lot, had been fitted with blank cartridges designed to fire in the heat.

Once again, the Myerses and Wechslers had a good hunch who was behind it. That day in the *Levittown Times*, in fact, an ad appeared signed by Newell. The ad solicited members for the group he chaired, the Levittown Betterment Association, and read: "The L.B.A. objectives are to promote the general welfare and secure for the community the former status of limitations by peaceful means. The L.B.A. has not, does not, and will not advocate violence in any form. Ours is not hate which we feel but one of encroachment upon our rights as a limited community. Those who would question the desire of the L.B.A. labor under a false, biased, and derogatory tale [by those] bating our influence who seek to deny and disparage our heritage. Nero fiddled while Rome burned. We do not propose to do likewise. From this we take our stand."

That afternoon, the Wechslers and Myerses saw exactly what kind of stand Newell and his group had decided to take. They heard the sound of a bugle coming from the empty house on 30 Darkleaf Lane. How could there be more mob members outside, they wondered, when the cops were still supposedly guarding their homes? The Wechslers and Myerses had feared who might take over the house and tip the balance of the neighborhood. As they rushed outside, their worst nightmare had come true.

The home had been transformed into a clubhouse. Men and women, disorderly and drunk, cavorted on the lawn. Noticing the attention of the Myerses, the women hoisted up their dresses, revealing their snow-white legs with a laugh. A loudspeaker in the window blasted the song "Dixie." An American flag flapped on the roof. Beside it flew a Confederate flag.

The Myerses and Wechslers recognized in horror the familiar faces of their tormentors, including Newell, and even the mailman who had started the riot after he'd delivered the first letter to Daisy Myers on that August day. Outside, the caretaker of the house, Eldred Williams, walked his black dog up and down the yard. He had renamed the pet in honor of this day. "Here, Nigger," he called to the dog, "come here you, Nigger." The neighbors had arrived.

Fifteen

DANDELIONS AND BAYONETS

ABE LEVITT HATED weeds. Weeds were an imperfection on his perfectly produced lawns. During his working years at Levitt & Sons, the legacy of the "vice president of grass seed" loomed large across the country. As one sociologist put it, Abe was "the man chiefly responsible [for inventing] the mass produced landscape to go along with its ready-built housing." Abe had created a host of grass-cutting rules. He provided free fertilization and reseeding to keep Levittown lawns green and weed-free. It wasn't just ego, it was a moral imperative.

"This is the first spring in Levittown. We want to present to the nation a model community in every respect," he said in 1948. And that model started with the Levittowners: "A fine carpet of green grass stamps the inhabitants as good neighbors, as desirable citizens." You could tell a lot about a community by the state of its lawns, he believed. "No single feature of a suburban residential community contributes as much to the charm and beauty of the individual home and locality as a well-kept lawn," he once wrote. Or, as he liked to say, "Grass is the very foundation of life."

But in September 1957, the grass around Levittown was dead. Dandelions shot from the dry, brown earth like dust balls. The record-breaking drought of the summer had taken its toll. The Levittowners were either losing their battle to the weeds or had simply stopped caring enough to try to win. As one reporter put it that month, the dandelions and other weeds were "running wild" and violating the town ordinances. With Abe

out of the picture and Bill off building his empire, no one was left to enforce the rules. One local borough tried to take matters into its own
hands, launching a plan called Operation Weed Removal to restore the
community to its original splendor.

Daisy Myers took up the charge on her own. She was determined to
weed her lawn. But as she walked outside, a more terrible scourge awaited
her. Behind her house, she saw the rebel flag flapping over the roof of what
had been dubbed the Confederate House. The house was quiet now. As
soon as Daisy started pulling weeds from the flower bed, however, she
heard the telephone ring inside. Putting down her things, she went in to
answer it.

"Hello?" She said, but the caller hung up.

Daisy returned to her work, only to hear the phone ring again. Once
more, Daisy put down her things and went in to answer it. This time, a
woman at the other end said, "There's no point to pulling weeds because
you won't be here that long." Then the line went dead.

Daisy glanced furtively outside her window. She was being watched. But
she would not be swayed. She went right back outside and put on her
gloves and began pulling out dandelions. The phone rang again. Daisy
went back to pick it up, but no one was there. The routine kept
happening—outside, inside, ring and hang up. The mob was tormenting
her, testing her will. But, she resolved more than ever, they would not
break her. The next time her phone rang, she picked up the receiver and
left it off the line. Then she put back on her gloves and got back to work.

Bill Myers wanted more protection. Outraged and fearful for his family,
he called the police. At the precinct, Bristol Township police chief Stewart
told him he could do nothing because the township couldn't afford to provide "round-the-clock" protection. Bill pleaded but was turned away.

While Stewart declined Myers's plea, other cops felt conflicted. A sergeant named Ernest F. Nuskey felt his stomach turn as the harassment
of the Myerses and Wechslers continued without the police's intervention. Nuskey had been on the force for six years and acted as chief before Stewart's arrival. He reeled because the police weren't doing more
to help the families on Deepgreen Lane. But what, he wondered, could
he do?

By the following Monday morning, the Myerses and the Wechslers had had enough. Daisy, Bill, Bea, Lew, Selma Von Blum (who had had a cross burned on her and her husband Peter's lawn weeks before), and Thomas Colgan of the Friends Service Association decided to drive up to Harrisburg, Pennsylvania, to tell Attorney General Thomas McBride that they wanted the state to step in and end this nightmare. Newell and his racist mob had long talked about their alleged desire to seek "legal means" to boot the Myerses from Levittown, but where was the law for them? Crosses burned and Confederate flags waved in plain view of the police. Where was the peace for the victims of this harassment?

As lifelong activists, Bea and Lew had been in sociopolitical causes long enough to know how to play this game. On the drive up they hatched a plan for how to get leverage. They said that if the state would not intervene, then they would pack up and leave Levittown once and for all. It was a calculated threat directed against the Pennsylvania government. Bea and Lew had a hunch that there wouldn't be any worse press for these liberal leaders than to have it be known that racists were successfully driving taxpaying citizens from their homes.

As they drove up together, the Wechslers and Myerses reflected on the events of the past month. This had not been what any of them had anticipated. The Myerses were simply looking for a good home, but never wanted to change the world. The Wechslers had always wanted to change the world, but had never been in a position to have such a chance. Now both families were cast in this drama in the most unlikely of places together. They realized that their personal quests, their desires for a home and for change, were intertwined with the greater good. The Levitts had built and sold the dream of the model town to America, but now these neighbors from different backgrounds had the opportunity to make Levittown a real model town for all.

As they arrived at and entered the state building together, Colgan saw Attorney General McBride down the hall. Colgan approached him and explained they had traveled up from Levittown to tell him about the crisis they were facing. The Wechslers sat watching with a sense of relief. McBride, they knew, was a good man. Not long before when he was a practicing attorney, McBride had gone out on a limb to become chief counsel to a group of Communist Party leaders who were under arrest for their activities. Bea and Lew were sure he would now do the right thing too.

When Colgan came back, he told the group that McBride would see them to discuss matters. But when Bea and Lew stood to join the group, Colgan had to stop them. What's going on? they wanted to know.

With a downcast gaze, Colgan sadly explained that McBride did not want the Wechslers to come inside. Bea and Lew were aghast. Why not? Colgan told them what he said McBride had told him: "Because I've heard that they are Communists, and it's best not to get that issue involved."

Bea and Lew felt crushed. McCarthyism still haunted them, and now even this man whom they considered liberal and courageous had succumbed to such fears too. Were their efforts for nothing? What was happening to the world around them? They had taken a stand and risked their lives, had a cross burned on their lawn, and yet they were being treated like criminals. "Are we now more dangerous than the leaders of the Communist Party?" they asked themselves, as they watched the rest of the group follow McBride down the hall. "That's certainly what it seems."

By the time the Wechslers arrived back alone in Levittown, they didn't have reason to be encouraged. The Confederate House was still flying its flags, and blasting African-American spirituals from loudspeakers. The bugle playing continued, and dozens of men and women were now boisterously cavorting on the dead brown lawn. Williams seized upon the moment to walk his dog Nigger up and down the property line as the Wechslers watched. "Come here, Nigger," he drawled, "good boy."

Just as Bea and Lew were about to lose hope, they heard a siren outside. At four P.M., a state police guard pulled up by the house. The plea to McBride had worked. As McBride later informed a reporter, he had spoken with the state police after the visit from the Myerses and others and suggested that the police resume a twenty-four-hour watch. As Bill Myers himself said upon returning home that evening, the state police "are here to do the job the local police did not do."

There was just one problem. The state police had no impact on the harassment from next door. Despite the cops parked along the streets, the rabble-rousers in the Confederate House only grew more obnoxious as night fell on Deepgreen Lane—and the police did nothing to stop them. At one point, Williams piled with friends into his gray station wagon with the Confederate flag in the window and led a caravan of cars up and down the streets alongside the Myerses' and Wechslers' homes. Williams's cohort Howard Bentcliff positioned himself in one of the parked cars, and Daisy saw him scribbling down the license-plate numbers of her friends' cars when they came for a visit. What retribution, she feared, did he have in mind?

At all hours of the night, the mob members played a bugle or took turns slamming the mailbox shut on the corner near the Myerses' and Wechslers' homes. Some, to the Wechslers' horror, even employed old union techniques of harassment—shuffling their feet noisily outside their windows as the Myerses' children struggled to sleep. A spotlight had been affixed to the roof to better illuminate the Confederate flag and kept them up late into the night.

Daisy Myers later appealed to a reporter: "What they're doing has all the earmarks of the Ku Klux Klan." When a reporter for the *Philadelphia Bulletin* wandered over to investigate late that night, he found a group of people listening to a championship boxing match on the radio. "We're just a group of neighbors," one of the men told him. "We have no meetings. It's open to all Levittown visitors. You might say that this is just Dogwood neighbors and their Levittown friends."

They called themselves the Dogwood Hollow Social Club. Inside, the home had been converted into a makeshift clubhouse. Twenty-five men and women milled about the house, serving and drinking coffee from a hot pot on the stove. They sat at mismatched tables and chairs. As visitors came in, they were offered coffee and asked to sign a registration book on a table. The living room had been transformed into the clubhouse center. A record player spun the same song, "Ol' Man River," over and over, as visitors joined in. "Niggers all work on the Mississippi," they sang, "Niggers all work while the white folks play."

Benches were lined up facing the center of the room, a reporter observed, "similar to church pews." Two large Confederate flags and one yellow one with the words DON'T TREAD ON ME were propped up against the window facing the Myerses' home. More Confederate flags were for sale in the corner, just like the ones that had been for sale at the Levittown shopping mall. Purchasers could pay for the flags in a wooden box on a table. The price: a donation of sixty cents for adults. Children got a break: They could buy the flags for thirty cents.

From a corner of the room, a scrappy, thin man with a cigarette appeared. He identified himself as the caretaker of the house, Eldred Williams. "We're going to keep up the appearance of the home and grounds," Williams told the reporter, but then quickly turned the questioning around. "Why are the white people on the defensive? Myers is causing all this trouble. What hold does this man have on Harrisburg that he can get state police protection and we can't?"

After the reporter left, a group inside the home convened to discuss how they might take matters into their own hands. A batch of lots was produced. Howard Bentcliff and four others took turns plucking lots from a hat. The first two men drew blanks. But Bentcliff and the fourth man drew the lots with the special marks.

They knew what they had to do.

While the standoff continued in Levittown, the crisis in Little Rock was reaching an apex. On Tuesday, September 24, three weeks after school began, President Eisenhower took what one reporter called "the most drastic action ever used by a president to enforce a federal court decree on school desegregation." He ordered the 101st Airborne Division to escort the nine African-American students to their first day of classes.

"The interest of the nation in the proper fulfillment of the law's requirements cannot yield to the opposition and demonstrations by some few persons," Eisenhower said. He cited the charter of the United Nations to affirm " 'faith in fundamental human rights and in the dignity and worth of the human person . . . without distinction as to race, sex, language, or religion.' "

The words rang across the country, as the burgeoning civil rights struggle took hold. From *Brown v. Board of Education* through Rosa Parks, Emmett Till, and now Little Rock, a new kind of battle had gripped the country. Martin Luther King Jr. was at the forefront of the struggle, advocating nonviolence in the face of growing threats.

But when the Myerses and Wechslers awoke on September 25, the morning after Eisenhower's order in Little Rock, they would find no such peace in Levittown. In the wee hours of the morning, they were awoken by the police. While the families slept, someone had painted the letters KKK, eighteen inches high, on the wall of the Wechslers' home on the exterior wall facing the Myerses' house. Next to the letters, a small poster entitled CONQUER AND BREED was framed in thick red paint.

The poster showed a crude drawing of voluptuous white woman in a strapless dress with thick red lips and flowing hair. At her feet were the words SOUTHERN WOMANHOOD. She looked fearfully back over her shoulder at a fat, shirtless African-American man with a tribal necklace and menacing hands. A label on his pants read INTEGRATION. At the bottom of the poster were two quotes attributed to spokespersons for the NAACP: "The association of the Races in public schools leads to friendship, love and marriage" and "Integration will result in White girls being associated with Negro boys . . . Naturally intermarriage would result. We of the NAACP are committed to a program of full integration." At the bottom of the page read the warning THE SOUTH MUST FIGHT OR PERISH. Someone had added in the margin, scrawled in red crayon, "We're right here in Levittown. We know every move you make." Someone had added the letters "K.K.K." under the heading of the poster, CONQUER AND BREED.

That same morning, a cross had been burned nearby at the home of man who had sold a car to Bill Myers and whose friend's thirteen-year-old daughter had brought flowers to the Myerses on the day of their arrival. A similar note was included at the cross-burning site, along with the warning "Keep your mouth shut. The KKK has eyes on you."

Bea and Lew struggled to decide what to do. On the one hand, they knew they had support. In the morning paper, an ad by the Levittown Citizens Committee came out quoting lines from Eisenhower's speech the day before: "These truths were spoken by President Eisenhower on

Sept. 24 . . . They refer to Little Rock, but they also apply directly to Levittown, PA."

But it was hard to take solace. For years, the Wechslers had stood in the face of opposition, but they had never been targets themselves. A person can only endure so much. "We just can't take it," Lew told one reporter who stopped by their house. "The fear in this town is enough to curl your hair. Those who were neutral before are afraid to open their mouths now. The troublemakers are as brazen as can be. The place is cluttered with Confederate flags. [Their] plans are to dress up in white sheets Ku Klux Klan–style for Halloween." Rumors were that they were going to blow up the Myerses' house on October 31.

And the Wechslers and Myerses weren't getting any help from the authorities. Where was the law? Levitt had defied the Supreme Court to foster this hateful environment, and nobody was stopping him. In fact, he was now building another Levittown just up the road with the same plan in mind. The local police had sat by and watched the harassment now for weeks. And even the state police had failed to help during their twenty-four-hour coverage, as the crosses were burned just yards from where they were parked on guard. Even the call to the attorney general had led to nothing.

For advice, Bea and Lew contacted their local state representative, A. Patrick Brennan, who had been pushing for help for them from the start. "Pat, we just don't know what do anymore," Lew said. "The police let these bigots congregate, abuse the Myers family with racial epithets, and call us 'nigger-loving Jews.' What do you think I should do?"

"If it was my house," Brennan said, "I'd have a half dozen friends come in, openly carrying their shotguns. Then, the first son of a bitch who stepped on my property, I'd shoot."

As these words ran through Bea's and Lew's minds, the Myerses were taking matters into their own hands. Despite the support, the "war of nerves," as Bill Myers had put it, was wounding him. Frequent visits to the doctor for nervous tension didn't alleviate his stress. He was chain-smoking now, his knee bobbing uncontrollably when he sat. He had told Daisy before that he had wanted to give up, to move out and find the life they had dreamed of when they'd parked on the shores of the Chesapeake in Virginia. Daisy had always been the strong one, but now he had to find the strength in himself.

Bill fished a letter from the pile of mail with a return address from Hampton, Virginia. Curious, he opened it to find a note from his alma mater. "We, the Faculty of Hampton Institute, wish to express our admiration for your quiet courage and forbearance under the trying circumstances," it read. They praised his embodiment of "every American's right to establish a home and rear a family without regard to discrimination based on race, color, or creed. While the ugly head of racial violence is being raised on several fronts of the national scene and when the tendency to meet violence with violence is a growing danger, your behavior is exemplary. It is with great pride that we commend you."

We face battles every day, Bill knew, little ones and big ones. We can fight them in two ways, with violence—physical and emotional—or quiet strength. It was time for the Myerses and Wechslers to choose. Bill took one last drag of his cigarette and put it out in an ashtray. Then he went to his garage and pulled out his bayonet. When Daisy asked where he was going, he lit another cigarette and said he had to pull some weeds. Bill stepped outside with the bayonet as the strains of "Ol' Man River" blasted from the Confederate House.

Eyeing Bill, a man in the Confederate House hollered, "You better keep on your side of the line or else."

Then Eldred Williams joined in. "This is it, we are here now. This is the boundary."

The mob spilled out of the house and began roaming their grounds around him. Others pulled up in cars with Confederate flags affixed to join their stand. Bill gripped his bayonet. With determined strokes, he thrust the weapon into the ground, ripping up the dandelions from their roots as his neighbors watched.

Sixteen

FREEDOM FIGHTERS

THE *SPUTNIK I* satellite was just twenty-three inches in diameter, but when the Russians launched it into space on October 4, 1957, it left a planet of fear in its wake. By putting the first human-made object into orbit, the Russians shot an icy chill into the Cold War with America.

It was a psychologically shattering moment for a country still trying to enjoy the postwar glow. If the Russians ruled space, then it seemed they had the ultimate power—the ability to track our every move, drop nuclear bombs from the sky, descend and vaporize happy families like the aliens depicted in the black-and-white sci-fi movies that ruled the box office of the day. As Senate majority leader Lyndon Johnson put it, the Soviets "will be dropping bombs on us from space like kids dropping rocks onto cars from freeway overpasses."

The news fired the imaginations and nightmares of the residents of Levittown, just as it did in other suburbs across the country. For years, people had flocked to these neighborhoods to escape the problems of the cities, but now that seemed increasingly futile. Whether it was the Cold War or the civil rights struggle, not even the highest white picket fence could keep out the rapidly changing times. In Levittown, it was not just *Sputnik* that threw the community into panic, it was the agents of change on Deepgreen Lane: the Myerses and Wechslers.

By October, the crisis had reached frightening heights—with the KKK graffiti, and the Confederate House raging despite the alleged 24-7 protection of the cops, who claimed not to have seen the crimes take place. The Myerses and Wechslers realized they couldn't expect the police or Levitt or even the Supreme Court of America to protect their safety or rights anymore. They had to find the strength within themselves, just as others across the land engaged in the civil rights struggles would have to find theirs. They weren't mere neighbors anymore. They were, as the activist paper the *Militant* dubbed them, "Levittown's Freedom Fighters."

And they weren't alone. As the Confederate flag waved in the house nearby, the Myerses and Wechslers experienced the flip side of hate: the love and support of their neighbors who came to their aid. After the KKK slogan was painted on the Wechslers' home, local community groups including the Quakers, the William Penn Center, the American Jewish Congress, and the neighboring communities of Bryn Gweled and Concord Park organized a 24-7 citizen patrol.

One night at three A.M., Lew got up to go to the bathroom when he heard voices in his kitchen. He walked down the hall to find a gray-haired woman and a teenage kid keeping guard. A pot of coffee steamed on the counter next to plates of cookies and cakes. "There they sat, holding the Klan at bay," Lew later effused, "a gray-haired 65-year-old woman and a 16-year-old boy!" Outside the house, Bea and Lew posted a letter of support in the place of the KKK poster that had been hung in a makeshift frame of bloodred paint. "Dear Sir," the letter read, "Thank you for being a good neighbor. The enclosed [money] is for some paint to help cover somebody's dirty work on your house." Wechsler posted the five-dollar bill sent with the letter on his wall too.

Next door, volunteer guards stood watch at the Myerses too all day and night. White couples arrived to babysit the children or lend a hand cleaning up. The outpouring moved the Myerses, and they took pains to point out how this awful standoff brought out the best in Levittown as well as the worst. "I doubt there were one hundred Levittown trouble-makers in [the mob's] crowd," Bill told the reporter from the *Militant*, "that speaks for a very small percentage. On the other hand, it was inspiring to see how many friends rallied to my defense. I felt it was unnecessary but the people themselves decided they wanted to stay through the night and give us protection. Most people here live in fear. The township police joked with the racist crowd, encouraging them."

Bill, once visibly shaking from nervous tension, had a newfound sense of power. When asked by a reporter for the umpteenth time if he would be run out of town, he replied more firmly than ever, "I definitely do not plan to leave. I think this neighborhood will change. I just painted the garage but haven't got to the cinder blocks yet."

"We'll leave you to your peace," the reporter said on his way out to see the Wechslers.

"We have no peace." Bill replied.

After all they'd been through, the Wechslers had finally become just as resolute. "I am not going to let some scum drive me out," Bea told the *Militant* reporter. "I was very upset when they burnt a cross in front of our house. But you reach a point where you get mad. It's much better to be mad than scared. I used to cringe when this first started, now I look them in the eye and feel I could spit."

The kids agreed. "I'm not leaving till I graduate," Katy said, "and nobody better bother me."

Outside, darkness began to fall. The Wechslers had taken to leaving their spotlights on all night, despite the protest of their neighbor next door, the FBI agent. The Wechslers found it hard to believe that the agent had complained to the cops about the spotlight, but not the Confederate House. As the sky turned black, Lew jokingly told Nick, "It's about time to light the Christmas tree." Nick flicked the light switch, and the spotlights blared on the yard.

"I'll tell you something," Lew said to the reporter. "To get the real story, you have to see William Levitt. He built this whole town with the clear understanding that Negroes would be kept out."

As the Levittown newspaper cheerily reported on October 9, however, the iconic builder had another story in mind: expanding his dream across the river. The paper was still ignoring the crisis in the community's backyard in favor of trumpeting their leader's momentous plans. WORKERS BUSY IN LEVITTOWN, N.J. read the headline, and the story, once again, spun Levitt's press releases into fairy-tale prose. The first Levittown had sprung from potato fields; the second, broccoli; and now this one, like some Jack-and-the-Beanstalk fantasy, would come from corn. "Across the Delaware on New Jersey's sandy soil," the article read, "the third planned miracle of Levitt and Sons is starting to burst forth from a Burlington County corn field."

Despite the racial tensions in Levittown, Pennsylvania, nothing could distract Bill Levitt from his own grand sense of his miraculous adventure— just like the fantastic tales of Captain Kidd that his father, Abe, had told him so long ago. Though still married to his wife, Rhoda, Bill Levitt continued to carry on his affair with his secretary Alice in the secret castle just a mile from Deepgreen Lane. His next empire in New Jersey would be his greatest yet, he promised.

Bill had plenty to prove. Since his brother had left the company, Alfred had been making a name for himself with his new projects in Long Island. Alfred, along with the help of his son Jon, was building an innovative "apartment colony" on the waterfront of Queens called Levitt House. The identical thirty-two eight-story-high buildings had his trademark blend of uniformity with openness and simple innovation. Each apartment had twenty feet of glass walls, and the exteriors were painted in whimsical shades of yellow and blue and brown. The kitchens were separated from the living rooms by a food bar and sliding wall. The *New York Times* praised Levitt House as having "some of the freshest ideas in design and construction."

With Alfred out of the picture, Bill could focus on making his New Jersey project any way he pleased. Still stung by attacks on his ticky-tacky towns by critics such as Lewis Mumford, he vowed to put the skeptics in their place. In Pennsylvania, he had been entangled in local politics because the community was built across four townships, but in Jersey, he worked within one township, Willingboro, which gave him freer rein.

With the four-thousand-acre Levittown, New Jersey, he would break away from any of Alfred's conventions. "Known for his low opinion of the city planning profession, however, and lacking Alfred's interest in its concepts and schemes, he had no intention of building the community to please the planners," wrote sociologist Herbert Gans. ". . . Unlike his father, he had no desire to involve the firm in the life of the community or to uplift the cultural level and civic performance of the residents. He wanted only to build what he deemed to be a better Levittown, what he often called 'a showplace.'"

At the same time, he was also making grand statements about his community in Bowie, Maryland, which would be open in 1960. He hyped that he built without plaster walls and predicted a future of new and technologically advanced materials. "In twenty-five years," he said, "people won't know what the word *plaster* means." And he derided so-called modern innovations favored by people like his brother, such as ovens built directly into walls. "I've got them in my [Levittown] houses because women want them," he said, "but it's ridiculous. Ovens ought to be down someplace near the floor and out of the way and out of sight. A woman bends over and puts something in and four hours later she bends over to take it out, so what's so hard about that that the oven needs to be in the wall?"

Levitt surrounded himself with his veteran executives, who were separated into philosophical camps called the realists and the idealists. Levitt fielded their pitches and concerns in his office and, as Gans put it, had an easy way of choosing which to back: the ones who "agreed with his own ideas." In Levittown, New Jersey, there would be areas set aside for churches. He hired renowned architects to design the shopping center with parking for more than six thousand cars. Each neighborhood would have around fifteen hundred homes with a park, a school, a swimming pool, and a baseball field.

Gone would be the days of communities with cookie-cutter homes, he promised. Instead, on the suggestion of his wife, Rhoda, he would have a mix of Cape Cods, ranchers, and colonials on the same block. The move to colonials was done "with a suddenness that almost took the breath away form his closest associates," one reporter wrote. "After years of building the contemporary type of house, the firm of Levitt and Sons is turning back to the traditional." As one of his execs put it, "Now Lewis Mumford can't criticize us anymore." In a press release, Levitt wrote, "We are ending once and for all the old bugaboo of uniformity."

As Bill Levitt was busy creating the fantasy of Levittown, New Jersey, reality was crashing in on Pennsylvania. On October 9, the same day the local paper celebrated the news of Levittown, New Jersey, a letter from Thomas McBride to the Bristol Township commissioners was made public through the press. In it, McBride was responding to an inquiry from the commissioners into why he had meddled by sending the state police back to Levittown.

McBride wrote that he was "somewhat surprised" by the tone of the township commissioners' letter given the extreme nature of the attacks. "I thought it to be of tremendous importance for this situation to be solved by local action," he continued, "and that if it was so solved, you would take pride in the accomplishment. Nevertheless, it remains true that I cannot, even if I would avoid the obligation that falls upon me as the chief law-enforcement officer of the Commonwealth; nor, in assuming my burden, does the responsibility fall from you of living up to yours." He concluded by writing, "I am convinced your police force did not do all that could have been expected."

McBride was not the only one who felt that way. On the heels of his letter, Sergeant Nuskey, the veteran Levittown police officer who had long been troubled by the police's inaction, put himself—and his career—on the line for his beliefs. It happened when he, along with his other officers, was awarded a citation by the township for their heroic service in protecting the Myerses.

But Nuskey returned the citation along with a letter of explanation: "I was not permitted to do my duty as my conscience dictated. I was ordered by my immediate superior not to take action. This was, to me, ignoring my responsibility. Although the board acted in good faith when it awarded the citation, I cannot accept it in good conscience. Therefore, I am taking a dignified step toward improving the department by returning it [the citation] to your charge."

Police Chief Stewart denied the allegation and found support from the township manager, Henry Rolfe, who said, "I do not consider the letters [from McBride and Nuskey] valid" because they contained "inaccurate information." And Nuskey would pay the price. The following week, Stewart demoted him to the rank of patrolman for allegedly violating a township police regulation against releasing police matters to the press.

Soon after, Sam Snipes, the Quaker attorney, heard his telephone ring. It was McBride, who invited Snipes to his home to discuss the Myerses' situation. "Why haven't you sought an injunction against the mob?" McBride asked. Snipes explained that the Myerses and their defenders lacked the resources, and the local police were as much a part of the problem. There was nothing they could do. McBride said, "I'll seek an injunction on behalf of the Commonwealth of Pennsylvania." If Levittown couldn't solve the problem, the state would.

Hughes, who had leased his house for use as the Confederate House, was arrested by the township for violating a zoning ordinance by allowing public gatherings in a residential area. But the charges would be dropped, he was told, if he told Eldred Williams and the forty other club dwellers to leave his home. Hughes took the deal. When he went to the house to deliver the news, the crowd inside was defiant.

"This is nothing more than a police state!" someone shouted.

"We're the wrong color," said another.

Hughes was sympathetic. "The wishes of the property owners in this section have not been considered at all. This whole thing was a railroad job," he said, but "this is the only way to keep me from going to jail." The Confederate House was closed. Despite the mob's claims that whites wouldn't want to be neighbors with the Myerses, a white family from New York happily assumed the lease within days. "It's a nice house," said the new tenant. "The neighborhood has nice winding roads, lots of greenery—it's very pleasant . . . We don't give a darn if Negroes live next to it."

One by one, the chips began to fall. On Thursday, October 17, after more than two months of investigations, Howard Bentcliff was working at his job as an auto-service-station attendant on the Pennsylvania Turnpike when he saw police cars arrive. The officers told him he was under arrest for malicious mischief in the harassment of the Myerses in Levittown. Five days later, the police arrested Eldred Williams, along with Bentcliff, for burning the cross on the lawn of Peter Von Blum the previous month. They were both held and then released on $500 bail for grand jury action. The following day, October 23, a temporary injunction was granted against the group, including Williams; Bentcliff and his wife, Agnes; John R. Bentley; John T. Piechowski; Mary Brabazon; and the chairperson of the Levittown Betterment Association, James Newell.

The five-and-one-half-page complaint by the Commonwealth of Pennsylvania stated that the defendants had "entered into an unlawful, malicious and evil conspiracy . . . to force the said Myers family to leave Levittown; to harass, annoy, intimidate, silence and deprive of their rights to peaceable enjoyment of their property residents of Levittown who did not participate in the conspiracy or in any act designed to force the said Myers family to leave Levittown; to deprive the said Myers family and other residents of Levittown of their rights to personal security and equal protection of the laws; to interfere with and prevent law enforcement officers from performing their duties with the intent to deny the aforesaid residents of Levittown of the equal protection of the laws . . . said conspiracy and said purposes being in violation of the Constitution of the United States and the Federal Civil Rights Act."

It barred them from:

A. Burning or causing to be burned fiery crosses.
B. Trespassing and affixing to property of others or littering the streets with inflammatory posters, scurrilous pictures, leaflets and other printed matter.
C. Harassing or annoying residents of Levittown by organizing, instigating or participating in motorcades, loud slamming of mail boxes and setting off firecrackers.
D. Placing or causing to be placed in Levittown bombs or explosives of any kind whatsoever.
E. In any manner threatening or intimidating any individual or in any manner threatening the destruction of property.
F. Taking any acts of any kind whatever which seek by force, violence or intimidation to compel removal or withdrawal of the Myerses from Levittown.

Upon the issuing of the complaint, McBride said, "We cannot tolerate for a single minute these attempts to stir up racial hatred in defiance of our state and federal laws and constitutions." The message was clear. William Levitt and his followers had defied the laws for over a decade now to keep their utopian suburb whites-only. Since Levitt wouldn't change its policy, the state would step in.

A hearing in the case of the *Commonwealth of Pennsylvania v. Williams et al.* was scheduled for December 9, 1957, in Doylestown, Pennsylvania, the county seat of Bucks County, twenty miles away. The state would seek a permanent injunction against the leaders of the mob, dubbed the Levittown 7. The battle had begun on Deepgreen Lane, but the fate of America's suburb would be decided in court.

Seventeen

THE STAND

THE SNOW WAS falling hard on December 5, as up to eight inches accumulated in Levittown, Pennsylvania. But that didn't stop someone from trudging through the slush to knock on the Wechslers' door. Bea opened it to find Sergeant Adrian McCarr of the local police towering over her. "I have a subpoena for Katy Wechsler," he said, handing her the document.

Bea eyed the paper addressed to her daughter. "We Command You," it read, "that all and every business, pretext and excuse set aside, you be and appear before our Judge, at Doylestown . . ."

Bea looked up at McCarr and snapped, "For Katy! She's fourteen years old! If anyone in this house is to be subpoenaed, it will be me or Lew, we are the adults here." Katy was one of forty-three people subpoenaed for the hearing, and Bea suspected why her daughter had been called. It was the red-baiting again. McBride and the others were simply afraid to have Bea and Lew, with their Communist backgrounds, take the stand. It was yet another snub, and worse, the state had the gall to put their daughter in the spotlight instead. Bea told McCarr to hit the road. Katy wasn't going anywhere.

The deputy attorney general called a few days later to admonish Bea about her "responsibility" to make her daughter testify. But Bea was having none of it. "If you need a Wechsler to take the stand, then it will have to be me or Lew," she said again. "Our children have withstood enough. They're not going to be cross-examined by an attorney representing

Klansmen." Bea hung up, and that was that. The state backed down, but no Wechslers were called.

Lew, nevertheless, decided to show up the first day of the hearing at the Court of Common Pleas of Bucks County, Pennsylvania. He found Daisy there as well. She would testify on behalf of her family. They arrived at the courthouse to find a chaotic scene. Reporters and onlookers crowded the door. Daisy dreaded seeing the mob up close after their months of tormenting her. Visions of the long, sleepless nights flashed before her—the feeling of being under siege by the group, the fear, the anxiety; Bill, chainsmoking and desperate.

After so many months, members of the mob had ceased to be human, Daisy thought. She had only taken a few steps into the hall when she saw them. There was the hulking Newell alongside the scrawny, skittish Williams and the others. Newell had an arrogant air as he tried in vain to keep a distance between himself and the others. They averted their eyes upon seeing Daisy. And something inside Daisy shifted. These people were not monsters after all. They were quite the opposite, she thought, "trapped mice seeking the nearest hole in which to hide."

As Attorney General McBride, who was conducting the trial for the state, came into the hall, one of the defendants went up to him and demanded to know if the court was going to pay him for the day of work he was missing because of the trial. "If I were you," McBride replied, "I'd be worrying whether or not I was going to jail."

The witnesses and the audience crammed into the small, stuffy courtroom as the judge, the Honorable Edwin H. Satterthwaite, took his seat on the stand. "Ready to proceed in the case of *Commonwealth versus Williams and others*?" he said.

"Ready for the Commonwealth," McBride replied.

"Gentlemen, will you please prepare for trial." Satterthwaite said. "Let's get under way."

One by one, the court called the names of the defendants, who rose from their seats in the crowd. They watched as the first witness made her way to the stand: Daisy Myers. "Mrs. Myers," McBride said, "since some of the defendants are seated in the back of the courtroom, it will be important that what you say should be heard by them. Please keep your voice up in answer to the questions that are asked."

In her slight Southern accent, Daisy recounted the story of her family's move to Levittown: her college background, her plans, the harassment, the mobs, the treatment of their visiting white friends. She told how she saw Bentcliff writing down the license-plate numbers of her friends and how he took to calling them hateful names. "They called [them] 'nigger lovers' and all types of disrespectful things," Daisy said.

This comment caused Newell's defense lawyer, H. Lyle Houpt, to rise from his seat. "I object to these statements at this time, because there is no showing any of the defendants were present at that time."

The judge wasn't having any of it. "Objection overruled."

But Houpt could not be restrained. Again and again he made his objections, as Newell sat nearby. At one point, he cross-examined Daisy about the notes she was referring to during her testimony, but was cut short again: "Your objection is overruled."

Daisy felt more than ready to face the defendants down. As she was describing the time Williams roamed her property line with the dog he called Nigger, McBride interrupted. "Will you stand, Mr. Williams?" he asked. Williams stood. With the press and crowd watching, Daisy found herself in the same position as Emmett Till's grandfather, who had courageously pointed out the white man who'd murdered his grandson. Williams stood. "Is this the gentlemen of whom you speak?" McBride asked.

Daisy stared at the small man. "That is."

Daisy went on, explaining how Williams also led motorcades of racists in front of her house. In addition, while Newell had made public efforts to distance himself from the militant side of the mob, Daisy knew otherwise, and testified to having seen him enter the Confederate House, where Williams reigned. "Just a moment," McBride interrupted. "Mr. Newell, would you stand up?" The lumbering North Carolinian stood. "Is that the Mr. Newell to whom you refer?"

"That's the Mr. Newell," Daisy replied.

But as courageous as it was to face down and single out these men,

Daisy would soon have to endure the worst indecency of all: being questioned by two members of the mob. Williams and Bentcliff had both chosen to defend themselves in court and were given their turn to cross-examine her. As McBride concluded his questioning, Williams rose to face Daisy. "You stated that I was the leader of these motor-cades?" Williams said.

Yes, she said, he was there "with the Confederate flag on one side of the automobile and some other flag on the other side, which I failed to bring out in the other testimony."

"I went to that home every day?" Williams continued.

"You were there every day."

After Williams haplessly concluded his questioning, which only served to implicate himself more, Bentcliff took his turn. "How did you know I was taking license numbers?" he asked Daisy.

"[You had a] pad, pencil, and wrote something down," Daisy replied.

"You could see that from your house?"

"Sure I could."

"You could see the car parked outside, and the man writing down something on a pad?"

"I saw you drive up, because I thought it was somebody coming to visit."

"And you can see from there he is writing?"

"Look right down and you can."

Bentcliff was dubious. "I can't see from my house into a car that somebody is writing."

"I don't know your house."

"Situated the same," Bentcliff said.

"Now, Mr. Bentcliff," the judge interrupted, "I warned you once. I won't warn you again. Don't interrupt while the witness is still talking."

Daisy didn't waver for the rest of her testimony. Finally McBride came back to the stand to ask her a few final questions about the mob. "Were there often times in which there was a Confederate flag flying on automo-biles?"

"Oh, yes, every day," Daisy said.

"Any of them have an American flag along with the Confederate flag?"

"I didn't see one."

The state's first witness was done.

One by one the witnesses took the stand following Daisy Myers's testimony, and it became clear that while the trial was against the Levittown 7, others were coming under scrutiny: the police and the various officials, all the way up to William Levitt, who had brazenly ignored the laws. "I thought when I bought the home there was—what would you say?—an understanding," said defendant Mary Brabazon. "Of course it wasn't on paper that it would be an all-white community."

"And that was your understanding when you purchased your home?" McBride asked.

"That is right."

"Now, when the Myers family moved into Levittown, did you consider that was contrary to your understanding?"

"We were quite shocked."

The ensuing riot had become integrated into the daily lives of Levittown residents, she explained. Brabazon testified that the proliferation of Confederate flags around town was a sign of their popularity.

"What was the purpose of the Confederate flag?" McBride asked.

"I think it was just like a fad," she said, "because all the people were buying them at the Levittown Shopping Center."

"When did this fad start? After the Myers family moved in or before?"

"Afterwards."

Again and again the defendants cloaked themselves in the flag of freedom, saying they were simply seeking their right, as Americans, to legally extricate the Myerses from their suburb. But McBride saw them for what they were—racists. And the local police had been complicit by not enforcing the rights of the Myerses and Wechslers. For months now, the local and state police had been ostensibly watching and protecting the Myerses and Wechslers from the mob violence, but to what effect? How had the cross burnings, the Molotov cocktails, the letters KKK painted on the home unfolded just a few feet from their watch?

When Peter Von Blum, the friend of the Wechslers' who had the

cross with blank cartridges burned on his lawn, took the stand, he testified to the response he got when he phoned his township manager for
help on the first night the violence broke out. "I described to him the
situation," Von Blum said, "and I asked him please to send some police,
somebody was in danger of getting beaten up, and he said, 'Well, the
township police knows what it's doing. We don't see any need for it at
present.' "

When a corporal named Keith R. Dane was sworn in on the stand,
McBride questioned the behavior of the police: "Now, in your opinion,
was the presence and action of the police necessary to prevent mob violence?"

"Objection!" said one defense attorney.

"Objection!" said another.

"Objection overruled," the judge said.

"Yes, sir," Corporal Dane continued in response to the question, "in
my opinion it was." Yet nothing had been done.

As testimonies continued, Levittown's summer of hate unfolded in
detail. At one point, a child, fourteen-year-old W. Paul Von Blum, the
son of Peter and Selma, testified to the harassment he faced one day
while he was playing outside the Wechslers' at a cookout party: "Mr.
Newell rode past in his car, and he called out several names, among
them 'nigger lovers.' "

"Do you see Mr. Newell in court?" McBride asked.

Von Blum looked into the sea of faces until his eyes landed on the
mountainous man with the square head. "Yes, I do."

"Will you identify him?"

"Right over there." Von Blum pointed to Newell.

"Is that the man who called you 'nigger lover'?"

"Yes, it is."

It became clear that the mob went way beyond the people on trial when
it was revealed that twelve hundred people in Levittown had signed up as
members of the Levittown Betterment Association. In the South they had
lynchings, but in Levittown the racism took the shape of a suburban committee with Confederate flags for sale at the local Shop-O-Rama. The
racists came from all walks of life—housewives and mothers, a candidate

for county commissioner, a tax collector, and Bentley, a Democratic committeeman.

One by one, the defendants hid behind the pretense of nonviolence, saying that all they were doing was looking for "legal means" to get the Myerses out of town. The rationale evoked strong emotions from the prosecution, and a surprising confession from the man who had led volunteers on the Myerses' behalf, the Reverend Ray Harwick. Over the summer, Harwick had proved inconsistent and complicated—defending the Myerses' rights on one hand, but leading a red-baiting inquisition of their main sympathizers, the Wechslers, on the other. His family had been threatened late at night to the point he shipped them off for protection. And the experience had left him changed.

"Reverend Harwick," McBride asked, "am I correct that you have certain strong convictions concerning this matter?"

"I do now."

"What do you mean you do *now*, Reverend?"

"Well, the implication made here before, it was a misnomer, of course, that I was an integrationalist [*sic*]. It is rather ironical, and I am ashamed to say it, that in six and a half years of my ministry until this time, that I definitely"—Harwick hesitated—"I had never preached a sermon on brotherhood."

"Do you want to explain the present view that you take on these things?"

"The present view that I take is stated, of course, very effectively in Paul's letter to the Romans, where in the first place he talks about the laws, man having derived from the laws of God, and, of course, in the book Genesis, we read that man was created in the image of God, and our Bill of Rights is, of course, very strong; the constitution of our Commonwealth, the Constitution of our nation makes no bones about its stand in this matter. The stand of our denomination is extremely clear and strong in this matter, and if I am in any way to live up to the vows that I took when I was ordained a Christian minister, I could not possibly do anything but be obedient and take a very strong stand on integration.

"Prior to this time, it never really seemed much of a problem to me.

I had never run into any controversial matter before, and certainly not this. My relations with Negroes prior to this time had for the most part been very good, except for a while I was in the service, but I never considered it too much of an issue, the areas in the country were pretty far removed from me personally, and they had never affected me before, but this did."

"Now, Reverend," McBride continued, "I think quite a few people in this courtroom would agree with many of the conclusions that you have reached. I would like to ask you whether or not you think these people, these defendants, are guilty?"

"You are asking me to pronounce judgment?"

"Yes, sir."

Harwick's mind reeled. The harassing calls. The intimidation. It was all there. But who was he to judge? Wasn't his role to forgive? Harwick looked out into the crowd. "I do think they are guilty," he finally said, "because they have said one thing with their mouths and actually gone ahead and done something else. They said they are opposed to violence, and yet they provided the leadership, and at that time the only leadership that was available apparently in the community for the group that was opposed to Myers moving, whether it was openly and clearly and concisely stated or not, there could have been no other purpose to be served by the Betterment Committee or any of those who engaged in any acts of harassment or intimidation in order to remove them from the community, which, in effect, of course, is a deprivation of their rights."

McBride then got to the crux of the issue, that the pursuit of these so-called "legal means" of evicting the Myerses was just a mask for racism. He did this when John Bentley, the Democratic committeeman and mob member took the stand. "Is it your thought that the majority should rule in Levittown," McBride asked, "that if a majority were against a colored person moving in, that colored person should not move in, because the majority have the right to rule?"

"I felt this way about it," Bentley said, "that if it could be shown to Mr. Myers that a majority of the people did not want him in Levittown, that he should accept it." Bentley later explained why: "I went to school with Negroes. I sent my son to school with Negroes. I worked with

Negroes. I am sometimes forced to eat with Negroes, but I do not want to live with them."

"And therefore," McBride said, "you joined the Betterment Committee to prevent that from occurring in the future?"

"If there was any way legally to prevent it, yes, sir."

McBride went on. "You said that you wanted to exert legal means to remove . . . the Myers family from Levittown?"

"We were attempting to find some solution to the problem, yes, sir."

"Legally?"

"Yes, sir."

"By then the windows, at least the pane of glass, had been broken at the Myers home, had it not?" McBride said.

"Yes, so I read in the newspapers."

"Did you take any stand that breaking their windows was a dirty deed, or that it was wrong and should be stopped?"

"No, sir, I didn't take any stand at all."

"You wouldn't consider that legal means, would you?"

"The breaking of windows?"

"Yes."

"No, sir."

"Did you later hear of the burning of the fiery crosses?"

"Yes, sir."

"Would you consider that legal means?"

"No, sir."

"Would you consider that the throwing of firecrackers on the lawn were legal means?"

"No, sir."

"Would you consider the terror that comes from anonymous telephone calls in the middle of the night legal means?"

"No, sir."

McBride was through. "This pious pretense of acting legally is just what it seems to be from the witness stand, a sham to get these people out of their home. How can there be any legal means of depriving a citizen of a constitutional right? How can there be any legal way of doing it under the sun? They may say they wanted to act legally, but when the

Supreme Court of the United States spoke authoritatively in *Shelly versus Kraemer* outlawing covenants which would debar Negroes from purchasing property, and outlawed even state action taken to enforce such covenants in deeds, how can anyone further pretend that here is any legal means of enforcing a proposition that would deprive these American citizens of the right to purchase property and live where they can and wish to do? Simply [there] are no legal means that could be adopted to the purpose that this evidence discloses, that is, getting the Myerses out of Levittown. Nobody has the right to get the Myerses out of Levittown by any means."

And though Bentley and the others did not agree with this, Bentley ultimately admitted that their cause was lost after all. "I am of the firm belief now, Mr. McBride," Bentley said, "that there isn't anything that can be done to keep Negroes out of Levittown."

After the first trial in December, which sought a permanent injunction against the Levittown 7 from harassing the Myerses or their supporters, a second trial began on January 31, 1958. Williams and his fellow mob member Howard Bentcliff had been charged with harassment for burning the cross on the Wechslers' lawn. Once again a standing-room-only audience packed the stuffy upstairs courtroom. The evidence against the two was damning. Williams himself had admitted to building the cross that was burned on the Von Blums' lawn. Sergeant Adrian McCarr testified that in Bentcliff's car he had found a carbon copy of the letter that Lew had received after the cross burning, telling him to "pull out while you can."

The police had also confiscated copies of a newsletter called the *Levittown Defender*, which was written on October 10, the day after McBride's attack on the Levittown police force's inaction had been made public. Five hundred copies were made, and one turned up in the United States Steel Company close by. "Levittown, Penna. Proved to the world the public demand for segregation in the north," it read. "Here 60,000 non negroes settled in five short years in 17,500 homes because negroes were excluded as buyers. Mr. Levitt has stated that 'through various means we have found that if we sell to negroes 90 to 95% of the whites will not

buy.' The will of the majority is being ignored. American Indians be-
ware; your reservation may be next! Support the Back-to-Africa plan! It
helps the negro to help himself." And, it concluded, "You can't blame Bill
M. for moving out of his former colored neighborhood; after all, who
wants to live amongst negroes?"

Literature on the "Back-to-Africa" movement was found, along with
other "propaganda," McCarr said, in Newell's home. Something more in-
criminating was found in Bentcliff's car: correspondence from E. L. Edwards, the imperial wizard of the Ku Klux Klan. The police found KKK
membership applications inside Bentcliff's car, which Bentcliff had
mimeographed along with Williams to hand out to their followers. The
letter from Edwards had come in response to an inquiry from Bentcliff.

"The content of the letter dealt with the fact that he had received
some communication from Bentcliff," McCarr testified, "and was sending some literature. I questioned Bentcliff upon what office he held, and
he claimed he did not hold an office, that they were getting the Klan together, and they had one hundred members, and when the Klan had
gathered, when they had gotten sufficient members, Mr. Edwards would
come up from Georgia, and they would initiate the group." America's
legendary suburb was harboring the Ku Klux Klan.

When it came time for the defense to present its case, Bentcliff sheepishly rose to defend himself, as he had done in the previous trial. His
wife and sixteen-year-old daughter watched from the audience. But just
as he took a few steps forward, he began to look dazed. Then, all at once,
he collapsed face-first against the ground. Those in court gasped as he lay
motionless. Lew watched in shock in the eerie silence. Had the guy just
died of a heart attack? No one was coming to his aid, not even his friend
Williams.

From out of the crowd came Peter Von Blum, the man who'd woken
up to find a burning cross with blank cartridges exploding on his lawn.
Von Blum began taking off his overcoat to cover Bentcliff, then someone
else was there to help: Lew Wechsler. It was a striking moment: The two
victims of Bentcliff's abuse were not above lending a hand.

Bentcliff had fainted—a doctor said he suffered from a heart condition. But that couldn't stop justice. When the first ruling eventually

came, Williams was found guilty of conspiracy and fined $50 for the burning of the cross. Then Bentcliff who had admitted to burning the crosses on the Von Blums' and another Levittowner's lawns, painting *KKK* on the Wechslers' home, and possessing the threatening letters—was put on probation for a year and fined $250 as well as court costs. "I'm giving you a break because of your health," Bucks County judge Edwin Satterthwaite told him. "You should go to jail."

But once the trials were done, the final verdict—the official ruling in the case against the entire Levittown 7—would take months to come. Across the Delaware River in New Jersey, the builder of Levittown was digging in for one last fight.

Eighteen

THE PROMISE

THE NEW POSTWAR suburbs are stereotyped, drab, and dull. The people who live in them, adapting like chameleons to the color of their surroundings, tend to become stereotyped, drab, and dull. There is no privacy. To get along with neighbors, conformity is a must. Not only does living in these new suburbs rob people of their individuality and bounce, but special kinds of neighborhood pressure tend to debase their values, warp their judgment, force them into unworthy behavior patterns, and interfere with the proper rearing of their children."

Not long after the Levittown trials concluded in early 1958, Bill Levitt sat at his desk reading these words. The harsh critique was aimed directly at him and the model town he and his family had set out to create just a decade before. And the words were his own. Fed up with the criticisms against his town, he had agreed to write an article for *Good Housekeeping* magazine in which he would recount and answer his critics' charges.

Some complained about the lack of privacy in his towns. But not so, Levitt wrote: "People can really have all the privacy they wish, all they have to do is hang draperies and maintain a decent reserve in personal matters." Levittowners are drab and dull? "This is the greatest foolishness of all. People who live in the suburbs are pretty much like people who live elsewhere. There are so many of them, differing in so many ways, that no capsule classifications can apply. If these people represent anything, I should say it is a cross section of the middle generation of American citizens today."

Finally, he took aim at the heart of the critique itself: "It seems to me incredibly myopic to focus on the thread of uniformity in housing and fail to see the broad fabric of which it is a part—the mass production culture of America today." Mass production was not just the rage with Levitt, it was changing the landscape of America in the 1950s: from the first franchise of Holiday Inn hotels dotting the roadways to the new McDonald's fast-food restaurants nearby. "This isn't something to grieve over," Levitt continued. "It's something to glory in—just so long as we keep in mind the difference between material values and those of the mind and spirit."

In the past decade, his town had become synonymous with America's mass-produced culture in the 1950s—the good, and the bad. The critique had run through popular entertainment from *The Crack in the Picture Window* to *Invasion of the Body Snatchers*. But now, on the heels of the Myerses' case—which dovetailed with the explosion of the civil rights movement—the fight against Levittown, and everything it represented, took on a new sense of urgency.

Levitt hadn't publicly addressed the Myers incident since it had unfolded the previous summer. Instead, he had tried to let his long history of justifications speak for the racial covenants he had so stubbornly enforced. It had been easier for him to do this in the past, when he had created Levittown in the postwar glow. But now, America was changing, and the promise of an integrated Levittown took on a new meaning.

As sociologist Herbert Gans put it, "Levittown had become a national symbol of suburbia and a brand name in housing generally, so that the publicity value of its integration would be considerable. One could even argue that the firm had attracted more purchasers and profit because its communities had become national symbols, and that it therefore deserved being singled out."

As the ruling against the Levittown 7 was awaited, a private battle was being waged among Bill Levitt's closest allies and advisers to turn him—and his towns—around. It was time for Levitt to open his communities' doors to blacks, they said. Chief among these advisers were John Reagan "Tex" McCrary, the high-powered publicist who had coined the "I Like

Ike" slogan in aid of General Eisenhower's presidential bid, and the liberal Republican senator from New York, Jacob Javits.

As Levitt hemmed and hawed, Javits reached out to leaders of the NAACP to plan for the integration of the next Levittown—the one set to open in New Jersey later in 1958. The idea was not to have a big announcement but to integrate quietly and without fanfare, to avoid the kind of violence that had broken out in Levittown, Pennsylvania. In his private conversations, Bill Levitt again voiced his concern that opening the doors to blacks would drive away the whites—and his sales. But Javits and the others tried to convince him that a controlled and managed integration would not affect his business at all, and that after the stand of the Myerses, the time to change was upon him.

At times, Bill Levitt seemed to be coming around. His son William Levitt Jr., who had come to work with the company in 1957 after graduating from Wharton Business School, was pleased to hear his father say as much to NAACP leaders when discussing the incident in Levittown, Pennsylvania. "It's unfortunate that this happened there," Bill Levitt said, "but you folks are going to be pretty happy soon because we're going to open our doors" to blacks.

After his self-congratulatory article appeared in *Good Housekeeping* magazine, Levitt decided to answer his critics in the boldest possible way: with a press conference in June 1958 officially announcing the charter of his latest master-planned community, Levittown, New Jersey. There was just one problem. His closest associates were desperately pleading for him not to make a public statement. The delicate plans to integrate Levittown, New Jersey, were being orchestrated by Javits and McCrary, and they, along with others close to Levitt, feared what might happen when Levitt took the microphone. Surely he would be questioned on the integration, and they worried about how the legendarily brash titan would reply. "There's a great danger in having a press conference," said his son William. "He'll be severely questioned about matters better left not spoken about. He's going to dig a hole for himself."

But Levitt insisted, and as always he got his way. On June 5, 1958, as the ruling in the Myerses' case still pended, and with Javits, McCrary, and William Jr. watching, reporters packed a conference room in Washington, D.C., to hear William Levitt's speech. William Levitt Jr. observed the intensity of the crowd. He watched as his father regaled the media with news of the new town near Camden and Trenton, New Jersey: built on four thousand acres, fifteen thousand homes ranging from $11,490 to $13,990, and just ten dollars closing costs.

Levitt's Barnumesque razzle-dazzle was in full display; he'd mass-produce as many as one hundred new homes a week. Mortgages would come, once again, from the Federal Housing Administration. Evoking the fairy-tale legend of his Depression-era roots, he promised to overcome any economic challenges along the way.

As the time came for questions, Javits and the others braced themselves. It didn't take long for the inevitable to happen. "Would the new community be segregated racially?" a reporter asked.

Bill Levitt looked out into the crowd for a moment, then said, "Our policy on that is unchanged. The two other Levittowns are white communities." And so, he promised, this one would be too.

Why did my father do it? William Levitt Jr. asked himself. He had his suspicions. Levitt's son had taken it upon himself to do his own due diligence on the viability of building a new Levittown in this area. He had hired an economist to prepare a report that he could show his father—and the findings weren't good. Willingboro, the location, was beyond the scope of the Philadelphia suburbs, and the demand for so much low-cost housing wasn't there.

William Levitt Jr. suspected that this news only further motivated his father to proceed. He was out to prove everyone wrong—and still harbored fears that selling to blacks would reduce his chances of selling to whites. "I think it was an aberration from his usual intelligence," William Jr. said. "Somehow in this conference he got upset and reacted badly. I think it was just a strange human reaction, he really knew better."

The fallout from the press conference was immediate, and dramatic. To his son's chagrin, his father had dug himself not just any hole, but the deepest one of his life. "I'd never seen him make a major mistake before or since," William Levitt Jr. said. It was a "crisis that he created."

After the talks with and promises to the NAACP, Levitt's closest advisers—Javits and McCrary—felt blindsided, embarrassed, and betrayed. McCrary resigned the account. "His major allies deserted him," said William Jr. "He was left without any allies at all on these issues, because anybody who'd been involved with him knew that he had double-crossed them."

After more than a decade of brazenly challenging the laws and the rights of black Americans, Levitt was no longer getting a free pass. The executive secretary of the NAACP telegrammed New Jersey governor Robert Meyner expressing outrage over "this flouting" of New Jersey law. Levitt, who had long been active and philanthropic with Jewish groups, was even abandoned by them; a joint statement from prominent Jewish organizations denounced Levitt for his "desecration of democracy and the basic ideals of the Judaic heritage." A prominent reverend who'd founded the Catholic Interracial Council urged the New Jersey governor to "do something about it" because, he said, "the front line of the racial problem in the United States" is in these communities. The American Civil Liberties Union joined the protest saying, "Mr. Levitt is not only promoting bigotry, he is proposing to create an entire township dedicated to the principle of segregation."

Community leaders, including a prominent senator in New Jersey and the New York–based chair of the National Committee Against Discrimination in Housing, called on the Federal Housing Administration to cut off Levitt's mortgages once and for all. The FHA commissioner said that if the New Jersey agency that enforced antidiscrimination laws determined that Levitt was breaking the law, then the FHA would reexamine its loans. The attorney general of New Jersey and the director of the State Division Against Discrimination began an investigation. And the state Assembly warned Levitt that discrimination would not be allowed in his community.

Levitt was under siege, and it was completely of his own doing. Though he had played a revolutionary role in providing homes for World War II veterans and popularizing the mass-produced suburban communities, the dark side of Levitt's perfect plan was finally seeping through. After decades of blindly praising him, people began to question why and how his exclusionary practice had even taken place.

"There is no question that Levitt's contemplated action violates the spirit if not the letter of the New Jersey housing and civil rights laws," one reporter wrote. "What is puzzling to us is the failure of state officials to carry out the specific provisions of the anti-discrimination laws when it was evident that these laws had been deliberately violated." But as the fight wore on, change began to occur. After Levitt's announcement, the New Jersey State Division Against Discrimination got the Veterans Administration to "withhold loan approvals from builders practicing discrimination because of race, creed, or color."

Now when Bill Levitt arrived at his model homes, he found groups of Quakers picketing outside. One night in July, 250 people crammed into a meeting room to establish the New Jersey Committee Against Discrimination in Housing, with a mission to "help preserve the advances in human rights so painfully won over recent years." As the group gathered, they watched a woman take the stage to share her experience with bias in Levittown: Daisy Myers. Daisy was still awaiting a final ruling in the case against the Levittown 7—which the judge, as with many rulings, was taking months to resolve—but she didn't hesitate to take up the fight. She was an activist now, and she would speak out against Levitt's racist plan. This "gives a go-ahead to the biggest race haters," she said.

On August 14, 1958, nearly one year to the date that the Myerses moved into their little pink house, Judge Satterthwaite handed down his final ruling against the leaders of the Levittown mob: guilty. Newell, Williams, Bentcliff, and the others were guilty of unlawful conduct toward the Myerses and of an attempted violation of the rights of them "and other peaceable residents of the area," the judge said. "Their unity of action, even though not spelled out in an express verbal or written understanding, constituted an unlawful conspiracy. Similar observations apply to those who engaged in the insidious and horror-inspiring secret machinations or burning of crosses, implied threats of KKK intervention, and malicious defacing of property by vile and opprobrious posters and paint daubing in the general Levittown area."

The harassment of the Myerses was forbidden by law. Back on Deep-green Lane, the Myerses and Wechslers rejoiced in the news, which quickly spread across the town and the region. The message was clear, as one paper put it: "Bitter racial prejudice is not confined to the Southern States. Those who take the law into their own hands in Bucks County are warned in advance by the Court that they can expect to pay conse-quences of their unlawful acts."

While the "war of nerves" against the mob had been won, one last battle was remaining in New Jersey. Two black veterans, William R. James and Franklin D. Todd, sued Levitt after being denied the right to buy a house in the New Jersey development. "The complainants argue that since the Federal Housing Administration has agreed to guarantee mort-gage payments for the Levittown development, that the project is bound by the anti-discrimination law," the *New York Times* reported. "The builder maintains it is not covered by the law, which it says applies only to quasi public or public housing."

As the months passed and Levitt buckled down for his fight in court, the waves of change continued to rise against him. On May 21, 1959, the House Law and Order Committee met in Harrisburg, Pennsylvania, for a hearing on a fair-housing bill. The AFL-CIO human rights committee representative called a surprise witness, Daisy Myers, "a case in point in housing discrimination," he said. Daisy took to the stand and called for action to protect families like hers from such persecution in the future. "Had the housing measure been on the books" when she had moved to Levittown, she said, "I believe there never would have been trouble."

Two months later, the Appellate Division of the Superior Court in New Jersey handed down its decision—upholding the law against Levitt's plan. State law barred discrimination in "all housing financed in whole or in part by a loan whether or not secured by mortgage, the repayment of which is guaranteed by the Federal government or any agency thereof." Astonishingly, Levitt still refused to back down. He held out hope that the state's highest court—the Supreme Court—would rule in his favor. It didn't. On February 9, 1960, the state Supreme Court ruled unanimously that African-Americans would be permitted to buy homes in Levittown, New Jersey. But Levitt remained defiant, and his lawyer promised to appeal the ruling to the U.S. Supreme Court. This, he said, "raises serious questions about constitutional law."

For decades, Levitt had leaned on his stature to, as his PR once said, disobey the law and ignore red tape. He had become a symbol for what was now a staggering migration to suburbia, whose population had grown from 31.1 million in 1941 to 60.1 million by this time in 1960. The landscape across America had changed. Trees had been taken down to make room for houses, highways, hotels, car dealerships, and the country's favorite invention: shopping centers. In 1945, there had been only eight shopping centers in the entire country; by 1960 there were 3,840. But the most stunning statistic of all was how, from 1934 through 1960, less than 2 percent of the $120 billion in new housing underwritten by the U.S. government went to minorities.

Ultimately, Levitt's role in the transformation of America could not save him from the changes in civil rights. One day in March 1960, he called a number of township officials and clergy to his office. Soon after, on Sunday, March 27, the ministers read a statement from Levitt to their congregants: "Sooner or later present New Jersey law or some other law will be upheld and enforced no matter how present litigation turns out and Negro families will move into Levittown."

While Levitt tried to save face in the public eye, he was still pursuing a legal victory in this case by taking his appeal to the U.S. Supreme Court. The next June, however, the Court, which refused to hear Levitt's appeal, made it official. Levittown would be integrated once and for all. The New Jersey Division Against Discrimination issued a formal order to William J. Levitt "to cease and desist from discrimination, receive from the two Negro families and report back within 45 days on what progress has been made in processing the applications." One of the black veterans, Willie R. James, eagerly sat down and wrote a letter, at last, requesting an application to live in Levittown. "I plan to buy a house and move into Levittown as fast as I possibly can," he said. "I have never had any hesitancy about moving there."

It was a picture-perfect day on Deepgreen Lane. Toddlers played in kiddie pools. Children sold lemonade from a stand. Nick and Katy Wechsler were playing around inside their home with their dog Biff, when Lew came in. Long ago when they'd decided to move to Levittown, he'd made the children two promises: they would get a dog, and he'd take them to see Jackie Robinson. Now it was time to fulfill the second promise.

By standing up for their rights, and for each other, the Myerses and Wechslers—two families from different worlds—showed the power that neighbors can conjure up when they choose to come together. The Myerses, who never expected or wanted to be leading a political struggle, discovered that the personal is the political, that they could lead by example. The Wechslers, who came to Levittown after a lifetime of struggles to change the world, learned that they too could make a difference after all. Sometimes the greatest strength can't be found on one's own, the two families realized. The power comes when ordinary people join to take an extraordinary stand. And it was a power available to all.

They would soon learn how far word of their actions had traveled. One day months after the ordeal, Bill and Daisy were invited by a Philadelphia reverend to a special dinner. These sort of invitations were becoming more common as the two were elevated to the roles of heroes. Some would take to calling Daisy "the Rosa Parks of the North." Bill and Daisy got into the same blue-and-white Mercury that they had once packed so eagerly to move to their new home in Levittown and headed out of Dogwood Hollow. They passed the Wechslers, passed the site of the burning cross. They passed what had been the Confederate House, where their tormenters had tried to drive them out.

When they arrived at the dinner, they were greeted by many well-wishers. But the reverend politely pushed his way through the crowd and said he had someone special he'd like the Myerses to meet. Bill and Daisy followed him as a warm twenty-eight-year-old man with a mustache stood there to greet them: Martin Luther King. "It's so nice to meet you," Daisy said.

Dr. King smiled, but deferred. "No, it's so nice to meet *you*." He knew all about the Myerses' fight in Levittown and was happy to be thanking them.

Bill recounted this story as they drove with the Wechslers one day to see Jackie Robinson. They pulled up to a building in Camden, New Jersey.

Nick and Katy looked out the car windows and were confused when they
didn't see a baseball stadium. They thought they were coming to see
Robinson in person. We are, Lew explained, as they headed inside. It was
a special meeting of the NAACP, and Robinson, the national membership chairman, was the featured speaker. After the speech, Bill led Lew
and the kids backstage. Nick anxiously clutched a new baseball, which
he hoped to have signed. As Robinson approached, Nick nervously said,
"You're my hero, Mr. Robinson, it's so incredible to meet you."

Robinson looked the boy in the eye, just as Martin Luther King had
when he'd met the Myerses. "I'm thrilled to meet *you*, Nick," he said
with a smile. "I know what you and your family did to help the Myerses,
and I'm proud of you."

He took Nick's ball and signed it.

Promise complete.

EPILOGUE

ON NOVEMBER 20, 1962, President John F. Kennedy signed Executive Order 11063, which banned racial discrimination in homes built, purchased, or financed with federal assistance. But it didn't stop William Levitt from making one last try to save his whites-only dream.

Despite the losses and opposition he faced in his three Levittowns—New York, Pennsylvania, and New Jersey—Levitt challenged President Kennedy's antidiscrimination order by refusing to sell homes to blacks in the community he had built in Bowie, Maryland. The fracas began after a Levitt salesperson wouldn't sell a home to a thirty-two-year-old economist with the U.S. Government's Bureau of the Budget because he was black. Bill Levitt had always contended that he could either fight for civil rights or be a builder. He had said that by opening his communities to blacks, his competitors would discriminate and leave him in the lurch. Levitt's defense was that he was simply abiding by local customs.

A series of protests followed in the fall of 1963. A government physicist and vice president of the Congress of Racial Equality told the protesters that Levitt is "the biggest builder of suburban housing and has the most noxious record on racial discrimination in the country." But Levitt had found a loophole—arguing that his financing was secured prior to Kennedy's order. The Federal Housing Administration agreed. Levitt's Maryland community would remain whites-only.

But after years of his fights, Levitt began to contradict himself too. In 1966 on the heels of a housing discrimination ban proposed by President

Lyndon Johnson, Levitt pledged his support for the measure. "We are for it one hundred percent," he told a House Judiciary subcommittee. "Any home builder who chooses to operate on an open-occupancy basis, where it is not customary or required by law, runs the grave risk of losing business to his competitor who chooses to discriminate. That, in a nutshell, is why we follow our present policy in Maryland." Once again, what he said and did were different—and after his testimony, he continued to turn blacks away in Bowie and at a seven-hundred-unit housing development near Dulles Airport in Virginia.

As the pressure built, Levitt no longer had his family to turn to for support—if they would even support him at all. His father, Abe, died in 1962, and his mother followed in 1965. The next year, his brother, Alfred, also passed away. Levitt was devastated and decided to no longer hang on to the past—he'd rather cash in. In February 1968, he sold his company to the International Telephone & Telegraph Corporation for ninety-two million dollars. Levitt pocketed sixty-two million dollars in ITT stock, but at a price—he agreed not to build in the United States for ten years and, more painfully, relinquished the Levitt name. "That never stopped bothering him," his accountant later told *Newsday*.

Levitt remained on as president of the company for about six months, however, and had one last unexpected order of business before he left for good. It began on April 4, 1968, when Martin Luther King was assassinated in Memphis, Tennessee. Six days later, a small story on page four of the *Wall Street Journal* bore the headline, LEVITT & SONS STARTS 'OPEN HOUSING' POLICY AS KING 'MEMORIAL.' The *Journal* reported that the proposal had been "drawn up by the Levitt management and approved by ITT," though failed to specify whether it had originated with Bill Levitt himself. Nevertheless, the announcement was viewed as a stunning admission of his past racist policies and the mark of sweeping changes to come. "Open housing was one of Dr. King's greatest hopes," said Levitt, "our action is a memorial to him."

African-Americans were already living in his three Levittown communities, but Levitt & Sons now had eighteen communities being constructed around the world, from Illinois to France, and the new policy would ensure open housing in each. "It is high time that we take this stand," Levitt said.

The company took out a full-page advertisement in cities including Washington, D.C., New York, Philadelphia, Baltimore, and Chicago to announce the plan as well. At the top of the ad was a large picture of Martin Luther King. Underneath the photo was the headline LEVITT PAYS TRIBUTE TO DR. KING IN DEED—NOT EMPTY PHRASES. The ad continued, "This Company has adopted a new policy—effective at once—eliminating segregation any place it builds . . . We ask all our colleagues to adopt a similar policy without delay. The forces of bigotry and prejudice must not be permitted to prevail any longer, and we urge all builders—large and small alike—to do their part in making America once again the ideal of the world."

But the damage to Levitt's name had been done. While some revered Levitt to the end, a backlash had begun. "Little Boxes," a song by folksinger Malvina Reynolds, indelibly branded the landscape of identical "ticky-tacky houses." In New Jersey, residents voted to change the name of their community back to Willingboro. Some said it was due to confusion over the mail's getting sent to the Levittown in Pennsylvania. When homeowners of Levittown, Pennsylvania, pushed, unsuccessfully, for a similar measure, one resident said what was on a lot of residents' minds: "*Levittown* is a dirty word."

But Levitt had found a distraction: a young, ravishing French art dealer named Simone Korchin. After leaving his first wife, Rhoda, Levitt divorced his second wife and former secretary, Alice, in 1969 to marry Korchin on November 19, 1969, and the two began living a life of decadent luxury. They celebrated their wedding anniversary monthly instead of yearly, and Levitt lavished Simone with gifts of diamonds, rubies, and gold.

They lived together in a twenty-six-room mansion called La Colline on sixty-eight acres in Mills Neck, Long Island, with their Rolls-Royce parked outside. The estate had an indoor tennis court, an elevator, and a staff of servants and maids. The Levitts raised red devon cattle and Bill bought a 237-foot yacht called *La Belle Simone*, for his wife, and transformed it into a hot spot for international jet-setters. Bill would stay up late into the night playing songs on the piano, drinking his favorite, Rob Roys.

But despite his fairy-tale lifestyle, his business was in trouble. Never a saver, he had borrowed against his ITT stock—only to lose 90 percent of the value when the company's stock tanked. To make matters worse, Levitt had to abide by a noncompete clause that prevented him from building in the United States. His attempts to build abroad in countries such as Nigeria and Venezuela went nowhere. He lost twenty million dollars trying to build a community in Iran. In 1978, with his noncompete clause expired, Levitt set his sights on a comeback: He would build a ten-thousand-home community in Florida aimed at the generation of Levittowners in New York and Pennsylvania who were getting ready to retire. He wanted to call it Levittown, but ITT, which had bought his name, refused to let him. He called it Williamsburg, after himself, instead.

That deal and two others in Florida fell apart—leaving the buyers, the contractors, and the builder in dire straits. Levitt had been using money from the homeowners' deposits to pay his mounting bills, yet no cash was coming in. People who had put their life savings into the deposits found themselves standing in empty fields of incomplete homes. "I lived in a Levitt house on Long Island for thirty years—just his name was like magic to us," said one jilted buyer, "[but] it's like a ghost town here. Levitt has been a tremendous disappointment to us." Another put it more bluntly: "I feel like I've been mugged."

Levitt, though, refused to change his extravagant ways. "His ego made him succeed," Simone Levitt said, "and his ego broke him because he could have stopped spending." To cover costs, Levitt illegally took eleven million dollars from his family's charitable foundation. After an investigation by the New York State attorney general's office, Levitt was forced in 1987 to pay back the money he had taken. Simone Levitt didn't know there was a problem until one day the people from Christie's came to take her husband's original Renoir and Monet paintings from the walls. She recalls seeing Bill sitting numbly at his desk as his favorite objects were being repossessed. "He was on Valium, he was like a zombie," she said, "he couldn't believe this was happening to him." The electricity got shut off, along with the phone. They had to sell the house, and the boat. When they were down to nothing but the last ring Bill had given Simone—a twenty-seven-carat diamond—Bill wanted to sell it too. "I promise I can make it into eight times its value," he told his wife.

"I'd rather swallow it," Simone replied, and kept it (she would sell it years after her husband's death to rebuild her life).

In his darkest hours, Levitt found new meaning in the legend he had created. One day in 1987, he returned to Levittown, New York, upon an invitation to celebrate the community's fortieth anniversary. As he rode along in the parade, he looked out upon the sea of people rushing up to greet him. As a child, his father used to read him stories about Captain Kidd sailing the high seas for adventure. Bill had grown to build and live his fantasy, traveling the world on his yacht. But, in the end, this life had left him dry. As he looked out upon the Levittowners, he began to cry. "The people of Levittown are much more my friends than the people of Park Avenue," he said he realized. "Oh, God, yes, more than most of those I entertained on my yacht."

When reality set in, Levitt was destitute. Unable to pay his debts, he pleaded with a judge for mercy. "I haven't bought a pair of shoes in ten years," he said. Before long, he ended up in North Shore University Hospital with his kidneys failing. Though he couldn't afford care, he was given a room because in his heyday he had donated millions to the hospital. In the fall of 1993, a sociologist from Hunter University filmed an interview with the once great titan. Though weak and raspy, Levitt still exuded the unbridled mix of optimism and denial for which he was famous. "I have a regular organization ready to punch in full-time," he said. "I need another six months." Three months later on January 28, 1994, eighty-six-year-old William Jaird Levitt was dead.

Levitt left behind a complex legacy—the man who both provided the American Dream to a generation of veterans and denied it to an entire race. As planned communities of seemingly identical homes spread across America, his legacy would continue to be debated for decades to come.

Some preferred to remember him for what he'd achieved. "What difference does it make if you die with a hundred million dollars in the bank or nothing in the bank if you had Bill Levitt's life?" his friend

Ralph Della Ratta told *Newsday* after Levitt's death. "He had a huge estate, a huge yacht, three gorgeous wives, and was generous to boot. What the hell more do you want? It was the American Dream."

Others divided over what he'd left behind. "Levitt bears a lot of responsibility, enormous responsibility, in that he was the pacesetter," said Rosalyn Baxandall, a professor at the State University of New York in Stonybrook. He and other builders "established a pattern of segregation that we still have" today. Others cautioned against overstating his role. "To paint Levitt as a villain would be unfair," said sociologist Herbert Gans. "The whole system was villainous. Levitt strictly reflected the times." For historian Kenneth Jackson, Levitt missed the chance to be truly heroic: "Levittown was an opportunity tragically lost. There was such a demand for houses—they had people waiting on lines—that even if they had said there will be some blacks living there, white people would still have moved in."

On June 13, 2007, the National Association of Home Builders enshrined Levitt, "the Father of Suburbia," as they called him, in their Hall of Fame. "The National Housing Hall of Fame recognizes individuals whose spirit, ingenuity, and determination have changed the face of housing history for the better," said the president of the group. "Except for the man who invented nails, no one man has had a greater effect on home building in America than William J. Levitt."

For the Wechslers, the experience in Levittown left them with a complicated legacy of their own. In the wake of the injunction, their community tried to heal itself. A neighborhood group, the Dogwood Hollow Neighbors, was established to heal the wounds. "We are ashamed of the terrible incidents that took place in our neighborhood," the group said in a statement. "We feel that they have seriously damaged the reputation of our community and of all Levittown. But we're also convinced that they were not at all representative of the vast majority of Dogwood Hollow residents and Levittowners. The great majority of our neighbors are decent, responsible, law abiding, and fair minded. During the heat of events it was hard for anyone to speak out. Now, however, we believe it is time for all responsible law-abiding people to come forward and express the true sentiments of our community."

In 1958, the Wechslers saw a second African-American family move into Levittown. Concerned about another breakout of violence, the police parked a school bus near the home and filled it with officers. But the family moved in without event. African-Americans were now part of the town once and for all.

But despite their victories, the Wechslers felt less and less welcomed. The chill of their experience lingered long after the court gavel fell. Friends and neighbors who had once stood by their side began to treat them like ghosts. Infighting within the liberal factions in town left them alienated. The "whispering campaign," as Lew put it, surely related to their political past, took hold.

Before long, the very groups that the Wechslers had rallied behind in their support of the Myerses left them behind, particularly the Human Relations Council. "They were delighted to keep us at the length of a very long arm," Lew would later note. The Friends Service Association, however, stuck by the Wechslers and invited Lew to join the board of directors. During his time there, he helped start a multicultural community center serving African-Americans, Latinos, and Italians.

Before long, Bea and Lew decided to leave Levittown for good. The two bought a home on the Jersey shore and moved there full-time in 1976. They spent their days tending to their house, and Lew would canoe into the bay for clams. But the events in Levittown always stayed in their hearts and minds. One day in 1991, Lew began jotting down his memories of that hot summer years before. It became his memoir, *The First Stone*, which his family self-published in 2004. Bea and Lew both continued to work until their late eighties. As of this writing in 2008, eighty-eight-year-old Bea and eighty-nine-year-old Lew are still there, alive and well.

As they settled into a quieter life, their children continued working for causes their parents had introduced them to so long ago. Katy remained active in civil rights and graduated from Lew's alma mater, Oberlin. Nick became a conscientious objector during the Vietnam War. When asked by the court if he believed in a supreme being, he replied, "Yes, the people." In his house in Chicago, Nick still has the ball that Jackie Robinson signed so proudly that day fifty years ago.

For the Myerses, in the aftermath of Levittown they were civil rights icons. They were featured in news stories and on *60 Minutes*; they attended honorary dinners and functions. But throughout it all they retained their quiet strength and humility. "It's heartening to see so many people sincerely interested in this problem," Bill Myers said. "Now we're just another normal family living in another normal community." Still, he said, it wasn't perfect. People drove by the house to gawk at them and their now famous home. "Of course there are some that still won't accept us," he said. "On the other hand, there are some that we don't find acceptable."

Though the leaders of the Levittown mob abided by the injunction, they were largely unrepentant. Howard Bentcliff spit on the sidewalk as Daisy Myers passed by one afternoon. The most brazen was James Newell, the Southerner who had been the group's ringleader. Despite his notoriety, Newell ran for the position of Levittown committeeman. Before the election, he drove through the neighborhood promoting himself over a loudspeaker. When he passed the Myerses' home, he saw Daisy in front and said, "I only did what people wanted me to do." Newell lost the election and faded out of sight.

Though the Myerses were now able to live in the town without harassment, Daisy and Bill often felt on edge. One day, Daisy went with a friend to shop for a washing machine. When the salesman learned her name, however, he quickly excused himself to the back. "Well, here it comes," Daisy whispered to her friend, assuming there would be some retribution. Instead, the salesman returned with his colleagues, who were proud to shake her hand for taking such a courageous stand. Daisy went home that night and resolved to look at life in a new way. "Bigots are a small minority," she wrote in her journal, "and the American people, for the most part, are kind and tolerant at heart."

But the Myerses wouldn't stay in Levittown for long. In June 1961, with a fourth child, Barry, now in tow, the family left Levittown for good. Bill had gotten a job as a superintendent in Harrisburg, and Daisy had decided to commute to York to teach sixth grade. The following year, they moved back to York. They enjoyed their lives back in their old town. Bill, always the fix-it man, took out his tools again and built a basketball hoop that all the local kids used for play.

Now and then, Daisy found herself having to fight again. Her daughter, Lynda, had become an honor student and earned a spot in an exchange program to Austria. Before she was to leave, however, the administrators called a meeting with her parents. They explained that they had never sent a black student before and worried that it wouldn't work out well if they did. They didn't know whom they were dealing with. "Well, if you don't send her," Daisy told them firmly, "you'll hear from me." The school complied.

Lynda Myers would go on to become a teacher, her brother Stephen, a police officer, and her brother William, the owner of a courier service. Daisy, who would complete two master's degrees in education, soon became a principal of a local elementary school, where she remained until her retirement in 1979. But after a lifetime of social and political activity, Daisy couldn't stay on the sidelines for long and went back to work for another two decades as a congressional assistant. In 1987, however, tragedy struck. Bill died of lung cancer. Daisy always kept him close to her heart. From the day they'd met in Virginia, he remained the love of her life.

Over the years, Daisy would often recall her experiences in Levittown, and one day, she decided to revisit them again. During the crisis of 1957, Daisy would steal time away to chronicle the events in her diary. But those pages would end up collecting dust in a box in her attic for decades. Not until 1999, with the encouragement of a local writers' group she had joined upon her retirement, did she dig up the pages again. Her friends were so moved by her recollections that they helped arrange for the local York County Heritage Trust to publish Daisy's journal, which she titled, *Sticks 'n Stones*.

As Daisy read over the words she had written so long ago, the scenes came rushing back. When she was through reading, she picked up a pen and added one last thought: "When I think back over all of this—what happened in Levittown—I wonder how we made it through those days,

[but] . . . what happened to me and to my family prepared us for who we are now—stronger human beings. The Myers family has not only survived but thrived while seeking a part of the American dream: to have a comfortable home. No one should ever be punished for that."

Later that year, the new generation of Levittowners wanted to show her how much they agreed. On December 7, 1999, more than forty years after her ordeal, seventy-four-year-old Daisy Myers returned for a special tribute in Levittown. As she arrived, she could plainly see that despite Levitt's fears blacks never did cause the white buyers in Levittown, Pennsylvania, to leave. If anything, the notoriety of the Myerses' experience kept other African-American families away.

According to a recent census, blacks represent only 2.45 percent of Levittown, Pennsylvania's residents. Of course, this isn't the only such suburb in the twenty-first century; millions of Americans still look outside their homes to see neighbors of the same race. After a 2000 census identified Levittown, New York, as being 94.1 percent Caucasian, the *New York Times* declared Long Island "the most racially segregated suburban region in the country."

In Levittown, Pennsylvania, the overwhelmingly white Levittowners had plenty of problems of their own. Levittown had become a haven for the home-brewed drug crystal methamphetamine. A Levittown-based biker gang running the largest crystal-meth operation in the area was busted. Nazi paraphernalia was found at one of the homes. Soon after, the Levittown high school valedictorian spent his graduation under police lockdown after a member of the Bloods gang threatened to kill him. The *New York Times* wrote, "Simple American rites of passage were not supposed to be this jarring in Levittown, a community that was designed in the early 1950's as an affordable refuge for returning World War II veterans eager to seek serenity in the suburbs."

But on this cold, wintry night, the people of Levittown had come to pay respects to a woman who had taken a stand here so long ago. As holiday lights twinkled in the streets, Daisy was escorted to where a crowd of hundreds had gathered around a sixteen-foot blue-spruce tree. The tree was being dedicated to her, and everything she had done. A plaque at the base bore her name, MISS DAISY.

"Tonight we want to welcome back a hero," the Bristol Township mayor told the crowd. "A hero is a person admired for qualities and deeds, and tonight a true hero stands in front of you—Mrs. Daisy Myers—a person of distinguished bravery, the principal figure in a story. She endured the worst kind of humiliation—racism. For that we are truly sorry."

As the crowd applauded Daisy, her emotions mixed. Though she appreciated the apology, she couldn't help but wonder where these people were when she'd really needed them most that summer so long ago. More than anything, she longed for her husband, Bill, to be here sharing this moment with her. "The tree will serve as a reminder that what happened in the past cannot be tolerated or accepted," the mayor continued. "What is happening here tonight is the welcome she should have received long ago."

On cue, Daisy flipped a switch and the lights on the tree came to life. Out in the crowd, the young families watched the display. Daisy would return to York, where she lives to this day. But this night would long be remembered. Whenever children in the future would ask for whom the tree was named, their parents would tell them the tale. There are stories that are true, and stories we want to believe. This, they'd say, is the story of Levittown.

ACKNOWLEDGMENTS

This is a true story, and like any true story, it's indebted to the people who have told pieces of it before. I'm grateful to Bea and Lew Wechsler for sharing their memories and archives. Lew wrote and self-published a wonderful memoir of Levittown called *The First Stone*, and I urge anyone who wants a firsthand account of the events of the summer of 1957 to read it.

Daisy Myers shared her recollections with me over many long conversations at her home in York. In August 1957, Daisy began keeping a remarkable journal of her experiences in Levittown, which, even more remarkably, spent decades afterward in her attic. I was fortunate to read an early draft of the manuscript, which was finally published in 2005 as *Sticks 'n Stones*. It should be required reading for anyone interested in the story of Levittown. Thanks, Daisy, for all your help.

I'm also grateful to the surviving members of the Levitt family who spoke with me: Bill Levitt's widow, Simone; his sons, William Jr. and James; as well as his stepdaughters, Gaby Altman and Nicole Bernstein. Alfred Levitt's son, Jon, was a wonderful resource for stories of his family too. Thanks to the many others who took time to talk with me. I'm also indebted to the librarians and archivists at the public libraries in Levittown, Pennsylvania, and Levittown, New York, as well as the Temple University Urban Archives in Philadelphia. Thanks to Dr. Ray Arsenault, John Hope Franklin Professor of Southern History at the University of South Florida, for reading and commenting on the book.

Big thanks to my editor, Kathy Belden, who connected with this story from the start and nurtured it to completion; my publisher, George Gibson of Walker & Company; my literary agent, Mary Ann Naples of the Creative Culture; my film/TV agent, Judi Farkas of Judi Farkas Management; and all the magazine editors I work with throughout the year.

Writing a book is a strange sort of disappearing act, especially since I don't let anyone read anything until I'm finished with my first draft. For that reason, it's all the more crucial to get support from family and friends as I'm deep into my work. So here's to Dad, Mom, Andy, Shelley, Alyssa, Howard, Harriett, Joanne, Sue, Sami, Mia, and everyone else who rooted me on.

Notes

Note: Some of the page numbers and publication titles were not listed on the archived materials. In addition to the following resources, my recreation of events in this book was culled from my own interviews with people, including Lew Wechsler, Bea Wechsler, Katy Wechsler, Nick Wechsler, Daisy Myers, William Myers III, Simone Levitt, William Levitt Jr., James Levitt, Jon Levitt, Gaby Altman, Nicole Bernstein, David Virgil Randall, Governor George Leader, Dave Matza, Samuel Snipes, Charles Biederman, Harriet and Paul Pushinsky, Roy Sheldon, Howard Kasman, Hal Lefcourt, Ralph Della Ratta, Ed Cortese, Diane Walker, and Bud Rubin.

Prologue

xii   "Our property seems": Kenneth Jackson, *Crabgrass Frontier: The Suburbanization of the United States* (New York: Oxford University Press, 1985), p. 12.

Chapter One

2   "The way to be happy": "Abraham Levitt Is Dead at 82; Developer of Three Levittowns; Lawyer Founded Firm That Built 60,000 Homes in East—Active in Philanthropies," *New York Times*, August 21, 1962, p. 33.

2   washing dishes at restaurants and selling newspapers: Ibid.

2   He started with magazines: Ibid.

3   As a sophomore: Ibid; and author interview, Jon Levitt.

3   As his family would later joke: Author interview, William Levitt Jr.

4   "Self-confidence waxed": *Current Biography Yearbook 1956* (New York: HW Wilson, 1956), p. 373.

4   Alfred, introspective: "Up from the Potato Fields," *Time*, July 3, 1950, http://www.time.com/time/magazine/article/0,9171,812779,00.html.

4   They dueled: Author interview, Jon Levitt.

4   At PS 44: "Dream Builder," *Newsday*, September 18, 1997, http://www .newsday.com/community/guide/lihistory/ny-levittown-hslevpro,0,721552 .story.

4   In one photo: Author interview, William Levitt Jr.

4   "Alfred is a genius": "Dream Builder."

5   "Where's your brother": Ibid.

5   At sixteen: Ibid.

5   "I got itchy": "Up from the Potato Fields."

5   Around that time: "William J. Levitt: Master Builder," *Horizons* 18 (1976).

5   The housing market: Nathaniel Schneider Keith, *Politics and the Housing Crisis Since 1930* (New York: Universe Books, 1973), p. 17, as cited in Rosalyn Baxandall and Elizabeth Ewen, *Picture Windows* (New York: Basic Books, 2000), p. 32.

5   With many losing money: Tom Bernard, "New Homes for $60 a Month," *American Magazine,* April 1948, p. 104.

5   "Bill wouldn't be a success": "Dream Builder."

6   Thomas Jefferson said: Jackson, *Crabgrass Frontier,* p. 68.

6   Llewellyn Park, New Jersey: Ibid., p. 78.

6   Brooklyn bard: Ibid., p. 50.

6   Frederick Law Olmstead: Ibid., p. 79.

6   One scribe: Ted Steinberg, *American Green: The Obsessive Quest for the Perfect Lawn* (New York: W. W. Norton & Company, 2006), p. 12.

7   And so that homeowners: Ibid.

7   "The city is doomed": Kenneth Jackson, *Crabgrass Frontier: The Suburbanization of the United States* (New York: Oxford University Press), p. 175.

7   883,000 homes: Ibid.

7   As the end of the decade: Baxandall and Ewen, *Picture Windows*, p. 30.

7   New housing: Ibid., p. 32.

8   As the head of: "William J. Levitt: Master Builder."

8   "Better come in": Ibid.

8   While the Depression loomed: "New Homes for $60 a Month," p. 104.

8   By 1934: Baxandall and Ewen, *Picture Windows*, p. 74.

8   He would bring: Ibid., p. 75.

8   Bill secured land: "Developers Defy Depression Years; Long Island Company Has Constructed and Sold 250 Dwellings Since 1929. New Group Under Way; Levitt & Sons Plan the Eventual Erection of 200 More Residences at Manhasset," *New York Times*, October 28, 1934, p. RE1.

8   "Alfred loves to draw": Eugene Rachlis and John E. Marqusee, *The Land Lords* (New York: Random House, 1963), p. 232.

8   He was the first: Author interview, William Levitt Jr.

8   The idea for Manhasset: Baxandall and Ewen, *Picture Windows*, p. 75.

9   No home would go: Ibid.

9   The homes were built: Barbara M. Kelly, *Expanding the American Dream: Building and Rebuilding Levittown* (Albany: State University of New York Press, 1993), p. 37.

9   It included a: "Manhasset Homes Have Novel Notes," *Washington Post*, April 8, 1934, p. R3.

9   Alfred said: "Levitt's Progress," *Fortune*, October 1952, p. 164.

9   They called it: "New Features Seen in Manhasset Home," *New York Times*, April 25, 1937, p. 190.

9   They converted a: "Club to Be Part of the Home Colony," *New York Times*, March 5, 1939, p RE1.

10 Even doghouses: Baxandall and Ewen, *Picture Windows*, p. 76.

11 The *New York Times*: "Developers Defy Depression Years," p. RE1.

11 Abe Levitt and his kids: Jackson, *Crabgrass Frontier*, p. 234.

11 Word spread: "Dream Builder."

11 "in the seventeenth century": "The House That Levitt Built," *Esquire*, December 1983, p. 5.

Chapter Two

16 While the U.S. Supreme Court: Rosalyn Baxandall and Elizabeth Ewen, *Picture Windows* (New York: Basic Books, 2000), p. 31.

16 Banks refused: Becky M. Nicolaides and Andrew Wiese, *The Suburb Reader* (New York: Routledge, 2006), p. 225.

16 Believing that blacks: Baxandall and Ewen, *Picture Windows*, p. 26.

17 One Long Island march: Ibid., p. 30.

17 The HOLC pumped: Kenneth Jackson, *Crabgrass Frontier: The Suburbanization of the United States* (New York: Oxford University Press, 1985). pp. 196–97.

17 A community in St. Louis: Ibid., 200.

17 Scholars and real-estate-textbook: Ibid., 198.

17 "Inharmonious groups of people": Nicolaides and Wiese, *Suburb Reader*, p. 237.

18 Bankers and Realtors: Jackson, *Crabgrass Frontier*, p. 203.

18 With the Federal Housing Administration's creation: James W. Loewen, *Sundown Towns: A Hidden Dimension of American Racism* (New York: The New Press, 2005), p. 129.

18 "If a neighborhood is": Federal Housing Administration, *Underwriting Manual: Underwriting and Valuation Procedure Under Title II of the National Housing Act with Revisions to April 1, 1936* (Washington, D.C.), pt. 2, sec. 2, "Rating of Location."

18 "Natural or artificially": Ibid.

18 The next provision: Federal Housing Administration, *Underwriting Man-*

ual: Underwriting and Valuation Procedure Under Title II of the National Housing Act with Revisions to February, 1938 (Washington, D.C.), pt. 2, sec. 9, "Rating of Location."

18   While the HOLC insured: Jackson, *Crabgrass Frontier*, 207.

18   "For perhaps the first": Ibid., 213.

18   "The national government": Ibid., 217.

21   She said it felt as if: Daisy D. Myers, *Sticks 'n Stones: The Myers Family in Levittown* (York, PA: York County Heritage Trust, 2005), p. 13.

21   "If integration works here": Ibid., p. 12.

Chapter Three

24   "Because, honey": Interview, Bea and Lew Wechsler.

25   Formed in 1931: Robert Cohen, "Student Activism in the 1930s," http://newdeal.feri.org/students/move.htm.

25   One letter writer: "Our Red Menace," *New York Times*, April 11, 1932, p. 14.

26   "The creation of the deeply": "Nation's Students Strike for Peace; Disorders Are Few," *New York Times*, April 13, 1935, p. 1.

26   few high school students: Ibid.

27   "It condemns the 'southern system'": "Students in a Union," *New York Times*, January 5, 1936, p. X9.

29   "Ownership of homes": Barbara M. Kelly, *Expanding the American Dream: Building and Rebuilding Levittown* (Albany: State University of New York Press, 1993), p. 48.

29   "A nation of homeowners": Ibid., 49.

29   At the New York World's Fair: Kenneth Jackson, *Crabgrass Frontier: The Suburbanization of the United States* (New York: Oxford University Press, 1985), p. 187.

29   Pop songs such as: Rosalyn Baxandall and Elizabeth Ewen, *Picture Windows* (New York: Basic Books, 2000), p. 22.

29   Magazines such as: Jackson, *Crabgrass Frontier*, p. 232.

29   "All the fighting power": Baxandall and Ewen, *Picture Windows*, p. 83.

30   Nineteen forty-five would be: Dolores Hayden, *Building Suburbia: Green Fields and Urban Growth, 1820–2000* (New York: Vintage Books, 2004), p. 131.

30   Six million moved in: Ibid.

30   "Most veterans said: "Homes in Barracks Attract Veterans; Applying for Homes in Former Military Installations," *New York Times*, December 4, 1945, p. 21.

30   A half million: Jackson, *Crabgrass Frontier*, p. 232.

30   One senator: Lomas Financial Corporation, p. 3, Levittown History Collection, Levittown Library, NY.

30   But their so-called: Hayden, *Building Suburbia*, p. 130.

30   It was "a deliberately created slum": Baxandall and Ewen, *Picture Windows*, p. 91.

31 "There are those who maintain": Ibid., p. 93.

31 Planes dropped flyers: Ibid., p. 94.

31 Painters and bricklayers: Ibid., p. 98.

Chapter Four

35 "a big car". "Up from the Potato Fields," *Time*, July 3, 1950, http://www.time.com/time/magazine/article/0,9171,812779,00.html.

35 And for the young, self-taught builders: "Revolutionizing an Industry: William J. Levitt," *Lessons of Leadership: 21 Leaders Speak Out on Creating, Developing, and Managing Success* (Garden City, NY: Doubleday, 1968), p. 56.

36 "It is part": "They'll Build Neighborhoods, Not Houses," *Saturday Evening Post*, October 28, 1946, pp. 11, 43–46.

36 Some in the company: "Up from the Potato Fields."

36 "That little branch": Eugene Rachlis and John E. Marqusee *The Land Lords* (New York: Random House, 1963), p. 233.

36 As the press later recounted: *Current Biography Yearbook 1956* (New York: HW Wilson, 1956), p. 374.

36 Levitt made sure: "Dream Builder," *Newsday*, September 18, 1987, http://www.newsday.com/community/guide/lihistory/ny-levittown-hslevpro,0,721552.story.

37 the demand, sixteen million: "The Six Thousand Houses That Levitt Built," *Harper's*, September 1948, p. 82.

37 While sitting with companions: Lomas Financial Corporation, "The First 10 Years," undated, p. 4, Levittown Public Library.

37 As Alfred put it: "A Community Builder Looks at Community Planning," *Journal of the American Institute of Planners*, Spring 1951, p. 88.

37 They would, he said: Ibid., p. 80.

38 "Access to a swimming pool": Rosalyn Baxandall and Elizabeth Ewen, *Picture Windows* (New York: Basic Books, 2000), p. 131.

38 "There will be no need": "They'll Build Neighborhoods," pp. 11, 43–46.

38 "Mrs. Kilroy Gets": "Mrs. Kilroy Gets the Best," *New York Times*, September 14, 1947, p. SM29.

39 "Alfred [draws] on": "The House That Levitt Built," *Newsday*, August 15, 1997, http://www.newsday.com/community/guide/lihistory/ny-levittown-hslevhou,0,7148676.story?coll=ny-lihistory-navigation.

39 "Teams of two or three": "New Homes for $60 a Month," *American Magazine*, April 1948, pp. 46–47, 104–7.

40 "A small builder": "Suburban Pioneers," *Newsday*, September 28, 1997, p. H23.

40 A photo spread: *Newsday*, May 28, 1947, p. 17.

41 "I wanted the new name": "Levitt Licks the Housing Shortage," *Coronet*, September 1948, p. 112–16.

41 "Milk wagons raced": "1st Vets Move in at Island Trees," *Newsday*, October 2, 1947, p. 2.

42 "An Accomplishment": "Six Thousand Houses That Levitt Built," p. 79.

42 *Newsday*, declared it: "Pride and Prejudice," *Newsday*, no date/page, Levittown History Collection, Levittown Library, NY.

42 "Cultivation, cultivation, cultivation!": "Chats on Gardening," *Levittown Tribune*, May 22, 1952, p. 6.

43 "They ride roughshod": "Chats on Gardening," *Levittown Tribune*, June 12, 1952, p. 8.

43 "The policy that has prevailed": "Rental Policy to Remain Unchanged at Levittown," *Newsday*, June 1, 1949.

44 "It's not me": Llewellyn M. Smith, "The House We Live In," *Race: The Power of an Illusion* (San Francisco: California Newsreel, 2004), http://www.newsreel.org/transcripts/race3.htm.

44 As she was led outside: "Say Negroes Got Levitt 'No,'" *Newsday*, June 7, 1949.

44 "Give me a chance": "An Interview with Levitt," *Building the American Dream*, documentary, 1993, transcript excerpt, http://www.uvm.edu/~jloewen/sundowntownsshow.php?id=272.

44 "We can solve": Kenneth Jackson, *Crabgrass Frontier: The Suburbanization of the United States.* (New York: Oxford University Press, 1985), p. 241.

44 "Despite the skeptics": "Suburban Pioneers," *Newsday*, September 28, 1997, http://www.newsday.com/community/guide/lihistory/ny-levittown-hslevone,0,7345274.story?coll=ny-lihistory-navigation.

44 Despite Levitt's claims: *To Stand and Fight: The Struggle for Civil Rights in Postwar New York City*, new ed. (Cambridge, MA: Harvard University Press, 2006), pp. 230–31.

44 "Organizations which appear": *Newsday*, editorial, March 12, 1949.

45 One morning: John Thomas Liell, "Levittown: A Study in Community Planning and Development" (Ph.D. diss., Yale University, 1952), p. 259.

46 "We've waited": "Home-Rush Mobs Levitt," *Newsday*, May 12, 1949, p. 5.

46 "In a scene": Ibid.

46 By November 1951: "Veteran Takes Title to Last L'town House," *Levittown Tribune*, November 22, 1951.

46 "I'm not going out on a limb": "Growing Pains," *Newsday*, http://www.newsday.com/community/guide/lihistory/ny-levittown-hslevtwo,0,2163353.story, accessed July 14, 2008.

46 "Only in America": "1951 Construction Last for This Area, Says Levitt Official," *Levittown Eagle*, May 31, 1951, no page number, Levittown History Collection.

47 "The success of a parent": "All Levittown Honors Abraham Levitt," *Levittown Eagle*, November 1, 1951, no page number, Levittown History Collection.

47   "Nation's Biggest Housebuilder": "Nation's Biggest Housebuilder," *Life*,
      August 23, 1948, p. 75.

Chapter Five

49   "You shouldn't feel bad": Author interview, Daisy Myers.
50   "Who are my neighbors?": Daisy D. Myers, *Sticks 'n Stones: The Myers
      Family in Levittown* (York, PA: York County Heritage Trust, 2005), p. 17
51   With every trip: Ibid., p. 18.
51   "There are many": Ibid.
52   Despite eventually winning: James W. Loewen, *Sundown Towns: A Hidden
      Dimension of American Racism* (New York: The New Press, 2005), pp. 10–11.
52   There, Oliver Brown: Juan Williams, *Eyes on the Prize: America's Civil
      Rights Years, 1954–1965* (New York: Penguin Books, 1988), p. 21.
52   At the same time: Ibid.
54   "The word spread": Ibid., p. 45
55   "Mrs. Myers": Myers, *Sticks 'n Stones*, p. 18.
56   He supplemented his income: "Embattled Home Owner," *New York
      Times*, August 22, 1957, p. 16.

Chapter Six

60   "We bought five thousand acres": "Levittown, PA: Building the Suburban
      Dream," State Museum of Pennsylvania, 2003, http://server1.fandm.edu/
      levittown/one/c.html.
60   "Every store, filling station": Kenneth Jackson, *Crabgrass Frontier: The
      Suburbanization of the United States* (New York: Oxford University Press,
      1985), p. 237.
60   The second-largest steel mill: "Is All Fair at Fairless?; Will Negroes Live,
      Work in U.S. Steel's New Half Billion $$$ Industrial Town?" *Chicago De-
      fender* (national edition), January 23, 1954, p. 7.
60   Each neighborhood would: "Levittown, PA: Building the Suburban
      Dream," http://server1.fandm.edu/levittown/one/c.html.
60   Schools would be: Ibid.
60   In total: Ibid.
61   "It is hoped": "Dream Town—Large Economy Size," *New York Times*,
      December 14, 1952, p. 40.
61   More than sixteen hundred homes: "Levittown, PA: Building the Subur-
      ban Dream," http://server1.fandm.edu/levittown/one/f.html.
61   The *New York Times* called: As quoted in "Developer Levitt Dies," *Bucks
      County Courier*, January 30, 1994, p. 11A.
61   "There is no social strata": Linda Abby Fein, "Levittown, Pennsylvania: A
      Community Survey," January 6, 1965.
64   After a family there: Martha Biondi, *To Stand and Fight: The Struggle for*

Civil Rights in Postwar New York City (Cambridge, MA: Harvard University Press, 2006), pp. 230–31.

65 Cotter concluded: William Cotter, letter, Committee to End Discrimination in Levittown, 1951, Levittown History Collection, Levittown Library, NY.

66 "If we don't like": "Levittown Meet Marks Brotherhood Week," *Newsday*, February 20, 1952, no page number, Levittown History Collection.

66 When it opened: "Ronek Park, Equal Opportunity Suburb," *Newsday*, September 28, 1997, p. H19.

66 Not far from Levittown: Chad Kimmel, "Levittown, Pennsylvania: A Sociological History" (diss., University of Western Michigan, 2004), p. 179.

67 "A large majority of people moved": Ibid., p. 177.

67 As Blanshard promised: Ibid., p. 186.

67 As Blanshard put it: Friends Service Association semiannual meeting notes, October 29, 1955.

67 They called for meetings: Lewis Wechsler, *The First Stone: A Memoir of the Racial Integration of Levittown, Pennsylvania* (Chicago: Grounds for Growth Press, 2004), p. 15.

67 When Bill stood firm: Kimmel, "Levittown, Pennsylvania," p. 186.

68 The lawsuit came to pass: Wechsler, *First Stone*, p. 15.

68 In a statement: "Human Relations Group Supports NAACP Suit," *Levittown Times*, January 1955.

68 Representing the veterans: Ibid.

70 The song was never banned: "The Lonesome Train in Levittown," in Joseph F. Maloney, *State and Local Government: A Case Book* (University of Alabama Press, 1963), p. 47.

70 "When I walked through": "Levittown, PA: Negroes Not Wanted," *Buck's Traveler*, 5th year, no. 10 (June 1954): p. 12.

70 "Any evidence of": Ibid.

71 As one member of the group: Stockholders and Friends of Suburban Housing, Inc., newsletter, February 4, 1957.

Chapter Seven

73 Capps then either: "Ex-GI Confesses He Murdered Levittown Teenager," *Bristol Daily Courier*, January 26, 1954, p. 1.

73 When he was through: *Commonwealth of Pennsylvania v. George Capps*, May 23, 1955.

73 Betty Peart, stunned: Chad Kimmel, "Levittown, Pennsylvania: A Sociological History" (diss., University of Western Michigan, 2004), pp. 170–75.

74 Marta's grief-stricken: "Ex-GI Confesses," p. 2.

74 One time when Bradbury: Neal Gabler, *Walt Disney: The Triumph of the American Imagination* (New York: Alfred A. Knopf, 2006), p. 608.

75 "It is a one-class": "Levittown, PA: Building the Suburban Dream." State Museum of Pennsylvania, 2003, http://server1.fandm.edu/levittown/one/b.html.

75   Levitt, he argued: "Suburban Pioneers," *Newsday*, September 28, 1997, p. h25.

75   With his huge: Ibid.

75   "The plain fact": "Levittown, PA: Negroes Not Wanted," *Buck's Traveler*, 5th Year, no. 10 (June 1954): p. 29

76   "Strangely enough": "Up from the Potato Fields," *Time*, July 3, 1950, http://www.time.com/time/magazine/article/0,9171,812779,00.html.

76   While Bill cruised: Author interview, Jon Levitt.

76   Alfred "didn't give": Kimmel, "Levittown, Pennsylvania," p. 55.

77   The 675-acre: Herbert Gans, *The Levittowners: Ways of Life and Politics in a New Suburban Community* (New York: Columbia University Press, 1967), p. 4.

77   In 1953, he left: Author interview, Jon Levitt; and "Dream Builder," *Newsday*, September 18, 1997, http://www.newsday.com/community/guide/lihistory/ny-levittown-hslevpro,0,721552.story.

Chapter Eight

79   When he told Daisy: Daisy D. Myers, *Sticks 'n Stones: The Myers Family in Levittown* (York, PA: York County Heritage Trust, 2005), p. 23.

82   And at $12,150: Sam Snipes, "Racial Crisis in Levittown," *The Writs* 17, no. 2 (June 2006): p. 6.

82   "Would we be able": Myers, *Sticks 'n Stones*, p. 26.

83   "What can happen?": Lewis Wechsler, *The First Stone: A Memoir of the Racial Integration of Levittown, Pennsylvania* (Chicago: Grounds for Growth Press, 2004), p. 48.

84   "I can lend you": Ibid., p. 19.

84   "There is no depreciation": "Fair Housing in Bucks County," report, Lower Bucks County Council of Churches, July 9, 1957.

Chapter Nine

86   Rain had not fallen: "$5,000,000 Loss Seen in Drought," *Bristol Daily Courier*, August 15, 1957, pp. 1–2.

86   On the advice: Sam Snipes, "Racial Crisis in Levittown," *The Writs* 17, no. 2 (June 2006): p. 6.

86   "I will appreciate": Letter archives, Sam Snipes.

88   Though they wanted: Daisy D. Myers, *Sticks 'n Stones: The Myers Family in Levittown* (York, PA: York County Heritage Trust, 2005), p. 5.

88   FIRST NEGRO FAMILY: "First Negro Family Moves into Levittown," *Levittown Times*, August 13, 1957, p. 2.

89   Just fifteen minutes after: *Commonwealth of Pennsylvania v. Eldred Williams, James E. Newell, Howard H. Bentcliffe, Mrs. Agnes Bentcliffe, John R. Bentley, David L. Heller, John Thomas Piechowski, Mrs. John Brabazon*, September term, 1957, p. 11.

89   The traffic built: Ibid.

90   "I only wanted": "Stones Break Windows in Home of First Negro Family in Levittown," *Philadelphia Evening Bulletin*, August 14, 1957, p. G3.

92   "It's up to the local" Myers, *Sticks 'n Stones*, p. 7.

92   The police made no move: Snipes, "Racial Crisis in Levittown," p. 6.

92   He was James E. Newell: "Bias Mob Stones Cop in Levittown, PA," *Newsday*, August 21, 1957, p. 4.

93   One of the people: *Commonwealth v. Williams et al.*, p. 245.

93   "Thirty pieces of silver!": Snipes, "Racial Crisis in Levittown," p. 6.

94   It was the first time in: "Five Arrested in Levittown Disorder," *Bristol Daily Courier*, August 14, 1957, p. 1.

94   As the police were: Ibid., p. 3.

Chapter Ten

95   The Levitt & Sons representative: "Five Arrested in Levittown Disorder," *Bristol Daily Courier*, August 14, 1957, p. 3.

95   The Levitt exhibit center was packed: "Legal Means Sought to Force Negroes to Leave Levittown," *Bristol Daily Courier*, Levittown edition, August 16, 1957, p. 2.

95   Representatives from the mob: Ibid., p. 2.

95   "The right to live": "Group Blasts Mob Violence," *Bristol Daily Courier*, August 15, 1957, p. 1.

96   A Concord Park spokesperson: "Legal Means Sought," p. 2.

96   The plan: to construct: "Fantastic Triangle Poses Big Problem," *Washington Post and Times-Herald*, October 5, 1957, p. D1.

97   He bragged: *Current Biography Yearbook 1956* (New York: HW Wilson, 1956), p. 375.

97   He would be the first: Author interview, Roy Sheldon.

97   With eighty dollars from his friends: "Dream Builder," *Newsday*, September 18, 1997, http://www.newsday.com/community/guide/lihistory/ny-levittown-hslevpro,0,721552.story.

97   On the right rose: "For Sale: Special Levitt Home," *Philadelphia Inquirer*, Levittown Public Library, Levittown, PA.

98   "What toll would:" Daisy D. Myers, *Sticks 'n Stones: The Myers Family in Levittown* (York, PA: York County Heritage Trust, 2005), p. 8.

99   Why had this: Ibid., p. 30.

99   The Myerses even: Ibid.

100   "As soon as": "Protest over Negro Family Ends Meeting," *Bristol Daily Courier*, August 15, 1957, p. 1.

100   "They have a right": "Police Guard Site of Race Violence," *New York Times*, August 15, 1957, p. 14.

101   To their astonishment: Ibid.

102   "Do something!": "Protest over Negro Family Ends Meeting," p. 1.

102   "Disturbing the peace": "Negro Family Insist They'll Move into Levit-

town Home Despite Crowds," *Philadelphia Evening Bulletin*, August 15, 1957, p. 5.

102   "You tell that black": Author interview, Hal Lefcourt.

103   Because this was August: "Legal Means Sought," p. 2.

103   "We regret the violence": Lewis Wechsler, *The First Stone: A Memoir of the Racial Integration of Levittown, Pennsylvania*. (Chicago: Grounds for Growth Press, 2004), p. 26.

104   "I am ashamed": "Levittown Group Seeks to Oust Negro Home Buyer," *Philadelphia Evening Bulletin*, August 16, 1957, p. 2.

105   As the former commander: "Anti-Negro Group Seeks Legal Bolster," *Bristol Daily Courier*, August 16, 1957, p. 1.

105   One man in the mob: *Commonwealth of Pennsylvania v. Eldred Williams, James E. Newell, Howard H. Bentcliffe, Mrs. Agnes Bentcliffe, John R. Bentley, David L. Heller, John Thomas Piechowski, Mrs. John Brabazon*, September term, 1957, p. 150.

105   Volunteers were picked: "Legal Means Sought," p. 2.

105   It belonged to: *Commonwealth v. Williams et al.*, p. 328.

106   Anyone who wanted: Ibid., p. 325.

106   "But if it doesn't": Ibid., p. 211.

106   "Burn them out!": "Anti-Negro Group Seeks Legal Bolster," p. 1.

107   Drawing from union techniques: "Negro Home Gets Expanded Guard," *New York Times*, August 17, 1957, p. 7.

107   And it was burning: "Anti-Negro Group Seeks Legal Bolster," p. 1

Chapter Eleven

109   What had happened: Daisy D. Myers, *Sticks 'n Stones: The Myers Family in Levittown* (York, PA: York County Heritage Trust, 2005), p. 33.

109   "Nothing whatever will": "Levittown Group Signs Petition on New Owner," *Philadelphia Inquirer*, August 17, 1957.

109   News spread: San Snipes, "Racial Crisis in Levittown," *The Writs* 17, no. 2 (June 2006): p. 7.

110   "Our committee works": "Levittown a Disgrace to America," *Philadelphia Tribune*, August 17, 1957, p. 2.

111   "If you come in peace": *Commonwealth of Pennsylvania v. Eldred Williams, James E. Newell, Howard H. Bentcliffe, Mrs. Agnes Bentcliffe, John R. Bentley, David L. Heller, John Thomas Piechowski, Mrs. John Brabazon*, September term, 1957, p. 204.

112   Nearby, a disheveled: "Battle of Levittown," *New Jersey Afro American*, August 24, 1957, p. 1.

114   Newell stared down: Ibid., p. 2.

114   "As long as": "Both Factions Seek Peaceful Solution," *Levittown Times*, August 17, 1957, p. 3.

114   "Well, what's": *Commonwealth v. Williams et al.*, p. 294.

115 That night, the ice cream: Ibid.

116 There was no need: Ibid., p. 127.

116 Sam Snipes: Sam Snipes, author interview.

117 "As a sailor can": "The Pastor Speaks," *Bristol Courier Levittown Times*, August 17, 1957, p. 8.

117 The first thing he did: *Commonwealth v. Williams et al.*, p. 146.

117 When a local reporter: "Negro Couple Back at Home in Levittown," *Philadelphia Evening Bulletin*, August 19, 1957.

117 "This is no longer": "More Meetings Planned on Levittown Issue," *Bristol Daily Courier*, August 19, 1957, p. 3.

117 The Lower Bucks County Council of Churches: "Statement Concerning Fair Housing Practices," Lower Bucks County Council of Churches, August 16, 1957.

118 "We regret the violence": "Declaration of Conscience," August 18, 1957.

119 "Do you think": Myers, *Sticks 'n Stones*, p. 39.

Chapter Twelve

121 Levittown, New York, was: Barbara M. Kelly, *Expanding the American Dream: Building and Rebuilding Levittown* (Albany: State University of New York Press, 1993), p. 100.

121 "All is all right": Author interview, Jon Levitt.

123 "Levittown is a new": "Levittown's Shame," *Trenton Evening Times*, August 16, 1957, p. 4.

123 Lew's United Steelworkers: "Steelworkers Union Urges Halt of Levittown Bigotry," *Philadelphia Evening Bulletin*, August 20, 1957.

124 The president of the group: "The Shame of Levittown," *Union Reporter*, September 1957.

124 "You look toward": "Street Scene in Levittown," *Philadelphia Evening Bulletin*, August 20, 1957.

125 It was, she resolved: Daisy D. Myers, *Sticks 'n Stones: The Myers Family in Levittown* (York, PA: York County Heritage Trust, 2005), p. 43.

126 As one housewife: *Commonwealth of Pennsylvania v. Eldred Williams, James E. Newell, Howard H. Bentcliffe, Mrs. Agnes Bentcliffe, John R. Bentley, David L. Heller, John Thomas Piechowski, Mrs. John Brabazon*, September term, 1957, p. 462.

127 Advisers from: Ibid., p. 45.

128 "I knew all the reaction": "Negro Family Takes Over House in White Section," Associated Press, August 19, 1957.

128 And he added: "State Police Swings Clubs in Levittown," *Philadelphia Evening Bulletin*, August 20, 1957.

128 Bill looked the reporter: Ibid.

128 "I realize you have": "Troopers Repel Unruly Crowd at Levittown Home," *Philadelphia Evening Bulletin*, August 20, 1957.

128   "You have to take": "State Police Swings Clubs in Levittown."

129   "I give you ten minutes": "Troopers Break Up Crowd; Man Arrested," *Bristol Daily Courier*, August 20, 1957, p. 1.

129   They pulled him: "State Police Swings Clubs in Levittown."

129   "America!" they sang: "Troopers Break Up Crowd," p. 1.

130   "You don't have": Lewis Wechsler, *The First Stone: A Memoir of the Racial Integration of Levittown, Pennsylvania* (Chicago: Grounds for Growth Press, 2004), p. 43.

130   "Mr. Lewis (I love)": Ibid., p. 60.

132   And any further statements: "State Troopers Ban Crowd; Township Officer Felled," *Bristol Daily Courier*, August 21, 1957, p. 2.

132   He had battled: "Out of Control," *Bucks County Courier Times*, August 14, 1997, p. 15a.

133   One young boy: "Rock Injures Policeman in Levittown Row," *Philadelphia Evening Bulletin*, August 21, 1957.

Chapter Thirteen

134   "In addition to": "Levittown to Mark Ten Years on L.I.," *New York Times*, September 19, 1957, p. 24.

135   As one writer: Barbara M. Kelly, *Expanding the American Dream: Building and Rebuilding Levittown* (Albany: State University of New York Press, 1993), p. 101.

136   As for the three-story: "Levitt Enters Highest Bid on Maryland Farm," *Bristol Daily Courier*, August 28, 1957, p. 1.

136   And it would: "Levitt Firm 'On the Move' in Jersey," *Bristol Daily Courier*, August 22, 1957, p. 1.

136   But they wanted: "Bucks' Attorney Offered to Buy Negro's Home," *Philadelphia Evening Bulletin*, August 23, 1957.

137   Sorry, Bill said: "Crowds Stay Away from Dogwood," *Bristol Daily Courier*, August 22, 1957, p. 1.

137   A meeting would: Ibid.

137   The wooden cross: Ibid.

138   "I've been contacted": *Commonwealth of Pennsylvania v. Eldred Williams, James E. Newell, Howard H. Bentcliffe, Mrs. Agnes Bentcliffe, John R. Bentley, David L. Heller, John Thomas Piechowski, Mrs. John Brabazon*, September term, 1957, p. 385.

139   "It will be": "Betterment Meeting Set," *Bristol Daily Courier*, August 30, 1957, p. 2.

140   One day, Harwick: Lewis Wechsler, *The First Stone: A Memoir of the Racial Integration of Levittown, Pennsylvania* (Chicago: Grounds for Growth Press, 2004), p. 64.

141   "I knew Negroes": Daisy D. Myers, *Sticks 'n Stones: The Myers Family in Levittown*. (York, PA: York County Heritage Trust, 2005), p. 55.

141   Daisy, who on the advice: Ibid.

142   Joseph Segal: "Crowds Stay Away from Dogwood," p. 3.

142   "I don't like": Ibid.

142   "Go home to": Wechsler, *First Stone*, p. 155.

143   It pained him: Ibid., p. 24.

143   The owner of the house: *Commonwealth v. Williams, et al.*, p. 403.

Chapter Fourteen

145   "Now's the time": "Back to School," *Bristol Daily Courier*, August 26, 1957, p. 1.

145   A small item: "Negro Is Teacher in Levittown, PA," *New York Times*, September 17, 1957, p. 21.

147   "They burned a cross": Lewis Wechsler, *The First Stone: A Memoir of the Racial Integration of Levittown, Pennsylvania* (Chicago: Grounds for Growth Press, 2004), p. 61.

147   A broken jar: "Cross Burned in Levittown," *Philadelphia Evening Bulletin*, September 6, 1957.

148   Such intimations: Wechsler, *First Stone*, pp. 61–63.

148   A story in: "Two Lonely Little Boys in Levittown," *New York Post*, September 3, 1957

149   As Lew later noted: Wechsler, *First Stone*, p. 67.

150   "I expected some": "Levittown Deals with Integration: A Study in Contrasts," *New York Post*, September 17, 1957.

151   Bea and Lew agreed and left: Wechsler, *First Stone*, p. 82.

152   "Here, Nigger": Ibid., p. 65.

Chapter Fifteen

153   "No single feature": Ted Steinberg, *American Green: The Obsessive Quest for the Perfect Lawn* (New York: W. W. Norton & Company, 2006), p. 19.

153   Or, as he: Ibid., p. 17.

154   One local borough: "Operation Weed Removal Almost Done," *Bristol Daily Courier*, September 9, 1957.

154   Then she put back on: *Commonwealth of Pennsylvania v. Eldred Williams, James E. Newell, Howard H. Bentcliffe, Mrs. Agnes Bentcliffe, John R. Bentley, David L. Heller, John Thomas Piechowski, Mrs. John Brabazon*, September term, 1957, p. 88–89.

154   Outraged and fearful: "Myers Neighbor's Home Is Crayoned," *Levittown Times*, September 26, 1957.

156   Colgan told them what: Lewis Wechsler, *The First Stone: A Memoir of the Racial Integration of Levittown, Pennsylvania* (Chicago: Grounds for Growth Press, 2004), p. 84.

157   What retribution, she feared: *Commonwealth v. Williams et al.*, p. 32.

157   Daisy Myers later appealed: "Night and Day Watch Kept by State Police in Levittown Disorder," *Philadelphia Inquirer*, September 25, 1957.

158   They knew what they had: "Levittown Man Held in Bail on Malicious Mischief Charges," *Bristol Daily Courier*, October 18, 1957, p. 2.

158   He ordered the 101st: "Levittown Owner Told to End Noise at Negro's Home," *Philadelphia Inquirer*, September 26, 1957, p. H27.

159   A similar note: Wechsler, *First Stone*, p. 90.

160   "We just can't take it": "Levittown, PA, Revisited," *New York Post*, September 30, 1957, p. 3.

161   "This is it": *Commonwealth v. Williams et al.*, p. 25.

Chapter Sixteen

162   As Senate majority leader: "Ike's Wise Restrained Response to *Sputnik*," History News Network, http://hnn.us/articles/43173.html.

163   They were, as the activist: "An Evening with Levittown's Freedom Fighters," *Militant*, October 14, 1957, p. 1.

163   "There they sat": Lewis Wechsler, *The First Stone: A Memoir of the Racial Integration of Levittown, Pennsylvania* (Chicago: Grounds for Growth Press, 2004), p. 97.

165   The *New York Times* praised: "Apartments with Levitt Touch Rise on Waterfront in Queens," *New York Times*, February 24, 1957, p. 292.

165   "Known for his low": Herbert Gans, *The Levittowners: Ways of Life and Politics in a New Suburban Community* (New York: Columbia University Press, 1967), p. 6.

166   "I've got them in": "Levitt's Belair Homes Will Be Ready in '60," *Washington Post and Times-Herald*, December 18, 1957, p. D1.

166   The move to colonials: "Home-Building Firm Shifts to Traditional Styling in Third Huge Project," *Christian Science Monitor*, August 15, 1958, p. 12.

166   As one of his: Ibid., p. 9.

167   Police Chief Stewart denied: "Police Sergeant Raps Levittown Orders, Rejects Citation," *Philadelphia Inquirer*, October 9, 1957, p. H29.

167   The following week: "Demote Sergeant in Police Row on Levittown Duty," *Philadelphia Inquirer*, October 16, 1957, p. H49.

168   "I'll seek an": Sam Snipes "Racial Crisis in Levittown," *The Writs* 17, no. 2 (June 2006): p. 7.

168   "This is nothing": "House Party Protest Halted at Levittown," *Philadelphia Inquirer*, September 27, 1957.

168   "The wishes of": "Gatherings Halted in House Next to Negro's in Levittown," *Philadelphia Evening Bulletin*, September 27, 1957.

168   Despite the mob's claims: "Large Crowd Hears Talk in Myers' Case," *Levittown Times*, October 7, 1957, p. 2.

168 On Thursday, October 17: "Bucks Man Seized in KKK Painting," *Philadelphia Inquirer*, October 18, 1957.

Chapter Seventeen

171 "For Katy!": Lewis Wechsler, *The First Stone: A Memoir of the Racial Integration of Levittown, Pennsylvania* (Chicago: Grounds for Growth Press, 2004), p. 114.

172 They were quite the opposite: Daisy D. Myers, *Sticks 'n Stones: The Myers Family in Levittown.* (York, PA: York County Heritage Trust, 2005), p. 83.

172 "If I were": Ibid., p. 84.

172 "Mrs. Myers, McBride said": *Commonwealth of Pennsylvania v. Eldred Williams, James E. Newell, Howard H. Bentcliffe, Mrs. Agnes Bentcliffe, John R. Bentley, David L. Heller, John Thomas Piechowski, Mrs. John Brabazon,* September term, 1957, p. 7.

174 "Now, Mr. Bentcliff": Ibid., p. 49.

175 The state's first: Ibid., p. 59.

175 "We were quite": Ibid., p. 443.

175 "Afterwards": Ibid., p. 462.

176 "Yes, sir," Corporal Dane: Ibid., p. 195.

176 "Yes, it is": Ibid., p. 173.

177 "Reverend Harwick," McBride: Ibid., pp. 164–65.

178 "I do think": Ibid., p. 166.

178 "I felt this way": Ibid., p. 357.

179 "Yes, sir": Ibid., p. 346.

179 "No, sir": Ibid., p. 352.

179 "This pious pretense": Ibid., p. 317.

181 And, it concluded: Ibid., p. 86.

181 Those in court: "Defendant Collapses in Myers Case," *Bucks Daily Courier*, February 1, 1958.

182 "I'm giving you": "Bentcliff Is Fined, Put on Probation," *Bristol Daily Courier*, February 27, 1958, p. 2.

Chapter Eighteen

183 "The new postwar": "What! Live in a Levittown?" *Good Housekeeping*, July 1958, p. 47.

184 As sociologist Herbert: Herbert Gans, *The Levittowners: Ways of Life and Politics in a New Suburban Community* (New York: Columbia University Press, 1967), p. 373.

184 a private battle was being waged: Author interview, William Levitt Jr.

186 Levitt's Barnumesque: "New Levittown with 15,000 Homes to Open in New Jersey," *Wall Street Journal*, June 6, 1958, p. 8.

186 "Our policy on that": "Third Levittown Gets Underway," *New York Times*, June 6, 1958, p. 28.

187   Levitt, who had long been: "Levittown Builder Hit on Racial Policy," *New York Times*, June 7, 1958, p. 10.

187   A prominent reverend: "Catholic Editor Sees Peril in Segregation at Third Levittown," *New York Times*, June 13, 1958, p. 24.

187   The American Civil Liberties: "Joins Levitt Protest: Civil Liberties Union Asks Jersey to Disavow Charters," *New York Times*, July 3, 1958, p. 26.

187   And the state Assembly: "Bias Charge Threatens U.S. Aid to Levittown Housing in Jersey," *New York Times*, June 20, 1958, p. 21.

188   "There is no question": "Racial Strife Can Be Resolved," *Daily Defender*, July 9, 1958, p. 35.

188   After Levitt's announcement: "V.A. to Help Jersey Fight Housing Bias by Curbing Loans," *New York Times*, July 9, 1958, p. 29.

188   Now when Bill Levitt: Gans, *Levittowners*, p. 372.

188   This "gives a go-ahead": "Fight Proposed All-White Levittown for New Jersey," *Chicago Defender*, July 12, 1958, p. 9.

189   "Bitter racial prejudice": "Warning to Lawbreakers," *Philadelphia Inquirer*, August 18, 1958.

189   "The complainants argue": "Jersey Levittown to Sell to Negroes if Law Is Upheld," *New York Times*, November 11, 1959, p. 31.

189   "Had the housing measure": "Levittown Negro Woman Testifies for Fair Housing," *Philadelphia Inquirer*, May 21, 1958.

189   State law barred discrimination: "New Jersey Upholds the Law," *Chicago Defender*, July 27, 1959, p. 11.

190   In 1945, there had been: "Suburbanization, Post World-War II," *Encyclopedia of American History: Postwar United States, 1946–1968*, vol. 9, Facts on File Database Center, www.fofweb.com/.

190   Soon after, on: "Integration Near in Levittown, New Jersey: Builder Cites Losing Fight—Asks Council for Negroes," *New York Times*, March 27, 1960, p. 31.

190   "I plan to buy": "Order Levittown to Consider 2 Negroes," *Chicago Defender*, July 30, 1960, p. 21.

191   "No, it's so nice": "We Shall Not Be Judged by What We Might Have Been. What We Have Been," *Bucks County Courier Times*, August 15, 1997.

Epilogue

193   The fracas began: "Levitt Excludes Negroes, Testing U.S. Housing Ban," *New York Times*, March 27, 1963, p. 1.

193   A government physicist: "Rights Groups to Picket Levitt," *New York Times*, November 13, 1963, p. 14.

193   But Levitt had: "Can't Crack Belair Ban, FHA Says," *Washington Post and Times-Herald*, June 16, 1963, p. B10.

194   "Any home builder": "Levitt's Defenses of Racist Policies," "Long Island: Our Story," Levittown History Collection, p. 413, Levittown Library, NY.

194   "That never stopped": "Dream Builder," *Newsday*, September 18, 1997, http://www.newsday.com/community/guide/lihistory/ny-levittown-hslevpro ,0,721552.story.

194   Six days later: "Levitt & Sons Starts 'Open Housing' Policy as King 'Memorial,' *Wall Street Journal*, April 10, 1968, p. 4.

195   At the top: "Levitt Drops Sales Ban to Subdivision Negroes," *Washington Post*, April 10, 1968, p. B1.

195   "*Levittown* is a dirty": "Another Levittown Studies Possibility of Changing Name," *New York Times*, November 23, 1963, p. 16.

196   He lost twenty million: "Too Long at the Party," *Forbes*, May 4, 1987, p. 40.

196   "I lived in a Levitt": "They Banked, and Lost, on Levitt's Good Name," *Newsday*, February 18, 1986, p. 7.

196   Another put it: Ibid., p. 24.

196   After an investigation: "Levitt to Repay Family Charity $11 Million," *Newsday*, January 23, 1987, p. 7.

197   "The people of": Ibid.

197   Unable to pay: "Levittown's Builder in Straits," *Newsday*, October 27, 1990, p. 11.

198   "Levitt bears a lot": "Shut Out in the Suburbs," *Newsday*, May 19, 2003, p. B6.

198   "To paint Levitt": "At 50, Levittown Contends with Its Legacy of Bias," *New York Times*, December 28, 1997, p. 1.23.

198   "Levittown was an": Ibid.

198   "The National Housing Hall": "Father of Suburbia William J. Levitt Named to National Housing Hall of Fame," National Association of Home Builders, June 13, 2007, www.nahb.org/nets.

198   "We are ashamed": "Levittown Negro Invited to Join Neighborhood Group," *Philadelphia Inquirer*, December 14, 1957.

200   "Of course there are some": "First Negroes in Levittown Are 'Making Out Fine' Now," *Philadelphia Evening Bulletin*, December 14, 1958.

202   After a 2000 census: "Memories of Segregation in Levittown," *New York Times*, May 11, 2003, p. L13.

202   The *New York Times* wrote: "After Gang Threat, It's Cap, Gown and Lockdown," *New York Times*, June 10, 2006, p. A1.

203   "Tonight we want": Daisy D. Myers *Sticks 'n Stones: The Myers Family in Levittown* (York, PA: York County Heritage Trust, 2005), xiii.

BIBLIOGRAPHY

These books were helpful in my research.

Ambrose, Stephen E. *Eisenhower: Soldier and President*. New York: Simon & Schuster, 1990.

Bailey, Beth, David Farber, et al. *The Fifties Chronicle*. Lincolnwood, IL: Legacy Publishing, 2006.

Baxandall, Rosalyn, and Elizabeth Ewen. *Picture Windows: How the Suburbs Happened*. New York: Basic Books, 2000.

Beuka, Robert. *SuburbiaNation: Reading Suburban Landscape in Twentieth-Century American Fiction and Film*. New York: Palgrave Macmillan, 2004.

Branch, Taylor. *Parting the Waters: America in the King Years, 1954–63*. New York: Simon & Schuster, 1988.

Carson, Clayborne, David J. Garrow, Gerald Gill, Vincent Harding, and Darlene Hine Clark. *The Eyes on the Prize Civil Rights Reader: Documents, Speeches, and Firsthand Accounts from the Black Freedom Struggle*. New York: Penguin Books, 1991.

Cohen, Robert. *When the Old Left Was Young: Student Radicals and America's First Mass Student Movement, 1929–1941*. New York: Oxford University Press, 1997.

Coontz, Stephanie. *The Way We Never Were: American Families and the Nostalgia Trap*. New York: Basic Books, 2000.

Duany, Andres, Elizabeth Plater-Zybrek, and Jeff Speck. *Suburban Nation: The Rise of Sprawl and the Decline of the American Dream*. New York: North Point Press, 2001.

Ferrer, Margaret Lundrigan, and Tova Navarra. *Levittown: The First 50 Years*. Dover, DE: Arcadia Publishing, 1997.

———. *Levittown: Volume II*. Dover, DE: Arcadia Publishing, 1999.

Gabler, Neal. *Walt Disney: The Triumph of the American Imagination*. New York: Alfred A. Knopf, 2006.

Gans, Herbert. *The Levittowners: Ways of Life and Politics in a New Suburban Community.* New York: Columbia University Press, 1967.

Garrow, David J. *Bearing the Cross: Martin Luther King, Jr., and the Southern Christian Leadership Conference.* New York: First Perennial Classics, 2004.

Halberstam, David. *The Fifties.* New York: Villard Books, 1993.

Hayden, Dolores. *Building Suburbia: Green Fields and Urban Growth, 1820–2000.* New York: Vintage Books, 2004.

Jackson, Kenneth. *Crabgrass Frontier: The Suburbanization of the United States.* New York: Oxford University Press, 1985.

Kaplan, Judy, and Linn Shapiro. *Red Diapers: Growing Up in the Communist Left.* Chicago: University of Illinois Press, 1998.

Keats, John C. *The Crack in the Picture Window.* Boston, MA: Houghton Mifflin Company, 1956.

Kelly, Barbara M. *Expanding the American Dream: Building and Rebuilding Levittown.* Albany: State University of New York Press, 1993.

Kimmel, Chad. "Levittown, Pennsylvania: A Sociological History." Diss., University of Western Michigan, 2004.

Labovitz, Sherman. *Being Red in Philadelphia: A Memoir of the McCarthy Era.* Philadelphia, PA: Camino Books, 1998.

Liell, John Thomas. "Levittown: A Study in Community Planning and Development." Ph.D. diss., Yale University, 1952.

Loewen, James W. *Sundown Towns: A Hidden Dimension of American Racism.* New York: The New Press, 2005.

Matarrese, Lynne. *The History of Levittown, New York.* Levittown, NY: Levittown Historical Society, 1997.

McCullough, David. *Truman.* New York: Simon & Schuster, 1992.

Mumford, Lewis. *The City in History: Its Origins, Its Transformations, and Its Prospects.* New York: Harcourt Brace & Company, 1968.

Myers, Daisy D. *Sticks 'n Stones: The Myers Family in Levittown.* York, PA: York County Heritage Trust, 2005.

Nicolaides, Becky M., and Andrew Wiese. *The Suburb Reader.* New York: Routledge, 2006.

Roberts, Gene, and Hank Klibanoff. *The Race Beat: The Press, the Civil Rights Struggle, and the Awakening of a Nation.* New York: Alfred A. Knopf, 2006.

Robinson, Jackie. *Jackie Robinson: I Never Had It Made, an Autobiography.* New York: HarperCollins, 1995.

Rovere, Richard H. *Senator Joe McCarthy.* Berkeley: University of California Press, 1996.

Steinberg, Ted. *American Green: The Obsessive Quest for the Perfect Lawn.* New York: W. W. Norton & Company, 2006.

Wechsler, Lewis. *The First Stone: A Memoir of the Racial Integration of Levittown, Pennsylvania.* Chicago: Grounds for Growth Press, 2004.

Williams, Juan. *Eyes on the Prize: America's Civil Rights Years, 1954–1965*. New York: Penguin Books, 1988.

Wilson, Sloan. *The Man in the Gray Flannel Suit*. New York: Four Walls Eight Windows, 2002.

Wright, Gwendolyn. *Building the Dream: A Social History of Housing in America*. Cambridge, MA: MIT Press, 2001.

INDEX

A Note on the Author

David Kushner is the author of *Masters of Doom* and *Jonny Magic & the Card Shark Kids*. He is an essayist for National Public Radio, and a contributing editor at *Rolling Stone* and *Wired*. His writing has also appeared elsewhere, including the *New York Times Magazine*, *GQ*, *New York*, and *Mother Jones*. He is an adjunct professor of journalism at New York University.